"Michael Rota's book is an ingenious, readable expansion of Pascal's hint ... — that commitment to God is worth making even if we can't be sure God exists. This is the rare book that makes a profoundly serious argument and does so in a wonderfully joyful way. Those who haven't yet taken the wager of Christian commitment will be challenged by this book. But so will others who haven't yet taken the wager of philosophy itself—to see how fun and even life-changing philosophical reasoning can be."

Andy Crouch, executive editor, Christianity Today, author of *Culture Making, Playing God* and *Strong and Weak*

"As a Pascal enthusiast, I am enthusiastic about *Taking Pascal's Wager*. Professor Rota presents a careful and cogent understanding of the wager and places it within a robust apologetic program. Bravo!"

Douglas Groothuis, Denver Seminary, author of *Christian Apologetics*

"The conventional wisdom is that Pascal's wager has been completely discredited: it is excessively self-interested, intellectually dishonest and stands in opposition to real faith. But Michael Rota shows that the conventional wisdom is wrong. In *Taking Pascal's Wager*, Rota confronts the usual objections to the wager and argues that they all miss the point. For those who say that 'more evidence' is needed before Christianity can be considered rational, Rota provides a solid response. But he also goes beyond the head and appeals to the heart. This is a book that should be read by any honest, thoughtful skeptic and that will also answer many of the questions of believers who are questioning their faith. As Rota shows, Pascal's wager can be as powerful an evangelistic tool today as it was in the seventeenth century."

Forrest E. Baird, Whitworth University

"*Taking Pascal's Wager* is a novel combination of Pascalian wagering with natural theology and Christian evidences. Rigorous but readable, this unusual book challenges the mind while appealing to the heart. Believers and unbelievers alike will find much in this book to challenge and inspire them. Truly a gem!"

William Lane Craig, Talbot School of Theology, Houston Baptist University

"Professor Rota offers a distinctive and persuasive case for the reasonableness of accepting the truth of the Christian faith. The book patiently develops a very strong case, considers numerous objections in a fair manner and develops several very illuminating analogies. The argument is thorough, cast in a personable manner and a joy to read."

Patrick Lee, John N. and Jamie D. McAleer Professor of Bioethics, Franciscan University of Steubenville

"Rota's well-crafted book is built around a purified form of Pascal's wager—one that emphasizes that taking a 'gamble' on God need not be motivated by selfishness. But it is much more than an excellent defense of the wager. Almost all the topics occupying center stage in contemporary philosophy of religion come in for serious attention, so that the book would work well as the core text of a survey course. Fortunately, it is not written like a textbook—far from it. Rota's style is winsome and personal. *Taking Pascal's Wager* is really an invitation to think carefully about whether the Christian story might be true and, if so, what one ought to do about it—an invitation that could be taken up with profit by anyone sincerely interested in whether God exists. Rota manages the incredibly difficult trick of explaining, in a way that the educated reader or the philosophical beginner can understand, the relevance of technical philosophical concepts to questions of great existential import. And he never loses sight of the personal and moral dimensions involved in accepting or rejecting a religious path. It is one of the very few books I will be both using in my classes and giving to my friends."

Dean Zimmerman, Rutgers University, director, Rutgers Center for the Philosophy of Religion

TAKING PASCAL'S WAGER

FAITH, EVIDENCE *and the* ABUNDANT LIFE

MICHAEL ROTA

IVP Academic
An imprint of InterVarsity Press
Downers Grove, Illinois

InterVarsity Press
P.O. Box 1400, Downers Grove, IL 60515-1426
ivpress.com
email@ivpress.com

InterVarsity Press® is the book-publishing division of InterVarsity Christian Fellowship/USA®, a movement of students and faculty active on campus at hundreds of universities, colleges and schools of nursing in the United States of America, and a member movement of the International Fellowship of Evangelical Students. For information about local and regional activities, visit intervarsity.org.

Scripture quotations, unless otherwise noted, are from the New Revised Standard Version of the Bible, copyright 1989 by the Division of Christian Education of the National Council of the Churches of Christ in the USA. Used by permission. All rights reserved.

Cover design: David Fassett
Interior design: Beth McGill
Images: ladder: jangeltun/iStockphoto
>*high diver: 1940s MAN POISED MIDAIR ARMS OUT JUMPING FROM DIVING BOARD INTO POOL*
>*(Photo by H. Armstrong Roberts/ClassicStock/Getty Images)*

ISBN 978-0-8308-5136-2 (print)
ISBN 978-0-8308-9999-9 (digital)

Printed in the United States of America ∞

 As a member of the Green Press Initiative, InterVarsity Press is committed to protecting the environment and to the responsible use of natural resources. To learn more, visit greenpressinitiative.org.

Library of Congress Cataloging-in-Publication Data

Names: Rota, Michael, 1975- author.
Title: Taking Pascal's wager : faith, evidence, and the abundant life /
  Michael Rota.
Description: Downers Grove : InterVarsity Press, 2016. | Includes
  bibliographical references and index.
Identifiers: LCCN 2016007922 (print) | LCCN 2016010662 (ebook) | ISBN
  9780830851362 (pbk. : alk. paper) | ISBN 9780830899999 (eBook)
Subjects: LCSH: Faith and reason--Christianity. | Apologetics. | Pascal,
  Blaise, 1623-1662. Pensâees. | Philosophical theology.
Classification: LCC BT50 .R645 2016 (print) | LCC BT50 (ebook) | DDC 239--dc23
LC record available at http://lccn.loc.gov/2016007922

P	23	22	21	20	19	18	17	16	15	14	13	12	11	10	9	8	7	6	5	4	3	2	1
Y	35	34	33	32	31	30	29	28	27	26	25	24	23	22	21	20	19	18	17	16			

To my parents

CONTENTS

ACKNOWLEDGMENTS

I'M VERY GRATEFUL TO THE MANY PEOPLE who have helped shape this book. Andy Crouch supplied crucial guidance early in the writing process, and Greg Boyd, Liz Kelly, Rebecca Konyndyk DeYoung, Michael Murray and Eleonore Stump assisted me in various ways with the proposal. A sabbatical fellowship from the University of St. Thomas during Fall 2013 provided uninterrupted time to begin work on the project in earnest.

I'm particularly appreciative of the insightful criticism of the manuscript (in whole or in part) offered by Luke Barnes, Lawrence Feingold, Matthews Grant, Andrew Le Peau, Neil Manson, Thomas Nechyba, Tim Pawl, Kenny Pearce, Ted Poston, Josh Rasmussen, Ann Rota, Erin Rota, Mary Ryan, Mark Spencer, James Taylor, David Tritelli, two external reviewers for InterVarsity Press, and especially by my editor at IVP, David McNutt.

I present a more technical but abbreviated version of the argument of part one in "A Better Version of Pascal's Wager," forthcoming in the *American Catholic Philosophical Quarterly*, and I thank the editor of that journal, David Clemenson, for permission to use sections of that article in this book. David Clemenson, Jeff Jordan, Liz Jackson, Michael Loux and two anonymous referees for *ACPQ* provided helpful comments on drafts of that paper, comments that influenced my treatment of the wager here.

I'm also thankful to the John Templeton Foundation, both for funding the Evolution and Theology of Cooperation project, through which I did a postdoctoral fellowship with Sarah Coakley and Martin Nowak at Harvard University, and for funding the St. Thomas Summer Seminars in Philosophy of Religion and Philosophical Theology, thanks to which I've had the opportunity to learn from my co-organizer Dean Zimmerman and a host of talented speakers and participants on most of the major topics discussed in this book. Especially formative were talks by or conversations with Luke Barnes, Nevin Climenhaga, Robin Collins, William Lane Craig, Andy Crouch, Brian Cutter, Evan Fales, Dan Greco, John Hawthorne, John Keller, Tom Kelly, Michael Licona, David Manley, Neil Manson, Bradley Monton, John Pittard, Al Plantinga, Alexander Pruss, John Schellenberg, Elliott Sober, Eleonore Stump and Peter van Inwagen. Michael Murray, John Churchill, Alex Arnold and Dan Martin at JTF have all been a pleasure to work with.

My able research assistants, Matt Sweeney and Kieran Driver, tracked down references with alacrity and located some helpful books I might not otherwise have found.

I owe a special debt of gratitude to my mentor, Eleonore Stump, who has contributed to my philosophical education more than anyone else, and to Peter Kreeft, from whose book *Fundamentals of the Faith* I first learned about Pascal's wager, as an undergraduate.

Most of all, I'm grateful to my caring wife, Ann, for her unfailing encouragement, and to my parents for their love and confidence in me.

INTRODUCTION

IS IT RATIONAL TO BELIEVE IN GOD? Is it reasonable to commit oneself to God—to live a deeply religious life? And how much certainty does one need before the time has come to decide? If you've pondered these questions before, this book is for you.

I was raised Catholic, although religion was not a major part of our family life. We prayed before meals and went to church on most Sundays, but there was little discussion of religious matters and no regular personal prayer, at least not on my part. Sometime in my early teens I began to wonder about the truth of the religion I had been born into. Does God really exist? If he does, then relationship with God is the most important part of human life. But if he doesn't, then the religious person is enmeshed in a massive deception. "We believe in one God, the Father, the Almighty . . . ," I found myself saying at Mass. But did I really mean it? I wasn't sure, and the fear that I was being dishonest concerned me.

I continued to wonder about God and the rationality of Christianity throughout high school, in college and in graduate school. Now, as a professor of philosophy, it's my job to think about these topics every day. My research focuses on the rationality of religious belief, and I wrestle with arguments for and against God, with classes full of students from every point of view, almost every semester. I have become convinced that it *is* rational to live a deeply religious Christian life. Indeed, it may be irrational not to.

When contemplating the choice to commit to living a Christian life, one might suppose that one should refrain from making a commitment in the absence of rock-solid evidence for the truth of Christianity. Reflection on personal relationships suggests otherwise. In *The Will to Believe*, William

James asks us to consider a man who hesitates "indefinitely to ask a certain woman to marry him because he [is] not perfectly sure that she would prove [to be] an angel after he brought her home. Would he not cut himself off from that particular angel-possibility as decisively as if he went and married some one else?"[1] In the area of romantic love, it can be reasonable to invest deeply in a relationship, and eventually make a lifelong commitment to the beloved, despite the absence of airtight evidence that the marriage will be a happy one. Because there is so much at stake, it can be reasonable to make a commitment to a personal relationship even when absolute certainty proves elusive. Applying this to the question of God: even if the evidence for God left some room for doubt, considerations about the possible value of a relationship with God might favor the decision to make a religious commitment.

Seventeenth-century French mathematician and theologian Blaise Pascal gave an argument that expands on this insight. Pascal's wager, as the argument has come to be known, addresses those who aren't sure whether Christianity is true but think that it *might* be true. The argument can be summed up in a single sentence: It is rational to seek a relationship with God and live a deeply Christian life, because there is very much to gain and relatively little to lose.

As the wager is usually presented, what's to gain is eternal happiness for the wagerer. An alternative and more powerful version of the argument, however, focuses not just on self-interest but also on goods that go beyond self-interest. If one commits to God and God does in fact exist, one brings joy to God, and one is better able to help others attain union with God. And if Jesus really is who he claimed to be, we may even have a moral duty to commit to living a Christian life. If Christianity is true, we have a duty to love God and have been called by God himself, who has given us everything good that we have, to live a deeply religious life. More than just self-interest can motivate one to take the wager.

On the other hand, if Christianity is false, the committed Christian has still lived a meaningful life, has pursued moral excellence and has enjoyed the many empirically well-attested benefits of belonging to a religious community. Much to gain, relatively little to lose.

In part one of this book (chapters one through four), I'll present an updated version of Pascal's wager, strengthened by cutting-edge research from psychologists, sociologists and philosophers. After introducing and laying out the basic argument in chapters one and two, I turn to objections to the wager in chapters three and four. These include the objections that committing to God on the basis of pragmatic considerations is immoral, that the cost of religious commitment is too high, that the existence of religions other than Christianity nullifies the argument and that Christian doctrine itself casts doubt on the wager. When addressing this last issue, I discuss grace, free will and predestination.

In part two (chapters five through twelve), I'll take a careful look at arguments for the existence of God and the truth of Christianity, showing how—once we no longer demand certainty—the available evidence is sufficient to make serious Christian commitment entirely reasonable. Together, parts one and two present the book's main argument, which can be summarized as follows:

> If Christianity has at least a 50 percent chance of being true, then it is rational to commit to living a Christian life (the conclusion of part one).
>
> Christianity does have at least a 50 percent chance of being true (the conclusion of part two).
>
> Thus, it is rational to commit to living a Christian life.

The argument of part two proceeds in two stages. First, I present evidence for theism (the view that there is a God); second, I present evidence for the more specific view of Christian theism. I begin by asking the question of why physical reality exists at all. Chapter five argues that there is at least one necessarily existing being, which explains the existence of contingent beings. (Contingent beings are things that reality didn't have to include, like all the physical objects we see around us.) Chapters six through eight then provide an argument that the cause of physical reality is an intelligent being. In the last several decades mainstream physicists and astronomers have come to realize that the life-permitting character of our universe is balanced on a knife's edge: if several features had been ever-so-slightly different from what they in fact are, then stable, self-reproducing life would not have been able to arise. Chapter six introduces some of the scientific evidence for this conclusion and gives a preliminary statement of what has come to be known as the *fine-tuning argument*. This argument has been summarized for non-specialists in several places, but not always with enough rigor and background for the strength of the case to be fully displayed. In chapter seven I explain the parts of probability theory required to appreciate the power of the evidence that our universe is the product of an intelligence. Chapter eight contains an original reply to the strongest alternative to design, the multiverse hypothesis. (This is the hypothesis that our universe is just one of a vast number of universes, most of which are not life permitting.) Taken together, chapters five through eight provide evidence for God, drawing on the best recent research but written so as to be accessible to the general reader.

In chapter nine I turn to specifically Christian doctrines, suggesting that the beauty and existential resonance of Christianity are clues to its truth. Chapter ten concerns the two most powerful arguments against theism, the argument from divine hiddenness and the argument from evil. (As arguments against all forms of theism, they are arguments against Christian theism as well.) These topics deserve not a single chapter but whole books of their own. And they have them. So in chapter ten I summarize what I take to be the strongest replies to the arguments from hiddenness and evil, focusing on the recent work of Peter van Inwagen and Eleonore Stump. Finally, in chapters eleven and twelve, I turn to arguments for the resurrection of Jesus. This is just one of many Christian doctrines, of course, but logically speaking it holds a special place. If one has reason to believe that Jesus rose from the dead, then one has reason to believe that Jesus' teachings have the divine stamp of approval and are therefore true. So an argument for the resurrection is an argument for the truth of Christianity (or at least the larger part of one). In this pair of chapters I draw on the most recent work on the issue by historians, theologians and philosophers. While I think that the evidence of part two is by itself sufficient to justify belief in Christianity, agreement on this point is not required for the main argument of the book to succeed. For, given the argument of part one, all that is required for a demonstration of the rationality of Christian commitment is that the evidence render Christianity at least as likely as not.

It's sometimes said that the longest distance in the world is the distance from the head to the heart. And so in part three I'll try to illustrate how a life of Christian commitment is not just reasonable but worth desiring as well—satisfying both the head and the heart. To do this, I'll tell the stories of three exemplary individuals who took Jesus up on his invitation to follow him. The lives of these individuals were enriched, and in turn enriched countless others, in ways all of us would want to be true for our own lives. Dietrich Bonhoeffer, Jean Vanier and Immaculée Ilibagiza show how heroic, noble and beautiful a Christian life can be. Jesus said, "I came that they may have life, and have it abundantly" (Jn 10:10). The abundance that so often characterizes a devout Christian life is not a matter of external goods or material wealth but is internal and spiritual, flowing from a close, personal relationship with God. Life focused on God offers comfort, inspiration and a peace that the vicissitudes of fortune need never take away.

The landscape of academic philosophy has changed significantly in the last forty or fifty years. In the 1960s and '70s it was taken for granted in many philosophical circles that traditional Christian belief is unjustified and irrational. Thanks to the work of philosophers such as Alvin Plantinga, Eleonore Stump, Peter van Inwagen and Richard Swinburne, things have changed.[2] Recent decades have been a time of enormous productivity for philosophers defending the rationality of Christian faith, answering objections to Christian doctrines, improving traditional arguments for the existence of God and formulating new ones. In the pages that follow, I'll explore some of the most important results of this body of work. I've written this book, though, without presupposing that the reader has had formal training in philosophy or theology. My hope is that it will be useful for anyone who is interested in the evidence for God, or the evidence for Christianity more particularly. I also hope that college students in philosophy and theology courses will find the material worthwhile.

Since this book is about evidence and reasons for religious belief, it's worth addressing at the outset the question of why people believe what they do on religious issues. Isn't religion a matter of the heart? Does anyone really believe on the basis of logic or argument? Many committed Christians believe in God not primarily because of *argument* but because of *experience*— they have an intuitive sense of God's presence. Perhaps not all the time, but certainly much of the time, it just seems that God is there, aware of what we do and think. This is how it is in my own case. But what if you don't happen to have such an experience yourself? Or what if you have it occasionally, but it is fleeting and open to serious doubt? In those cases, it makes good sense to spend some time examining arguments and publicly available evidence relating to questions about God and religion. According to Christianity, faith is a gift. But for the person who does not have faith, a careful look at arguments for (and against) Christianity is a natural and reasonable step to take. Examination of evidence can also be worthwhile for the person who does have faith, but has doubts, too. In what follows I give an extended presentation of evidence for the truth of Christianity and a rigorous argument for the reasonableness of Christian commitment.

While this book will focus on the rational case for Christianity, it's important to acknowledge that there are many factors involved in a decision to commit to a Christian way of life, factors that go beyond impersonal philosophical reasoning. One's upbringing, one's experiences with individual Christians, the attitudes and views of one's closest friends and family, one's emotional life, one's deep-seated hopes and fears and one's own particular way of viewing the world—all of these come into play when one encounters the message of Jesus. I believe that the philosophical argumentation contained in this book will be helpful to many people, but philosophical argumentation is only one part of a larger picture. When it comes to religion, logic may or may not be where one starts, but it's certainly not where one should end. Living a Christian life is an act of the whole person— mind and heart, body and soul. Still, precisely because a Christian life involves the *whole* person, there is a place for the mind, and thus for reason, evidence and logic.

Finally, a few words are called for regarding a concept that will play a key role in what follows: *probability*. Everyone has many beliefs, but some of those beliefs are held more confidently than others. For example, I believe that I'll still be alive twenty-four hours from now. I'm not absolutely certain I will be, but nonetheless I do believe it. I also believe I'll be alive twenty-four days from now. But I'm less confident in this belief than in my belief about being alive twenty-four hours from now. How about twenty-four *years* from now? In my case I wouldn't say that I believe I'll be alive twenty-four years from now. I also don't believe I *won't* be alive twenty-four years from now—there's just not enough information to form a belief one way or the other.

Philosophers sometimes use the language of "levels of confidence" when discussing beliefs and probability. Levels of confidence come in a scale from zero to one (or 0 percent to 100 percent). To be absolutely certain of something (e.g., 1 + 1 = 2) is to assign it a level of confidence of 1. To be absolutely certain a claim is false (e.g., 1 + 1 = 17) is to assign it a level of confidence of 0. In such a situation, one could say that the probability of the claim is 0 percent. There's just no chance that you've gotten confused and "1 + 1 = 17" is really true. What about a proposition like "this normal penny will come up heads when I flip it"? Here it's reasonable to assign equal levels of confidence both to this claim and to the claim that the penny will come up tails. So we'd assign both claims a level of confidence of 0.5, and we could say that the chance the coin will be heads is 50 percent. How confident am I that this six-sided die will show either a 1 or a 2 when I roll it? 33.3 percent. You get the idea.

The word *probability* will come up often in this book. I'll sometimes also talk about how *likely* something is, or what the *chance* is that such-and-such is true. Unless otherwise noted, these are all just different ways to talk about the same thing: what philosophers call epistemic probability. Roughly, the epistemic probability of a proposition (that is, a statement or a claim) is the level of confidence it's reasonable to assign to that proposition.[3]

Probability, evidence, moral heroism, commitment . . . all of these factors will enter into our discussion of the reasonableness of Christian theism. But enough with introductory matters. On to deeper waters!

Part One

UNCERTAINTY
and
COMMITMENT

1

A CURIOUS OFFER

IMAGINE THAT ONE DAY you receive a phone call from a fabulously wealthy individual—an eccentric billionaire known for spending his money in odd and trivial ways. He makes you a curious offer. You are to determine the religion you think most likely to be true and then practice that religion devoutly: attend religious services, read the sacred scriptures of that religion, pray as that religion prescribes and live out the religion's moral teachings. And he asks you to do this for the rest of your life. His part of the bargain will be to place $10 billion in an escrow account, to be deliverable on your death to whatever persons or causes you have named. You can leave the money to your family, or to a charitable organization, or to scientific research, or any combination of the above . . . whatever you think best. If you choose not to enter into the bargain, he adds, he will be using the money to hire tens of thousands of artists to paint millions and millions of mediocre oil paintings of his pet dog, Scout.

Of course if this actually happened to you, you'd be a mite skeptical. But imagine that after due diligence you became convinced that this was no joke. And the billionaire clarified that you did not have to lie or otherwise misrepresent yourself in order to fulfill your side of the bargain. If, for example, you chose Christianity as the religion you thought most likely to be true, you would not have to recite the creed during the liturgy if you did not believe it. And your prayers could be conditional, as in "If you're there, God, thank you for this, and please help me with that." An odd offer, to be sure, but also in all probability the only chance you'll ever have to direct $10 billion of wealth to persons or causes you care about. So what would you do? Would you accept the offer?

Perhaps the fact that the payoff is mere monetary gain gives you pause. Good for you; to trade one's religious devotion for money would be base. But remember that you can name whatever beneficiary you'd like, including charitable organizations that work with the poorest of the poor. You can trade your religious devotion for food for the starving, or education for impoverished children in the developing world. On board yet? Say that the billionaire adds that he doesn't want to make this offer if you already happen to be certain, or almost certain, that God does not exist. His offer is only for people who can say of some particular religion that there is at least a decent chance that it is true.

Now consider an alternative scenario. Suppose that, from the get-go, the billionaire had offered you a different bargain: the payoff is not a guaranteed $10 billion, but a 50 percent shot at $100 billion. That is, suppose the billionaire's side of the bargain is to put $100 billion in an escrow account. Then, after your death, a fair coin will be flipped. If it comes up heads, the entire $100 billion will be given to your named beneficiary or beneficiaries. If tails, then we'll have a lot of pictures of Scout. Would you accept this offer?

Hold on to that thought.

The overarching question of this book is the question of whether there is good reason to make a serious commitment to living a Christian life. In part two we'll take a tour of the evidence for Christianity. But before that, the question to ask first is, "How *much* evidence would be required to make a Christian commitment reasonable?" As I'll try to show here in part one, a serious Christian commitment is recommended by reason even if there is as little as a 50 percent chance that Christianity is true. In other words, if you are willing to grant that Christianity is at least as likely as not, then it is rational for you to commit to living a devout Christian life. Indeed, if you're in ordinary circumstances, it is irrational for you not to.[1]

Pascal's Wager

The argument I'll give for this conclusion has its roots in the reflections of seventeenth-century polymath Blaise Pascal. Pascal made important contributions in mathematics, probability theory and physics. His work on fluid mechanics was instrumental in the later invention of the hydraulic press, and he himself designed and built one of the first mechanical calculating machines, an early precursor to the digital computer. (Interestingly, the principles used in the machine are still employed in many automobile odometers.) Pascal was an inventor, an intellectual and a scientist. He was also a deeply religious man. At the age of thirty-one he had a powerful mystical experience of God. He described the experience in a note and stitched the note into his coat, keeping it close to him. He evidently transferred the paper note (together with a cleaner copy he put down on parchment) from coat to coat for the rest of his life—a servant found them after his death.

Pascal suffered from ill health, dying at only thirty-nine. In his final years he was drafting a work of apologetics. The disorganized fragments that were his notes for the project were published posthumously and quickly became a classic, Pascal's *Pensees* (French for "thoughts").[2] In one of those fragments Pascal gives an argument not for the theoretical conclusion that God exists but for the practical conclusion that one should live a devout Christian life. The argument is addressed to those who aren't sure whether Christianity is true or false, and has come to be known as Pascal's wager. To be precise, the fragment contains the seeds of four different arguments in support of religious commitment.[3] The strongest version comes down to this: It is rational to seek a relationship with God and live a deeply Christian life because there is very much to gain and relatively little to lose. In chapter two I'll present a strengthened and expanded version of this argument. If Christianity is indeed true, then by committing to live a Christian life one brings great joy to God and all others in heaven, raises the chance that one will be with God forever, raises the chance that one will help others attain union with God, expresses gratitude to God, and becomes more aware of God's love and more receptive to his help in the course of one's earthly life. On the other hand, if Christianity is false, the person who commits his or her life to Jesus' teachings has still lived a worthwhile life, striving for moral excellence and experiencing the benefits of religious community (benefits that contemporary sociological research reveals to be significant).

Pascal's pragmatic argument in support of religious commitment has had its share of critics. Thus the famous English philosopher G. E. Moore: "[Concerning Pascal's claim that] in our state of doubt, we should decide for that belief which promises the greater reward, I have nothing to say of it except that it seems to me absolutely wicked."[4] Voltaire thought the wager was "somewhat indecent and childish. The idea of gaming, of losing or winning, is quite unsuitable to the dignity of the subject."[5] In much the same vein, an earlier French critic had complained: "I lose patience listening to you treating the highest of all matters, and resting the most important truth in the world, the source of all truths, on an idea so base and puerile, on a comparison with a game of heads and tails more productive of mirth than persuasion."[6] More recently, Christopher Hitchens sees Pascal's theology as "not far short of sordid,"[7] remarking that "Pascal reminds me of the hypocrites and frauds who abound in Talmudic Jewish rationalization. Don't do any work on the Sabbath yourself, but pay someone else to do it. You obeyed the letter of the law: who's counting?"[8]

Are these objections fair? Mathematician James Franklin suggests that Pascal's actual view is often replaced with an unflattering caricature of the wager. Franklin contrasts these two views:

> *What Pascal said.* You have to choose whether to accept religion. Think of it as a coin toss, where you don't know the outcome. In this case, if you lose— there's no God—you have not lost much. But if you win, there is an infinite payoff. So, you should go to Mass, and pray for faith [Franklin's paraphrase].
>
> *Pascal caricatured.* Being base and greedy, we want lots of goodies in this life and, if possible, the next. So we are prepared to give up some pleasures now, on the off chance of a lot more later, if our eye to the main chance makes it look worth our while. Since the loot on offer is infinite, even a small chance of raking it in makes it worth a try to grovel to any deity that might do what we want.[9]

Franklin makes a good point. Pascal's argument is often interpreted in the worst possible light. Still, there are legitimate objections to consider, even when Pascal's reasoning is interpreted fairly. It may be that it is immoral to allow any considerations about cost and benefit to affect what we believe. Perhaps a respect for truth requires that our beliefs be determined by evidence and evidence alone. Second, we must consider whether the costs of committing to God are simply too high. And perhaps the most common criticism is that Pascal illicitly assumed there were only two options to consider: atheism and (Catholic) Christianity. The many gods objection, as it's often called, contends that the multitude of possibly true religions makes trouble for Pascal.

In chapters three and four I'll elaborate on these and additional objections and respond to them. But first we need to lay the basic argument out on the table, in more detail and with greater precision. In order to give the strongest argument possible, I'll set aside the analysis of Pascal's text and instead develop a Pascalian argument in my own way.[10] Just for the sake of having a handy title, I'll refer to my argument as "the wager," or even "Pascal's wager," but this title should be taken merely as a reference to its original inspiration, not as a claim that I am providing a verbatim reproduction of Pascal's thought. Indeed, the wager I'll present takes advantage of cutting-edge work in philosophy and psychology and recent sociological data unavailable to Pascal, and it is therefore able to greatly improve on his rather sketchy note. Since it's impossible to explain the wager clearly without using some concepts from decision theory, that's where we'll begin.

DECISION THEORY

Decision theory is about how to make good decisions in circumstances of risk or uncertainty. Three concepts are especially important: states, strategies and outcomes. A *state* is a possible way things might be (it will rain today, or it won't rain today); a *strategy* is a possible action the decider might take (bring my umbrella, or leave it at home). An *outcome* is a situation that results when a given strategy is taken and a certain state is actual (e.g., the situation of being stuck in the rain without an umbrella). In order to assess the suitability of the various available strategies, the decision maker attempts to form a judgment about how valuable the various outcomes are.

For example, suppose I offer you a bet. I ask a trusted third party to flip a fair coin but not to tell us whether it lands heads or tails. Then I ask you to decide either to play (that is, participate in the bet) or pass. If you choose to play, it will cost you one dollar, but if you play and the coin has come up heads, you will get your dollar back, and I will pay you two more dollars, so you will be up two dollars. If you choose to play and the coin comes up tails, however, I will keep your dollar, so you will be down one dollar. If, on the other hand, you choose to pass, no money will change hands either way. Would you take my bet?

I bet you would. Decision theory allows us to say precisely why the bet is favorable for you. There are two possible states for you to consider: it could be that the coin has come up heads, and it could be that it has come up tails. At the time you make your decision you don't know which state is the actual way things are, but you do know that it's one or the other. Next, there are two possible strategies you can adopt: play or pass. Corresponding to the four possible combinations of these states and strategies, there are four possible situations that may result—these are the outcomes: (1) you play the game and the coin is heads, and so you win two dollars; (2) you play the game and the coin is tails, so you lose one dollar; (3) you pass and the coin is heads, so you neither gain nor lose; and (4) you pass and the coin is tails, so you neither gain nor lose. In considering the question of what to do, the decision maker is invited to *evaluate* the outcomes. That is, the decision maker attempts to estimate how valuable the various outcomes are. In this case, the monetary value of outcome 1 for you is two dollars, for outcome 2 it is minus one dollar, and for outcomes 3 and 4, zero. In the case of most actual decisions, values other than money are at stake. But starting with an example using money is a good way to get an initial grasp of decision theory.

Decision theorists commonly use a "decision matrix" to sum up information relevant to a decision. In our case, we need a two-by-two matrix. The columns correspond to the two possible states of the world, and the rows correspond to the two strategies you might take. In the cells we write down the valuations of the resulting outcomes.

	Heads	**Tails**
Play	Outcome 1 $2	Outcome 2 $-1
Pass	Outcome 3 $0	Outcome 4 $0

Figure 1.1

Should you play or pass? If you only had one dollar to your name and needed it to buy food lest you starve, then it might not be wise to play. But if you're in ordinary circumstances and the loss of a dollar would be no great loss, then it's rational to play. Intuitively, this is because you've got an equal chance of gaining and losing, and if you gain, you gain twice what you would lose if you lost. More precisely, it's because the *expected value* of playing is higher than the expected value of passing. The expected value of a strategy, for a given game or bet, is the average value per game that would accrue to you if you played the game an infinite number of times and adopted that strategy every time. Here, the expected value of the strategy "play" can be calculated by multiplying the probability of each state by the value of its corresponding outcome and adding up the products. So, the expected value of "play" is equal to

$$(\tfrac{1}{2}) \times (2) + (\tfrac{1}{2}) \times (-1) = .50$$

If you were offered this bet a large number of times, and you chose "play" every time, you'd win an average of about fifty cents per game. The expected value of passing, by contrast is

$$(\tfrac{1}{2}) \times (0) + (\tfrac{1}{2}) \times (0) = 0$$

One reason playing is a good bet here is that the expected value of playing (fifty cents) is more than the expected value of passing (zero cents). Now, as it turns out, it's not *always* rational to take the strategy that maximizes one's expected value.[11] But maximizing expected value is often a good way to make decisions that involve risk.

For the sake of clarity, I've illustrated the concepts of a state, a strategy, an outcome and a decision matrix by giving an example with precise monetary values for outcomes and with definite probabilities assigned to the possible states in question. In real life, we usually don't have precise probabilities to assign to the states, and much (perhaps most) of what we care about can't be valued in monetary terms. Even in such cases, however, there are principles that can guide our decision making.

One such principle is at play when we say things like "I'll do X, because it can't hurt and it might help," or "You should do Y, because there's nothing to lose and maybe a lot to gain." Suppose you've borrowed your friend's bicycle and have cycled to a store on the edge of town. You put the lock around the bike and a parking sign, and as you're lifting the key to lock up the bike, it occurs to you that this part of town is very safe, and there's hardly any chance the bike will be stolen. Besides, when you're inside, the bike will be in your view through the store window. As you finish thinking this, you've also just put the key into the lock. So, should you lock up the bike? You don't have any precise knowledge about the probability of theft in the circumstances, and while you could estimate the value of the bike, there's no obvious way to calculate the disvalue your friend would experience if your negligence got his bike stolen. Despite your lack of knowledge on those points, though, it's clear enough what you should do: all you have to do to lock the bike is turn your wrist. A decision theorist could map out your situation like this:

	A thief will happen by	**A thief won't happen by**
Lock	Nothing bad happens	Nothing bad happens
Don't lock	Bike stolen (probably)	Nothing bad happens

Figure 1.2

If a motivated, capable thief is in fact coming along, the strategy of locking will result in a far better outcome, while if such a thief won't happen by, locking is no worse than unlocking (by the time of your decision, it's just so easy to lock that there's no cost to locking). In the language of game theory, we say that the strategy of locking "weakly dominates" the strategy of not locking. One strategy weakly dominates another if (and only if) there is at least one possible state of the world on which the first strategy delivers a better outcome than the second, and there are no possible states of the world on which the first strategy delivers a worse outcome than second. In other words, depending on how things turn out, adopting a weakly dominant strategy will either end up yielding a *better* result than adopting the other strategy would have, or it will end up yielding a result that is *just as good* as what you'd have gotten with the other strategy. In a situation of uncertainty, when we don't know which of several possible states of the world is the true one, it is always better to adopt a weakly dominant strategy instead of the strategy it dominates.

In case you're wondering, one strategy *strongly* dominates another strategy if and only if it delivers a better outcome on every possible state of the world. Of course strongly dominant strategies are even more preferable than weakly dominant strategies, when you can get them.

Decision theorists have other principles to help guide us in uncertainty. But it's worth noting that in some cases we don't need a general principle. Sometimes we can just see what the smart thing to do is, especially if we've laid out the information in a decision matrix. For example, suppose again that a trusted third party flips a coin for us but doesn't say whether it lands heads or tails. Now imagine that I credibly make you this offer: if you choose to play and it's heads, then I'll give you a million dollars, while you'll owe me one dollar if it's tails and you've chosen to play. If you choose to pass, no money is exchanged either way. We could represent this with the matrix:

	Heads	**Tails**
Play	Outcome 1 $1,000,000	Outcome 2 $-1
Pass	Outcome 3 $0	Outcome 4 $0

Figure 1.3

Here we can't say that *playing* weakly dominates *passing*, because if the coin is tails you do slightly better by passing. But it's one dollar we're talking about! Strictly speaking, *playing* is not a weakly dominant strategy here, but it's close enough. The payoff is so much greater if the coin is heads, and the loss is so little if it's tails, that it's clearly rational to play. Perhaps we could state a precise, universally valid principle that would apply in this case and tell us what to do, but we don't really need one: we can just see what the smart move is. This insight will prove helpful later on.

With these preliminaries behind us, we can now turn to the wager. A consideration of this argument will allow us to see that Christian commitment is recommended by reason, so long as the available evidence makes it at least as likely as not that the central claims of Christianity are true.

2

PASCAL'S WAGER

The Basic Argument

EITHER GOD EXISTS, OR NOT. These are two possible states of the world, two ways reality might be. And you can take different strategies about how you will live your life. Will you live your life as if God exists? Or not?

To be more precise, let's consider two possible ways the world might be. One is that Christianity is true.[1] God exists and offers you an eternal relationship with himself. The second possibility is that there is no God, or anything like God. There aren't any supernatural beings, we don't have souls and when we die it all goes black. Call this "naturalism." In chapter four we'll consider additional possibilities and different religions, but for now, just to get the basic argument in view, let's focus on Christianity and naturalism.

Next, consider two courses of action you might take: you might commit to God, or you might not. By "commit to God" I do not mean "decide to believe that God exists, right now!" When setting up a decision matrix, the strategies are supposed to be actions that the decider can choose between, actions that are within our direct voluntary control. Belief in the existence of God isn't like that. What one can choose to do is to seek God, to pursue a relationship with God.[2] This is the foundational component of what I mean here by "committing to God."

Committing to God is therefore a course of action that can be undertaken by one who already believes or by an inquiring agnostic. (An agnostic is a person who doesn't believe that God exists but also doesn't believe that God does not exist—they're just not sure either way.) While both believer and agnostic can commit to God, the strategy will look different for the two of them. For the person who already believes, committing to God will involve seeking a closer relationship with God and, indeed, putting one's goal of closeness with God at the center of one's life plans. It will involve prayer and the intention to live a life of moral excellence. It will involve attendance at religious services, association with other religious believers, the reading of sacred writings and perhaps study and discussion on religious questions.

For an agnostic, to seek a relationship with God is to seek a relationship with a being whose existence is in doubt. This is atypical but possible— compare a situation in which a person camping alone hears some ambiguous but possibly human sounds outside the circle of firelight and calls out, "Is that a person? If somebody's out there, you're welcome to come closer." For the agnostic, committing to God will involve prayer, likely in a similar conditional form; for example, "If you're there, God, please forgive me for that, and help me with this," and so on. An agnostic seeking God will probably also want to attend religious services, although full participation might be ruled out; no duplicitousness or hypocrisy should be involved in an agnostic's search for God. Association with religious believers, thought and discussion on religious matters, and the reading of sacred writings are all called for by the intention to seek a relationship with God. Most crucially, the inquiring agnostic will want to live a life that would be pleasing to God if God does indeed exist. If you're seeking a close relationship with God, then you'll want to live a life that is in harmony with what God would want.

The agnostic who makes a religious commitment need not turn a blind eye to counterevidence, and it may be that one day in the future he or she will decide to back out of religious commitment. Still, adopting the strategy involves a sincere openness to the possibility of God, a desire to search for him and a willingness to accept belief in God, should it come. If future experiences or arguments prove sufficient, an agnostic who is genuinely seeking a relationship with God won't resist the transition from agnosticism to belief.

Although committing to God will involve somewhat different things for the agnostic and the believer, the essential core is the same for believer and agnostic alike: the effort to form a close, personal relationship with God. This is not necessarily equivalent to faith. According to traditional Christian doctrine, the act of supernatural faith includes belief in God and the

revelation of Jesus, whereas the strategy of committing to God under discussion here does not necessarily include belief. At the same time, committing to God may serve as a crucial stage on the path toward a robust faith.

One strategy, then, is to commit one's life to God. The other is to not do
that. This could take a variety of forms. One need not join the local atheists
club to count as not committing to God. In the most common case, someone
who was not committing to God would be someone who just didn't pay
much mind to the question of God, and who lived his or her life focused on
the things of this world. He or she might even go to church on Christmas
and Easter. So we're defining this second strategy simply as an absence of
the first strategy. Defining it in this way ensures, as a point of logic, that there
is no third strategy available. You're either seeking a close relationship with
God or you're not.

Later I'll adjust the basic presentation of Pascal's wager to allow for the
fact that there are many different religions one might follow. But just for the
moment, simply in order to get clear on the basic argument, let's pretend
that the only way to commit to God is a Christian way. Of course this is
false—one can commit to God in a Jewish way, in a Muslim way and so on.
But, as I'll argue in chapter four, the wager still succeeds even after we've
discarded this false assumption and taken into account the multitude of
other religions. For ease of exposition, it's better to *begin* by considering just
the two states of Christianity and naturalism, and the two strategies of committing to God (in a Christian way) and not committing to God at all, and
then *later* add in the complication of additional states (e.g., Judaism is true)
and additional strategies (e.g., commit to God in a Jewish way). With all this
in mind, we can represent the wager, for now, with this decision matrix:

	Christianity is true	Naturalism is true
Commit to God	Outcome WC (**W**ager and **C**hristianity is true)	Outcome WN (**W**ager and **N**aturalism is true)
Refrain from committing to God	Outcome ~WC (Don't wager and Christianity is true)	Outcome ~WN (Don't wager and Naturalism is true)

Figure 2.1

FILLING IN THE BOXES

We've now reached the crucial stage of the argument: how does one fill in the boxes in this matrix? How should one evaluate the situation that would result if one has wagered for God and indeed Christianity is true (outcome WC)? How should one evaluate the situation that would result if naturalism were true and one has committed to God (outcome WN)? And so on for the other two possibilities.

Starting with outcome WC: what sort of value should one place on the outcome that results from committing to God, if Christianity is true? It might be tempting to write into our matrix "eternal life," perfect happiness with God and others, without end. But that would be to assume that salvation is guaranteed for anyone who embarks on the project of committing to God. Better to merely say that one has maximized one's chance at eternal life.

Yet there is much more to include in outcome WC. The benefits aren't just for the decision maker. If God exists and has offered you eternal life, he's there holding out his hand, so to speak, earnestly desiring that you won't reject his assistance. You can turn your back on him or you can reach out your hand. Being perfectly good, God loves you and wants what's best for you, and he knows that an everlasting relationship with him is the best and most satisfying thing possible for you. So by seeking closeness with God, you will bring joy to God and all others who are with God in heaven. Jesus expresses this thought in the parables of the lost sheep, the lost coin and the prodigal son (Lk 15). Christianity presents God as a father who cares for his children, and in another analogy, as a lover seeking his beloved.

Third, if God exists and you've committed to God, you've exhibited the virtue of gratitude to God. You've done something morally good. There is value in this. In a way, this third point is similar to the second point, but here we're looking at it from your side—not at the value of God's joy over your response to his offer but at the moral value of your response itself.

Fourth, it's very plausible to think that you are more likely to benefit from divine aid for moral and spiritual growth if you seek a relationship with God than if you don't. No doubt God would not leave you without grace if you didn't seek him, but it's reasonable to think that if you're more open to God's assistance in your life, then you'll end up resisting less when God sends help your way.

Fifth, you are more likely to be aware of God's love during this earthly life. If Christianity is true, a close relationship with God can begin now.

Sixth, if Christianity is true and you've attempted to follow a Christian way of life, you're more likely to be a help to others in their journey to God. Since the ultimate good for human beings will largely depend on their relationship with God, we can include in outcome WC the idea that you'll be more likely to help others *in the most important way possible*.

	Christianity is true	Naturalism is true
Commit to God	1. Maximize chance at eternal life 2. Bring joy to God and others 3. Express gratitude to God 4. More likely to benefit from divine aid 5. More likely to be aware of God's love in this life 6. More likely to help others attain salvation PLUS: This-worldly costs and benefits of outcome WN	Outcome WN
Refrain from committing to God	Outcome ~WC	Outcome ~WN

Figure 2.2

The six goods just mentioned are all goods specific to outcome WC; they are goods that won't also be present if Christianity is false, and thus are goods that won't be included in outcome WN. But there are certain *this-worldly* goods that should be included in both outcome WC (wager for God and Christianity is true) and outcome WN (wager for God but naturalism is true), like the benefits in this life of belonging to a religious community. The same goes for certain this-worldly costs, like the cost of time spent in pursuing a relationship with God. I'll discuss these costs and benefits at length in our examination of outcome WN. For now the thing to note is that, if Christianity is true, the overall value of these this-worldly costs and benefits tends to get swamped by the massive value of the goods specific to outcome WC. If Christianity is true, the cost of time "spent" in pursuing a relationship with God becomes negligible, if it is construed as a cost at all. So the value one places on outcome WC is almost entirely determined by the value of the goods specific to outcome WC, which are clearly of immense value.

At the end of the day, what should we write in the box for outcome WC? Shall we say that we have an infinitely valuable state of affairs here? That may be an acceptable way to put the point, but it isn't necessary to think of the value of outcome WC as a single infinite quantity. We make decisions all the time without quantifying the various possible outcomes. Here too, all we'll need to do is to hold the goods involved in mind for later comparison with the other outcomes.

OUTCOME WN

On the other hand, suppose you live your three-score years and ten committing to God, going to church, spending time in prayer, and then at death it's over. Have you wasted your life? Have you squandered your one chance at happiness? Pascal certainly didn't think so:

> But what harm will come to you from taking this course [committing to God]? You will be faithful, honest, humble, grateful, doing good, a sincere and true friend. It is, of course, true; you will not take part in corrupt pleasure, in glory, in the pleasures of high living. But will you not have others? I tell you that you will win thereby in this life.[3]

Famous early American psychologist William James held a similar view, writing that religion brings with it "a new zest which adds itself like a gift to life, and takes the form either of lyrical enchantment or of appeal to earnestness and heroism.... An assurance of safety and a temper of peace, and, in relation to others, a preponderance of loving affections."[4]

Could it be that if you commit to God, you will benefit even if there is no God? While Pascal and James say yes, others say no. Thus the philosopher Michael Martin: "There is little empirical reason to suppose that theists are happier and healthier, lead more rewarding lives, and so on than nontheists. ... Nor does it seem to be true that if one is a theist it is more likely that one will achieve happiness and so on in this life than if one is a nontheist."[5] Whether or not Martin had good grounds for these claims when he made them (in 1990), the psychological and sociological data now available show that he is seriously mistaken. Sociologists Rodney Stark (of Baylor

University) and Roger Finke (Pennsylvania State) describe research on the relationship between religion and health as "a huge and growing literature that finds religion to be a reliable source of better mental and even physical health."[6] In the most comprehensive review of research on the subject to date, Duke University's Harold Koenig and collaborators Dana King (Medical University of South Carolina) and Verna Benner Carson (Towson University) find strong evidence that religion and spirituality have both indirect and direct positive effects on well-being.[7]

Religious participation can indirectly affect well-being by directly affecting things like marital stability, social support and hope, which themselves in turn positively affect well-being. On this score, Koenig, King and Carson present evidence that religious persons are less likely to divorce and more likely to have stable families, have more social contacts and greater satisfaction with their social support, have higher self-esteem, have more optimism, are more hopeful, and have a greater sense of meaning and purpose in life. After a systematic review of seventy-nine quantitative studies examining the relationships between religion and marital stability, they summarize:

> No matter how marital stability is measured, whether by . . . attitudes toward divorce, likelihood of actual divorce, likelihood of infidelity, likelihood of domestic violence, or marital commitment, or whether that research is done in or outside of the United States, couples who are more R/S [religious/spiritual] or from the same religious background fare better. This has been demonstrated in cross-sectional studies and prospective studies following married couples for up to twenty-eight years.[8]

In a systematic review of seventy-four studies on religion and social support, Koenig et al. found that 82 percent of the studies showed "significant positive relationships between religiousness and social support." Their reviews also found that of sixty-nine studies examining the connection between religiousness and self-esteem, 61 percent "found significantly higher levels of self-esteem among individuals who were more religious," while only 3 percent found lower self-esteem. Eighty-one percent of relevant studies "reported significant positive relationships between religiousness and optimism." Seventy-three percent of relevant studies showed "significant positive relationships between religiousness and hope," while the rest found no correlation. Studies that investigated the connection between religiousness and a sense of purpose or meaning in life were even more consistent: "forty-two of forty-five studies (93 percent) reported significant positive relationships."[9]

Turning now to studies that examine the direct connection between religiousness and well-being, Koenig, King and Carson write:

> In the last ten years, 175 of 224 quantitative studies (78 percent) found positive associations between greater religiousness and greater well-being . . . ; eight (4 percent) reported mixed findings . . . ; two reported complex relationships difficult to interpret; thirty-eight (17 percent) reported no association; and two studies found a negative relationship.[10]

Similar results obtain for studies dating from 2000 and before.

Just how large is the effect of religiousness on well-being? Focusing on subjective well-being (i.e., self-reported happiness and satisfaction with one's life), sociologist Chaeyoon Lim of the University of Wisconsin-Madison and political scientist Robert Putnam (Harvard) tell us:

> Scholars who study the connection between religion and subjective well-being appear to agree on a few points. First, most studies find a positive association between religious involvement and individuals' well-being. . . . Second, studies find that the association between religion and subjective well-being is substantial (Inglehart 2010; Myers 2000; Witter et al. 1985). Witter and colleagues (1985) estimate that the gross effects of religious involvement account for 2 to 6 percent of the variation in subjective well-being. When compared with other correlates of well-being, religion is less potent than health and loneliness, but it is just as or more potent than education, marital status, social activity, age, gender, and race. Other studies find that religious involvement has an effect comparable to or stronger than income (Ellison, Gay, and Glass 1989).[11]

Lim and Putnam go on to report the results of their own analysis of 2006–2007 data. In an average case, and controlling for other variables,

> 28.2 percent of people who attend a service weekly are predicted to be "extremely satisfied" with their lives, compared with only 19.6 percent of those who never attend services. This result is roughly comparable to the difference between someone in "good" health and another in "very good" health, or the

difference between someone with family income of $10,000 and another with $100,000. Given that health and income are the strongest predictors in the model, this association between attendance and life satisfaction is notable.[12]

What should we conclude from all of this? Just because higher religiosity is statistically correlated with higher well-being, that doesn't necessarily mean that practicing a religion causes people to be happier. Maybe the causation runs the other way: maybe people who are happy are more likely to want to join or continue practicing a religion. Or maybe there is some third factor that explains both: maybe there is something that tends to make a person both happier and more religious. Given these two alternative explanations of the statistics, do we have any reason to think that a given, typical person will likely be happier if she or he practices a religion devoutly?

We do, for two reasons. First, sociologists and psychologists have plausible theories about the causal mechanisms that link religiosity and well-being. Lim and Putnam argue that the key factor is the friendships that committed religious people make and enjoy in their church communities. Interestingly, friendships in religious contexts seem to be special in an important way: even among respondents who had the same number of close friends, those with more close friends in their church community tended to have higher life satisfaction.[13]

Koenig, King and Carson attempt to offer a more comprehensive explanation than Putnam and Lim, presenting a complicated model according to which belief in and attachment to God is the source of a number of activities, commitments, experiences and behaviors (e.g., participation in worship services, prayer, commitments to a certain moral code or worldview, religious peer influences) that (a) have direct effects on mental health and (b) promote decisions, virtues, social relations and ways of thinking about the events of one's life that collectively tend to cause good mental health.[14]

As one examines these proposed causal mechanisms, it's easy to see how practicing a (mainstream) religion would typically lead to greater subjective well-being. To take just one example, consider the feeling of hope. Suppose you believe in God. Then you're liable to have both a hope in a glorious afterlife and a hope that even now God is actively concerned with people's lives, both your own and others'. Contrast this with the situation of a person who doesn't believe in God or an afterlife. On that view, you're liable to think that there are gross injustices in the world that will never be redressed. You get old and watch your health and beauty fade away; you realize there is no return to youth. Ultimately, nothing awaits you but the grave. There are certainly good things one can hope for if one is an atheist, but the point is that there are substantial grounds for hope available to theists that atheists simply do not have access to. So it's easy to see how practicing a religion would make it more likely that you have feelings of hope, which would in turn contribute to your well-being. Similar reasoning applies in other cases.

A second reason to think that religiosity causally influences well-being comes from studies in hedonic psychology, which examines questions about what makes life pleasant or unpleasant, satisfying or unsatisfying. Princeton's Daniel Kahneman and Alan Krueger have made important contributions in this area. Kahneman is a psychologist and winner of the 2002 Nobel Prize in economics; Krueger is a professor of economics and the former chairman of President Obama's Council of Economic Advisors. To gather data on how much people enjoy or dislike various activities, Krueger, Kahneman and their collaborators have developed a time-diary method that involves asking people to reconstruct their activities in the previous day and describe how they felt during those activities. In 2006 the Gallup organization adminis- tered the Princeton Affect and Time Survey, on Krueger et al.'s behalf, using a random-digit-dial telephone survey of US residents. Respondents were asked to describe the activities of their day and then to rate the extent to which they felt happy, sad, stressed, tired, in pain or interested during those activities. A zero through six rating scale was used, where zero meant "not at all" and six meant that the feeling was very strong. With respect to the question of religion, the results were striking. Out of the twenty categories of activity reported on, the average happiness rating for religious activity (4.97 out of 6) was the second highest, bested only by sports and exercise (5.08). The average for socializing was 4.74, childcare 4.63, eating and drinking 4.57, relaxing and leisure 4.34, and watching TV 3.91.[15]

Krueger and colleagues also compared different activities by calculating the percentage of time a person engaged in a given activity reported more stress, sadness or pain than happiness. (A lower percentage means that the activity is better.) On this score religious activity was best of all—those in- volved in religious activity reported feeling more stress, sadness or pain than happiness only 6.4 percent of the time, compared with 7.4 percent for sports and exercise, 9.7 percent for eating and drinking, 13.4 percent for relaxing and leisure, 13.5 percent for socializing, 15.6 percent for child care, 26.9 percent for working and 29.0 percent for medical care.[16] It appears that something about religious activities themselves affects the subjective well-being of the person at the time of the activity.

The Gallup studies on positive emotions provide similar evidence of causal influence.[17] All Americans, regardless of their frequency of church attendance, tend to have more positive emotions on Saturdays than they do on Mondays, Tuesdays, Wednesdays, Thursdays and Fridays. More frequent churchgoers have more positive emotions than their counterparts on every day of the week (and thus on Saturdays too). But while those who aren't frequent churchgoers (those who attend church never, seldom or about once a month) experience a drop in positive emotions on Sunday as compared to Saturday, those who attend religious services almost every week or at least once a week enjoy Sunday even more than Saturday. The effect is strongest for respondents who go to church at least once a week. Something frequent churchgoers do *on Sunday* gives them a boost in positive emotions. Since the vast majority of religious Americans are members of religious communities that set aside Sunday as a special day of worship, it's reasonable to conclude that frequent churchgoers experience a substantial boost from their spiritual practices on Sundays. And this is entirely what we would expect given the results found by Krueger, Kahneman and their colleagues.

Mortality. In addition to being happier, frequent churchgoers tend to live longer. In 2000, psychologist Mike McCullough (now at the University of Miami) and collaborators at Stanford, Iowa State, Duke Medical School and the National Institute for Healthcare Research conducted an analysis of twenty-nine studies on the connection between religious involvement and mortality.[18] After controlling for many other variables, they found that individuals involved in religion had a substantially higher chance of still being alive at the end of the studies. The size of the effect (an "odds ratio" of 1.23) amounts to this: Suppose we randomly selected one thousand highly religious people and one thousand who were not highly religious, and suppose we then tracked our group of two thousand until half had died (that is, until only one thousand were left). Given McCullough et al.'s conclusions, we would expect that at the end of our study 526 people from the highly religious group would still be alive and 474 of the less religious.[19] Not a trivial difference. More recent meta-analyses have yielded similar results.[20]

Civic virtues. Religious Americans also tend to volunteer more, give more to charitable causes (both religious and secular) and exhibit greater degrees of civic involvement as compared with their nonreligious counterparts. In a recent book, Robert Putnam and Notre Dame political scientist David Campbell present the evidence for these claims, which hold even after controlling for the possibly confounding variables of "gender, education, income, race, region, homeownership, length of residence, marital and parental status, ideology, and age."[21] To cite just a few of many statistics: of the most religious fifth of Americans, 61 percent report volunteering in the last year for a secular organization and 60 percent report volunteering in the last year for a religious organization. For the least religious fifth of Americans, the figures are 43 percent and 5 percent, respectively.[22] Americans in the most religious fifth of the population appear to give about three times more than those in the least religious fifth (roughly $3,000 versus $1,000 per year). And if we measure charitable giving as a fraction of income, "the average person in the most religious fifth of Americans is more than four times as generous as his or her counterpart in the least religious fifth, [giving] roughly 7 percent [of income] vs. roughly 1.5 percent."[23] Religious Americans give more generously to secular causes as well as to religious causes, and "this is especially true for organizations serving the needy."[24] Similarly substantial effects are found for measures of civic engagement. Religious Americans are considerably more likely to belong to community organizations, to work on community projects, to participate in local political life and to press for social or political reform.

When they investigate the possible causal mechanisms that might mediate this connection between religiosity and good neighborliness, Putnam and Campbell argue that a small portion of the difference between religious and nonreligious can be explained by differing levels of empathy and altruistic values: religious people tend to score higher on indexes of empathy and altruistic beliefs. But by far the most important factor has to do with friendships at church:

Having close friends at church, discussing religion frequently with your family and friends, and taking part in small groups at church are extremely powerful predictors of the entire range of generosity, good neighborliness, and civic engagement. . . .

In other words, devout people who sit alone in the pews are not much more neighborly than people who don't go to church at all. The real impact of religiosity on niceness or good neighborliness, it seems, comes through chatting with friends after service or joining a Bible study group, not from listening to the sermon or fervently believing in God.

In fact, the statistics suggest that even an atheist who happened to become involved in the social life of a congregation (perhaps through a spouse) is much more likely to volunteer in a soup kitchen than the most fervent believer who prays alone. It is religious belonging that matters for neighborliness, not religious believing.[25]

So, where are we? The person who commits to God will be a frequent churchgoer and is also more likely to acquire and/or maintain a belief in God (more likely than she or he would have been without a commitment to God). This in turn means she will probably experience greater life satisfaction and a sunnier emotional life than she would have if she had refrained from committing to God, other things being equal. The analogous conclusions hold for length of life, volunteering, charitable giving and civic engagement. Thus under outcome WN we should include "increased chance of higher subjective well-being and longer length of life" and "increased chance of exercising certain social virtues." Can committed atheists be satisfied with their lives and exhibit civic virtue? Of course they can. The point is only that religious involvement, over the course of time, is likely to give one an appreciable boost on the various positive dimensions discussed. This by itself isn't a reason to believe in God, and all by itself it's not a sufficient reason to make a religious commitment, but it is certainly *relevant* to the decision to make a religious commitment.

Outcome WN: Costs

We've seen that even if God does not exist, religious commitment can carry important benefits. But it also may have significant costs. If in reality there is no afterlife and no God, the person who has committed to God will never definitively realize he was wrong. But he still may have foregone certain goods that he would have valued. Let's now try to tabulate the costs that should be included in outcome WN.

A first possible cost is lost time: time spent in prayer, time spent in church, time spent studying religious teachings, etc. While these activities bring benefits even if God does not exist, it may also be true that there are other activities a given person might have derived greater benefit from. The economist's concept of an opportunity cost is helpful here. If you sit on the sofa navel-gazing for an hour when you might have been mowing someone's lawn for twenty dollars, the opportunity cost of sitting on the sofa is twenty dollars, even if you don't have to pay anything to gaze at your own navel. And we can think about opportunity costs in relation to goods other than money, like the satisfaction one misses out on by watching a bad movie rather than a good one. Returning to Pascal's wager, the point is that time spent on religious activities has an opportunity cost.

A second cost is psychological. The person transitioning from a nonreligious or only moderately religious lifestyle to a seriously religious lifestyle might experience a loss of a sense of control, a loss of the sense that he can do what he pleases with his life. The theist believes that God has authority over us. Some find that idea unpleasant.

Also worth considering is the possible disruption in one's personal relationships that might result from the transition to a seriously religious lifestyle. A person who previously was not living a religious life but begins to do so may find that not everyone she cares about approves of the change.

A different possible cost is mentioned by Richard Gale: "People morally ought not to live their worldly lives in a way that they deem inauthentic, no matter what possibilities it might open up" for other gains.[26] Perhaps the thought is this: for some agnostics, it would be inauthentic, dishonest or in contradiction to their deepest values to engage in Christian religious practices.

One can see how this could be true for a person who judges that the probability of Christianity is very low. But what about a person who thinks it is at least as likely as not that Christianity is true? This is the key question, for our purposes, because I am here arguing only that one should take the wager if one thinks Christianity is at least as likely as not. And for the person who does think this, it would not be inauthentic to engage in the sorts of religious practices described above. Imagine that a person had a serious health problem and learned that a certain regimen of diet and exercise had a 50 percent chance of curing it. (Suppose also that there was no other cure that had a higher chance of curing it.) Would such a person be inauthentic if he embarked on the regimen? Surely not. The same should be true for the person who thinks Christianity has at least a 50 percent probability of being true and makes a commitment to pray, attend religious services, do some reading on religious questions and so on. Of course, when it comes to the centrality of a practice in one's concept of self, there is a big difference between making a serious commitment to search for God and, say, taking up jogging. But it's hard to see why praying, going to church and so forth would be *inauthentic* for an agnostic inquirer. An inquirer should be able to *inquire*, after all, without being inauthentic; and for the agnostic the religious practices being suggested are precisely ways of inquiring, ways of searching for God.

When Pascal gestures at the costs of a devout life, he mentions abstaining from corrupt pleasure and high living. What does he have in mind? Certainly a person who commits to God can appreciate pleasure and enjoy food, drink, sex and relaxation. But only in the right contexts (e.g., marriage), in the right way, at the right times and while also realizing that pleasure is not the goal of life. The person who commits to God can't just follow his passions without regard for morality. Not that an atheist can or does either (more on that below). The point for now is just this: If you are seeking to live the life God would want you to live, you'll be seeking to guide your conduct according to what is best, for others as well as for yourself, and in the long term as well as the short term. Since human beings are naturally inclined to value their short-term well-being over their long-term well-being, to value positive feelings over more abstract moral goods (like keeping a promise), and to value their own well-being over the well-being of others, the effort to live a life of moral excellence is bound to involve painful sacrifice at times. This sacrifice will involve positive acts as well as abstention. In a world where millions of people suffer cruelly from lack of basic necessities or oppression by others, the person seeking moral excellence will avoid purchasing luxury goods where he could instead contribute his resources to those who really need help.[27]

A careful regard for morality, the renunciation of luxury and a focus on others will therefore be components of a devout life. But whether they should count as *costs* for a given wagerer will depend on what she would have been doing otherwise. If you would live just as virtuously whether or not you were committing to God, then you should leave out the costs of living virtuously when comparing outcome WN (commit to God but there is no God) and outcome ~WN (don't commit to God and there is no God). Or if you prefer to think of it this way, you could include these costs in both outcome WN and outcome ~WN. The point is that the costs we've been discussing won't constitute a reason not to commit to God, because you'd be facing them anyway.

On the other hand, if committing to God would involve for you a more comprehensive and demanding effort to live virtuously, then any costs of this extra effort at morality should be included in outcome WN for you. At the same time, whatever *benefits* come from your extra effort at morality should also be included. If you are more diligently striving for moral excellence, chances are you will be more responsible (and hence more successful in your work), and more honest and kind (and hence more successful in your personal relationships) and so forth. And chances are that you will feel better about yourself. You will be proud of who you are and the way you conduct your life. Those are big benefits. If one includes the loss of corrupt pleasures as a cost of committing to God, then one should also include the benefits of avoiding those corrupt pleasures as a benefit of committing to God.

In summary, for a typical person outcome WN should include (1) a modest but still appreciable increased chance at greater life satisfaction and happiness (along with myriad mediating states such as greater hope, optimism and social support), (2) an increased chance at a longer life, (3) an increased probability of exercising certain civic virtues, but also (4) the opportunity cost of time spent in religious activities, (5) the possible loss of a sense of being one's own master and (6) possible disruption to one's personal relationships. Finally, if the wagerer in question would be making greater efforts at moral excellence on the strategy of committing to God than on the alternative, then the benefits and costs of these extra efforts should also be included in outcome WN (3b and 6b).

	Christianity is true	Naturalism is true
Commit to God	Outcome WC 1. Maximize chance at eternal life 2. Bring joy to God and others 3. Express gratitude to God 4. More likely to benefit from divine aid 5. More likely to be aware of God's love in this life 6. More likely to help others attain salvation PLUS: This-worldly costs and benefits of outcome 2	Outcome WN 1. Increased chance of greater life satisfaction and happiness 2. Increased chance of a longer life 3. Increased chance of exercising certain civic virtues [3b. Benefits of extra efforts at moral excellence, if applicable] minus costs: 4. Opportunity cost of lost time 5. Possible loss of a sense of control over one's life 6. Possible disruption in one's personal relationships [6b. Costs of extra efforts at moral excellence, if applicable]
Refrain from committing to God	Outcome ~WC	Outcome ~WN

Figure 2.3

OUTCOMES ~WC AND ~WN

We can now draw the basic presentation of the wager to a close. Outcome ~WC is the flip side of outcome WC. That is, since maximizing one's chance of eternal life was a benefit of committing to God if he does exist, we should include minimizing one's chance of eternal life as a cost of not committing to God if he does exist. Relative to the strategy of committing to God, one reduces the probability that one will enjoy eternal life by not committing to God, supposing that Christianity is true. Each of the six benefits we listed in our discussion of outcome WC is not present in outcome ~WC. So, all in all, we should include in outcome ~WC a minimized chance of gaining eternal life, the bringing of sadness (or something analogous) to God and those in heaven, a failure to express gratitude to God, a lower receptivity to God's help in this life, a lower awareness of God's love throughout the course of one's earthly life and a lower chance of being a help to others in their journey to God.

In outcome ~WC, we should also add two additional items. The first is the regret one would feel on realizing, after death, that one has in a very important way misspent one's earthly life. The second concerns the possibility that if you don't commit to God, you may unwittingly make something else in your life a god substitute. You may find yourself trying, deep down and half-consciously, to find ultimate meaning in something that simply can't deliver the goods. Drawing on Søren Kierkegaard, Tim Keller expresses this point as follows:

- If you center your life and identity on your spouse or partner, you will be emotionally dependent, jealous and controlling. The other person's problems will be overwhelming to you.

- If you center your life and identity on your family and children, you will try to live your life through your children until they resent you or have no self of their own. At worst, you may abuse them when they displease you.

- If you center your life and identity on your work and career, you will be a driven workaholic and a boring, shallow person. At worst you will lose family and friends and, if your career goes poorly, develop deep depression.

- If you center your life on money and possessions, you'll be eaten up by worry or jealousy about money. You'll be willing to do unethical things to maintain your lifestyle, which will eventually blow up your life.

- If you center your life and identity on pleasure, gratification and comfort, you will find yourself getting addicted to something. You will become chained to the "escape strategies" by which you avoid the hardness of life.

- If you center your life and identity on relationships and approval, you will be constantly overly hurt by criticism and thus always losing friends.[28]

Are these exceptionless generalizations, laws of nature that apply to everyone? By no means. But there is a real risk here that's worth including in one's deliberations.

Moving on, outcome ~WN (don't commit and there is no God) is the flip side of outcome WN (commit but there is no God). For each cost one would incur by committing to God, we should consider the benefit that one would get by not incurring that cost because one did not commit to God. If God does not exist, and one has refrained from committing to God, one would have had extra time available for other activities, and possibly a greater sense of being in control of one's own life and reduced disruption to one's relationships (because of changes one never had to make). These are positives in outcome ~WN. As negatives we should include a slightly lower chance of greater life satisfaction, a lower chance of a longer life and so on. Plus, for any extra effort at morality that one wouldn't be exerting, there would be the consequent pleasures of moral laxity and the costs of vice. Thus we can summarize with the following matrix:

	Christianity is true	Naturalism is true
Commit to God	Outcome WC 1. Maximize chance of eternal life 2. Bring joy to God and others 3. Express gratitude to God 4. More likely to benefit from divine aid in this life 5. More likely to be aware of God's love in this life 6. More likely to help others attain salvation PLUS: This-worldly costs and benefits of Outcome WN	Outcome WN 1. Increased chance of greater life satisfaction and happiness 2. Increased chance of a longer life 3. Increased chance of exercising certain civic virtues [3b. Benefits of extra efforts at moral excellence, if applicable] **minus costs:** 4. Opportunity cost of lost time 5. Possible loss of a sense of control over one's life 6. Possible disruption in one's personal relationships [6b. Costs of extra efforts at moral excellence, if applicable]
Refrain from committing to God	Outcome ~WC 1. Minimize chance of eternal life 2. Bring sadness to God and others 3. Fail to express gratitude to God 4. Less likely to benefit from divine aid in this life 5. Less likely to be aware of God's love in this life 6. Less likely to help others attain salvation 7. Regret over having misspent earthly life 8. Increased chance of searching for ultimate meaning in the wrong place PLUS: This-worldly costs and benefits of Outcome ~WN	Outcome ~WN 1. Extra time not lost in religious activities 2. Possible increased sense of control over one's life 3. No disruption in relationships caused by changes involved in a serious religious commitment [3b. Benefits of decreased effort at moral excellence, if applicable] **minus costs:** 4. Increased chance of lower life satisfaction 5. Increased chance of a shorter life 6. Decreased chance of exercising certain civic virtues [6b. Costs of decreased effort at moral excellence, if applicable]

Figure 2.4

Finishing the Argument

To assess the rationality of committing to God using the decision matrix we've constructed, the decision maker needs to assess the value of all four outcomes. Clearly outcome WC is much more valuable than outcome ~WC. But what about the comparison between outcome WN and outcome ~WN? It seems to me that, for people in all but the most unusual circumstances, we can say this: outcome WN is either better than outcome ~WN, roughly equal or, if worse, then only worse by a small amount. If earthly life is the only life there is, then an increased chance at a longer and happier life is a huge benefit. True, the person who has committed to God spends a portion of her time engaging in religious activity, but if one finds the right church community, the time spent with that community can be fulfilling and meaningful. Personal prayer can be a burden, but it can also bring peace. Recent work in neuroscience indicates that prayer and meditation affect the brain in significant positive ways. Brain researcher Andrew Newberg and colleague Mark Waldman summarize: "religious and spiritual contemplation changes your brain in a profoundly different way [than other types of thinking or concentrating] because it strengthens a unique neural circuit that specifically enhances social awareness and empathy while subduing destructive feelings and emotions."[29]

What about the costs of moral excellence? We should all be striving for moral excellence anyway, so the costs of moral excellence shouldn't stand as a reason to refrain from committing to God. And once one is striving for moral excellence, there is a sense in which one is already not one's own master; the person striving for virtue recognizes that he is subject to its demands. Nor need this feel like a constraint; if we want to be good people, we *desire* to do what is right, even if at times we experience contrary desires warring within ourselves.

Now, if you believe that outcome WN is at least as valuable as outcome ~WN for you, then it is rational for you to commit to God. For to agree that outcome WN is at least as valuable as outcome ~WN is to think that if it turns out (unbeknownst to you) that God does not exist, then you're still no worse off for having committed to God than you would have been if you hadn't committed to God. And of course if God *does* exist, it's clearly much better to commit to God than not to. That is, outcome WC is much more valuable than outcome ~WC. Remember the definition of weak dominance? One strategy weakly dominates another when it yields a better outcome on at least one possible state of the world, and never a worse outcome. Thus for the person who thinks outcome WN is no worse than outcome ~WN, *committing to God* weakly dominates *not committing to God*.[30] It might be (a lot) better, and it's definitely not worse.

But even if one thinks the religious person misses out, all things considered, if naturalism is true (that is, even if one thinks that outcome ~WN is better than outcome WN), it's still rational to commit to God, so long as the difference between outcome ~WN and outcome WN is small, and the probability of Christianity is 50 percent or more. For if Christianity has a 50 percent or higher probability of being true, it would be exceedingly unwise to risk the loss of the goods involved in outcome WC merely for the *chance* of the small gain in benefit of outcome ~WN over outcome WN.

To see the logic here, imagine again that a trusted third party flips a coin but doesn't say whether it lands heads or tails. This time a wealthy person credibly makes you this offer: if you choose to play and it's heads, then she'll give you one million dollars, while she'll give you twenty-five dollars if it's tails and you've chosen to play. If you choose to pass and it's heads, no money will be exchanged, but if you choose to pass and it's tails, she'll give you one hundred dollars.

	Heads		Tails	
Play	Outcome 1	$1,000,000	Outcome 2	$25
Pass	Outcome 3	$0	Outcome 4	$100

Figure 2.5

In this situation, outcome 1 is much greater than outcome 3, and outcome 2 is a small amount less than outcome 4. Imagine a person saying he wanted to pass on such an offer on the grounds that he didn't want to risk losing the seventy-five-dollar difference between outcome 2 and outcome 4. What about the risk of losing one million dollars?

It is possible to think of a situation in which you *could* rationally pass on the offer here. If you happened to have good reason to believe that the coin was really a trick coin, and the probability of heads was extremely low, then you might rationally pass, especially if you were desperate for a small amount of money. But that sort of reasoning doesn't apply in the case of Christianity, as I'll try to show in part two, where I'll argue that there is good evidence for the truth of Christianity and that there is *at least* a 50 percent chance that Christianity is true. This is like showing the coin is either a fair coin or even biased in favor of heads.

For now—ignoring the arguments of part two—we can conclude this much from our reflection on the wager: because outcome WC is so much greater than outcome ~WC, and outcome WN is either better, equal or only a small amount worse than outcome ~WN, the strategy of committing to God weakly dominates (or close enough) the strategy of not committing to God. And for the person who thinks Christianity is at least as likely as not, this weak-dominance-or-close-enough is sufficient to make it entirely reasonable to commit to God. Indeed, it would be unreasonable for such a person not to commit. If Christianity is true, so much is gained, while if naturalism is true, not much is lost.

3

OBJECTIONS TO THE WAGER

Moral Reservations and the Cost of Commitment

MY OVERALL PROJECT IN THIS BOOK is to show that Christian commitment is rational, and not just in the sense that it is possible to be a Christian without being irrational but in the stronger sense that natural human reasoning reveals that we should commit to living a Christian life. I'm attempting to show this by breaking down the overall project into two tasks: first, using the wager, show that Christian commitment is rational *provided that* the truth of Christianity is at least as likely as not; second, using the arguments of part two, show that Christianity is indeed at least as likely as not. In part three I'll then try to convey the beauty and value of a committed Christian life by telling the stories of some exemplary Christian believers. If all three of these tasks are accomplished, then the rationality of Christian commitment will have been established and its desirability will have been illustrated. But let's not be hasty. Was the argument of chapter two successful? A number of objections have been made against Pascal's original arguments. Do any of these objections spell trouble for the updated formulation of the wager just given? Before proceeding to the arguments of part two, let's examine the wager with a critical eye.

One possible reaction to Pascal's original argument is moral disapproval: religious devotion based on a calculation of costs and benefits seems self-centered and mercenary, as morally repugnant as it is unworthy of God if he does exist. In this spirit, Richard Dawkins asks whether God might not respect a courageous skeptic on account of his honest search for truth "far more than he would respect Pascal for his cowardly bet-hedging."[1] As William James had remarked many years before: "We feel that a faith . . . adopted willfully after such a mechanical calculation would lack the inner soul of faith's reality, and if we were ourselves in the place of the Deity, we should probably take particular pleasure in cutting off believers of this pattern from their infinite reward."[2] I'll call the contention that Pascalian wagering is excessively self-interested and therefore immoral the "avarice objection."

To assess the avarice objection, it's worthwhile to note that different versions of the wager have been advanced by different thinkers. The avarice objection hits hardest against a version of the wager that makes one's own self-interest the sole motivating factor. But the wagerer need not be motivated merely or even mainly by self-interest. One might choose to commit to God largely because one wants to avoid the risk of disappointing God, or because one fervently desires to grow morally and therefore wants to live a life maximally open to the possibility of divine aid, or even because one might well have a moral duty to live a devout life. If one judges that there is a good chance Christianity is true, it's plausible to think that one has a moral duty to commit to living a Christian life, or at least a duty to look into it very seriously. If Christian doctrine is true, then we suffer from a spiritual cancer that, if left untreated, will result in our eternal separation from God. We have a duty to seek a remedy. And if Christianity is true, then we have a duty to love God, who has given us everything good that we have, and we have been called by God himself to live a deeply religious life. One could easily be motivated to commit to God not because of self-interest but because of concern for others or out of respect for a possible moral duty.

Still, suppose that an agnostic inquirer chose to commit to God mainly in order to maximize his own chance at eternal life. What precisely is wrong with this? Is it wrong to want to be happy? To be motivated by the goal of happiness is not in itself morally problematic. Is there perhaps something wrong with the way the wagerer goes about trying to reach this goal, with the actions he takes to attain it? Considering that the central action is *seeking a relationship with God*, and that this involves activities like reading the Bible, going to church and praying, it's hard to think there are any grounds for moral censure here. So the self-interested wagerer desires a good goal, and pursues it via actions that are themselves morally unobjectionable. Charges of selfishness are apt in situations where one focuses on one's own well-being in a way which involves neglect of others. But there's no reason the wagerer, even the self-interested wagerer, need be guilty of that. It is possible to love both oneself and others.

It might be thought that what is wrong with the wager is that the wagerer treats God as a mere means and adopts religious practices as so many tools to manipulate God. This would indeed be wrong. But the wagerer need not have this attitude. Rather than thinking of God as a means to the end of enjoying a heavenly "candy land," the Christian should view relationship with God as the ultimate goal. Religious practices are best conceived as ways of building that relationship or cultivating dispositions God would want us to have.

What of the charge that if God does exist, he won't be pleased by a wagerer motivated by self-interest? Jesus, for one, seems to disagree. The parable of the prodigal son (Lk 15:11-32) tells of a young man who asks his father to give him his inheritance at once, rather than at his father's death. The father acquiesces. The son abandons the family, travels to a distant land and squanders his money on prostitutes and revelry. Eventually he is reduced to extreme poverty and decides to return home. What motivates him to return? "But when he came to himself he said, 'How many of my father's hired hands have bread enough and to spare, but here I am dying of hunger! I will get up and go to my father'" (Lk 15:17-18). A natural reading of the story is that the son returns not primarily because of great repentance at his shameful behavior but first of all because he is hungry. Plain and simple. And yet the father welcomes him back with open arms.

There is, though, a valid and important insight at the core of the avarice objection: it is better to love God because of his goodness than to serve him out of fear or self-interest. Still, we all have to start somewhere. Recall that the Pascalian argument we're considering is addressed to someone who doesn't have a firm belief in God or who is wavering. If you're in that position, you have two options: either commit to God, or don't. And surely you're more likely to end up with the right sort of attitude toward God if you take the first option. An initial commitment to God based on considerations of self-interest could be an initial step on a journey to real faith and a purer love of God.

The avarice objection isn't particularly persuasive, then. But other, more powerful objections have been made against the wager. In this chapter and the next I'll examine the four strongest: First, committing to God on the basis of Pascal's wager involves a morally problematic attitude about the importance of truth. Second, the cost of living a seriously religious life is simply too high. Third, the fact that there are many possibly true religions invalidates Pascal's wager. And fourth, considerations from within Christianity itself raise trouble for the wager.

RESPECT FOR THE TRUTH

Suppose I offered you $10,000 if you would form the belief that the first person to set foot on Australia was left-handed. Besides thinking I'm strange, you might have two thoughts. First, it's just not possible to form a belief for which there is no good evidence. Second, even it were possible, it would be . . . seedy, somehow. Like letting someone pay you to go out to dinner with them. Both these criticisms are occasionally directed at Pascal's wager. Thus Sam Harris: "But the greatest problem with the wager—and it is a problem that infects religious thinking generally—is its suggestion that a rational person can knowingly will himself to believe a proposition for which he has no evidence."[3] And Antony Flew: "Deliberately to set about persuading yourself of the truth of a conclusion which is not warranted by the available evidence is flatly to reject . . . a principle fundamental to personal and intellectual integrity."[4] The charge, then, is that the wager asks the impossible, or the immoral, by asking the wagerer to voluntarily form a belief in the absence of good evidence.

Upon inspection, though, it's apparent that these objections don't precisely apply to the Pascalian argument presented in the previous chapter. For in that argument, the strategy suggested was not to form a belief that God exists or to deliberately try to form a belief that God exists but to take a certain action—to seek a relationship with God. So neither Harris's claim (that it is impossible to voluntarily form a belief in the absence of good evidence) nor Flew's (that it is wrong to do so) are directly relevant to the wager we are now considering.

Still, at a minimum the strategy of committing to God will include being open to theistic belief if it comes; it will probably also include some efforts at cultivating belief, for example, prayers for faith. And here there may be cause for concern. The worry is that because committing to God will involve some efforts at cultivating belief, the person who takes the wager will have to suppress his own critical mind and will therefore face the risk of self-deception. The late Oxford philosopher J. L. Mackie argues that taking Pascal's advice amounts to "playing tricks on oneself that are found by experience to work upon people's passions and to give rise to belief in non-rational ways," and that to do this "is to do violence to one's reason and understanding."[5]

I have a good deal of sympathy for Mackie's view here. If one honestly thought that the probability of Christianity's being true was, say, 1 percent, then it would be wrong to deliberately attempt to make oneself believe that Christianity is true. It just seems wrong to try to make yourself believe something you think is almost certainly false. We should love the truth more than that. But things aren't so clear in a situation where one thinks the evidence for an important claim is roughly balanced, or better yet where the evidence is in favor of the claim, even if not airtight. Likewise, some methods one might use to try to acquire a belief are more questionable than others. It would be one thing to subject oneself to subliminal messages or electro-shock therapy, and quite another to simply ask God to give oneself awareness of his existence, or more generally to put oneself in a situation where one might acquire new evidence for a belief. The strategy of committing to God should only include an effort to cultivate belief to this extent: one should ask God for faith, look at the evidence that is available and search for more, conduct one's life appropriately, and resist nonrational or emotional impulses to doubt or distance oneself from God. Nothing here requires the suppression of one's reason or the intention to deliberately acquire a belief, come what may.

That being said, it remains the case that the agnostic who embarks on a religious life will be taking a course of action that significantly raises the probability that she will one day form a belief in God. What if one ends up coming to believe simply for psychological reasons? According to a well-known psychological experiment, the act of choosing one consumer product rather than another seems to cause one to value the product chosen more highly than one valued it before choosing it and causes one to value the product not chosen less highly than one valued it before choosing it.[6] Suppose you're going to buy a computer and after some deliberation you end up buying a Mac rather than a PC. It's likely that *simply because* you've chosen the Mac you'll tend to value it more than you did before, perhaps to reduce a sense of discomfort about losing the good features of the PC, or to justify your own choice to yourself, or merely because you're regularly reminded of the Mac's good features through daily use.

And maybe what goes for choosing consumer products goes for choosing religions, too—aligning oneself with a particular belief, as the wagerer does with Christianity, may make one more likely to believe it, but not for reasons connected with evidence or truth. The agnostic contemplating the wager must take into account the fact that, by committing to God, she risks becoming ensnared in an illusion. Should this risk dissuade the agnostic contemplating a commitment to Christianity?

To address this question, consider an analogy. Suppose your brother has gone missing. He was backpacking in a foreign country, one lacking the rule of law and in a state of some turmoil. It's been a year now, and no one has heard from him. Then one day you receive a letter. It purports to be from your brother but is typed and so short that you can't tell one way or the other whether it is really from him. The letter states that he has been taken captive by a militant rebel group, who are using him for his knowledge of computer programming. They won't let him go but will let him receive letters. They won't let him write back. But he begs you to write with news from home, every week if possible. Suppose you judge that it's about as likely as not that this letter is really from him and that he really would be helped by your letters. What should you do? If you do write to him week after week, you may become so emotionally invested that you will end up believing that he's getting the letters and that they're helping him to cope. But that might be false. By writing, you face some risk that you will become ensnared in an illusion. Nonetheless, I think we can see that it wouldn't be wrong to write the letters. Indeed, writing the letters clearly seems like the right thing to do.

Of course, this example is in many way disanalogous to the situation of the would-be wagerer. But the point is just this: it's not always wrong to take a course of action that may result in the acquisition of a false belief. And once we put it that way, it's an obvious truth. When you so much as ask a stranger for directions, you risk forming a false belief. Now, in certain circumstances it may be wrong to expose oneself to the risk of false belief. But the case of wagering for God doesn't seem to be one of them. The decision matrix we examined in chapter two suggests that committing to God is the smart move, at least for the person who thinks Christianity is as likely as not. And for such a person both the decision to commit to God and the failure to make that decision carry risks. There is the risk of false belief on one side, and the risk of missing out on relationship with God on the other.

A final point on the question of respect for truth: Pascal's suggestion is that if you seek God you may gradually come to believe. And this won't necessarily be irrational. It may well be that because you are seeking God you will be given evidence. Perhaps God will give you an intuitive awareness of his presence, at least some of the time. Or perhaps you will have some other sort of religious experience that provides evidence for God. Or maybe you will simply come to see that there are good arguments for the existence of God and the truth of Christianity, arguments that you either did not know before or did not fully appreciate before. So even your love for truth might give you a reason to seek God—maybe you have to seek in order to get the evidence needed to know the truth.[7]

Is the Cost of a Devout Life Too High?

If I had to guess, I would suspect that for most people who find Christianity credible but still hold back from a serious commitment, the real reason is the feeling that the cost of committing to God is just too high. I argued in chapter two that even if there is no God, one loses little by committing to Christianity, all things considered. But is that really right? For there are indeed circumstances in which a person would lose much by committing to Christianity if God does not exist. Suppose one were the sole breadwinner in a family of eight, living in a country where the practice of Christianity carried a high risk of severe persecution, imprisonment or martyrdom. Or, to take a very different situation, imagine that one lived in a country with religious freedom but that one's conversion to Christianity would cause serious division within one's family or with one's spouse. No doubt there are circumstances in which a commitment to Christianity would have major negative consequences. Does the wager still apply in such a situation?

To address this question, we can begin by distinguishing three sorts of cases. First, some people are in situations in which Christian commitment will bring an appreciable risk of truly extreme costs—they probably comprise a relatively small proportion of the world's population, though the absolute number of such people may be large. Second, some people are in situations in which Christian commitment will bring an appreciable risk of major but not catastrophic consequences. And finally, there are many people (the majority in countries with religious freedom, I would argue) for whom Christian commitment will not bring major negative consequences all things considered, even if Christianity is in fact false. Let's consider these last two cases first.

How should a person living in typical circumstances in a country with religious freedom evaluate the costs and benefits of Christian commitment? That is, how should such a person evaluate outcome WN (you commit to God but in fact there is no God) and outcome ~WN (you don't commit to God and there is no God)? An initial thought is that outcome WN is very bad indeed, because if one commits one's life to God but God does not exist, then one is predicating one's entire life on a lie. This is indeed a real risk, but as noted above a risk just as serious comes with *not* committing to God: if one refrains from committing to God but God *does* exist, then one has missed out on a loving relationship with God in this life and perhaps in eternity. And because one is more likely to have and maintain a firm belief in God if one commits rather than not, it also follows that, if one refrains from commitment but God does exist, then one faces a much greater risk of missing out on the most important truth there is. The risk of being wrong and living a lie, on the one hand, and the risk of missing out on a loving relationship with God and not believing the most important truth, on the other, cancel each other out, so to speak. So the risk of being wrong isn't by itself a good reason to avoid religious commitment.

Perhaps it will be useful to consider the question from the point of view of someone who is not yet living a devout Christian life but is considering making a commitment to do so. It's easy to focus on the possible negatives. Will certain friends or family members disapprove? Will my relationships with those I am close to be jeopardized? Will I fit in within a church or religious community? How will I find the time for prayer and religious services?

Will others whose opinions I respect think me superstitious, irrational or untrue to my former self? Will I be called by God to a life I do not desire? Will I be called to acts of service or sacrifice that are too difficult?

These questions are worth asking. But it's important not to be guided here merely by fear. Conversion to Christianity *can* strain certain relationships. But when the convert lives out the Christian faith well, friends and family of goodwill tend to realize that the relationship can still flourish. Who can object if, instead of turning into the judgmental, narrow-minded religious fanatic who was anticipated, the convert is the same person as before, or, even better, if the convert becomes more kind, compassionate, forgiving, humble and so forth?

As for the worry that the sacrifices required by a religious life will leave one with a joyless existence, it should be kept in mind that human beings are not terribly good at predicting what will make them happy. Scholars who study our ability to predict our future emotional states, such as Harvard's Daniel Gilbert and the University of Virginia's Timothy Wilson, call their field "affective forecasting." Their work has uncovered a number of characteristic errors and biases that hinder our ability to judge accurately how we will react to a given event or change. Most relevant to the argument at hand: people tend to underestimate their ability to cope with negative events and so overestimate the duration of negative feelings they will experience because of such events.[8] Summarizing, Gilbert and colleagues write: "In our studies, students, professors, voters, newspaper readers, test takers, and job seekers overestimated the duration of their affective reactions to romantic disappointments, career difficulties, political defeats, distressing news, clinical devaluations, and personal rejections."[9] This suggests that as one considers the possible negatives attached to religious commitment, one should correct for the natural human bias to overestimate the impact of difficulties. Instead of relying on one's gut reaction, perhaps it's better to look to deeply religious people themselves. Are they happy? And if they are, why couldn't I be?

Such considerations may provide many people with sufficient reason to place themselves in the third category mentioned above, the category of people for whom a commitment to God won't bring major negatives overall. Now let us turn to the second category, the case of someone for whom outcome WN *is* significantly worse than outcome ~WN, though not cata-strophically worse. Suppose you place yourself in this category and thus think that if you commit to Christianity and God doesn't exist you will have lost a lot. The basic argument of chapter two won't then be convincing to you, since you won't agree with the premise that outcome WN is better, equally valuable or at least not much worse than outcome ~WN.

The basic argument was just that, however—a *basic* argument, suitable for getting the main ideas on the table. When we look deeper, there is still sufficient reason to commit to living a Christian life, so long as you think Christianity has an epistemic probability of at least one-half. If Christianity is at least as likely as not, then, while committing to God has a chance (50 percent or less) of leading to major and unredressed negatives, refraining from committing to God has a chance (50 percent or higher) of bringing even worse negatives: the negatives of turning your back on God, increasing your chance of eternal separation from God, being less helpful to others in reaching their ultimate happiness and so on.

A thought experiment will be helpful here—but it will take some work. Imagine a situation in which there is in fact no God and no afterlife, but in which you, not knowing these things, have made a serious commitment to live a devout Christian life. How much worse off would *you* be for having made that commitment? Call to mind all the costs of your religious commitment, supposing that there is no God.

Let's refer to those costs as the net costs of mistaken religious commitment, for you. I include the word *mistaken* because we are assessing the possible situation in which you commit to living a Christian life but Christianity is false. *Net* is a term used in accounting to talk about the amount of something after deductions or costs have been subtracted. So, for example, if you earn $100 but owe $25 in taxes, your net income is $75. Here I use the word *net* to highlight this point: the good that you would have lost by committing to Christianity (in a situation in which God does not exist) is equal to the value of outcome ~WN (the lower right-hand box of our decision matrix) *minus* the value of outcome WN (the upper right-hand box of our matrix). We are considering a person who thinks outcome ~WN is much more valuable than outcome WN. If we "subtract," so to speak, the value of outcome WN from the value of outcome ~WN, we get a measure of how much better outcome ~WN is and how much worse outcome WN is. So to think about the net costs of a mistaken religious commitment is to think about what you've lost by committing to God if God does not exist. Spend a moment and ask yourself, what are the net costs of a mistaken Christian commitment in your own case? I encourage the reader to put down this book and take a few minutes to ponder this question before proceeding.

Now to continue with the thought experiment: imagine that your best friend is dying of cancer.[10] The doctors say she only has a few days left to live. If for some reason you learned that your best friend would have a 50 percent chance of a miraculous cure if you committed to living a devout life, would you do it? Set aside concerns about how your friend's recovery could possibly be connected to your religious life—for the thought experiment we are simply imagining a situation in which you have good reason to believe that a religious commitment by you would increase your friend's chance of survival from around 0 percent all the way up to 50 percent.

Would you be willing to undergo a 50 percent risk of facing the net costs of mistaken religious commitment for the sake of a 50 percent shot at saving your best friend? If one answers yes to this question, then it seems that the costs of religion, high though they may be, are still deemed to be low enough that one is willing to face them for the sake of certain goods. To be more exact, consider this claim:

(1) It would be reasonable for me to undergo a 50 percent risk of suffering the net costs of mistaken religious commitment for the sake of having a 50 percent shot at saving the life of my best friend.

Those who agree to (1) should also agree that

(2) It is reasonable for me to undergo a 50 percent risk of suffering the net costs of mistaken religious commitment for the sake of having a 50 percent shot at any good that is as valuable or more valuable than saving the life of my best friend.

So now the question to ask is: is the net, total good that comes from committing to Christianity, if Christianity is true, as valuable or more valuable than saving the life of one's best friend? And here the answer is clearly "yes." In the context, by "saving the life of one's best friend," we really just mean "returning her to health so that she can live to a ripe old age." So we're talking about some additional dozens of years of life on earth. But if Christianity is true, the ultimate goal and highest good of human beings isn't just a happy life on earth; it's a loving, personal relationship with God (and others whom he has created) for eternity. By committing to Christianity, a person becomes empowered both to reach that goal and to help others reach it. As important as saving the earthly life of one's friend would be, helping that friend attain eternal salvation is not less important. All the more is it true that helping oneself and many others (including one's best friend) to attain salvation is at least as valuable as saving the earthly life of one's best friend. If Christianity is true, the net good that comes from committing to a devout life is not less valuable than the good of saving the earthly life of a loved one. But then it follows that those who agree to (1) and (2) should also agree to this:

> (3) It is reasonable for me to undergo a 50 percent risk of suffering the net costs of mistaken religious commitment for the sake of having a 50 percent shot at the net good that would come from committing to Christianity if Christianity is true.

In other words, even if you think you might lose a lot if Christianity is false, it's *still* rational to commit to living a Christian life (so long as you think the chance that Christianity is true is 50 percent or higher), because the net good that would come from a commitment, if Christianity is true, is so valuable.

I've just given an argument for (3) based on a comparison to a particular finite good (your best friend's earthly life). You don't have to agree with that argument to agree with (3), however. A different possible reason to agree with (3) is simply that, on careful consideration, one sees that the net good that would come from committing to Christianity if Christianity is true is much higher than the net cost of committing to Christianity if Christianity is false. If you accept (3) and you judge the probability of Christianity to be at least 50 percent, then it's rational for you to commit to Christianity and irrational not to, even if the costs of a devout life are very high.

Finally, let's turn to the unfortunate case of someone who faces a serious risk of *extreme* negative consequences if a commitment to God is made, that is, a person for whom conversion to Christianity would carry a high risk of serious physical harm or death. Now, in regions where a commitment to any given religion carries a high risk of martyrdom, it's likely that a person concerned for the human rights of all would almost necessarily find themselves in opposition to the perpetrators of such violence and thus would themselves faces serious risks of harm regardless of religious affiliation. So in such regions the risk of grievous harm may be present regardless of whether one commits to God. Still, what of the case where commitment to Christianity brings a high risk of martyrdom, whereas lack of such commitment really does leave one safe?

I grant that the force of the wager is less evident in such cases. But even so, it is far from obvious that the wager fails. Indeed, there is good reason to think that it still succeeds. For one must balance the negative of a life needlessly cut short by martyrdom (if Christianity is false) with all the negatives of ignoring God (if Christianity is true).[11] If Christianity is at least as likely as not, then, while committing to God brings a risk (50 percent or less) of leading to needless extreme negatives, not committing to God brings an even higher risk (50 percent or more) of something worse: lowering one's chances of eternal salvation, rejecting God, being less helpful to others in the most important way possible and so forth. Since it's rational to choose to face a high risk of a great cost in order to avoid a higher risk of a greater cost, it's still rational for the one at risk of martyrdom to take the wager, so long as he or she judges, after careful consideration, that the epistemic probability of Christianity is 50 percent or higher.

In this chapter we've examined the avarice objection, the objection that taking the wager is immoral because it disregards the importance of evidence and truth, and the objection that the cost of Christian commitment is simply too high. But all along I've been assuming that Christianity and naturalism are the only two games in town. What about other religions?

4

MORE OBJECTIONS TO THE WAGER

Other Religions and Christianity

SO FAR I HAVE IGNORED RELIGIONS other than Christianity for the purpose of presenting clearly the basic idea behind the wager. Now it's time to face this issue head-on. In chapter two I argued that for the person who judges Christianity to be at least as likely as not, it is rational to commit to living a devout Christian life, because doing so weakly dominates (or close enough) not doing so. But as we'll soon see, this conclusion no longer holds once we've taken into account the fact that there are other religions that also promise eternal life. Indeed, there are some other religions that promise infinite torment for those who reject them. According to the Qur'an, "Those who disbelieve among the People of the Book [this is taken to include Jews and Christians] and the idolaters will have the Fire of Hell, there to remain. They are the worst of creation."[1] On one interpretation, this implies that a person who has learned of Islam and its teachings but rejects it will be consigned to an eternal hell.

Just for the sake of getting a solid understanding of the challenge different religions offer to the basic argument of chapter two, let's for the moment pretend that Islam is the only rival religion to Christianity, and let's consider only a version of Islam that accepts the interpretation above that those who have rejected Islam will go to hell. Given all this, our decision matrix should not be the 2x2 matrix we examined in chapter two but the following 3x3 matrix:

	Christianity is true	Islam is true	Naturalism is true
Commit to God in a Christian way	Outcome 1	Outcome 2	Outcome 3
Commit to God in a Muslim way	Outcome 4	Outcome 5	Outcome 6
Do neither	Outcome 7	Outcome 8	Outcome 9

Figure 4.1

To further zero in on the issue, let's ignore the subtleties of previous chapters and fill in the valuations of the outcomes as follows:

	Christianity is true	Islam is true	Naturalism is true
Commit to God in a Christian way	Outcome 1 Higher chance of eternal happiness	Outcome 2 Eternal misery	Outcome 3 Finite this-worldly goods
Commit to God in a Muslim way	Outcome 4 Lower chance of eternal happiness	Outcome 5 Higher chance of eternal happiness	Outcome 6 Finite this-worldly goods
Do neither	Outcome 7 Lower chance of eternal happiness	Outcome 8 Eternal misery	Outcome 9 Finite this-worldly goods

Figure 4.2

Clearly we could do a better job of filling in the outcomes,[2] but for now the point is just to see how the possibility of Islam undermines the argument from chapter two. Before, with the 2x2 matrix of chapter two, I could argue that committing to God in a Christian way won't yield much of a loss, no matter which state of the world turns out to be right. But that's incorrect. For if the world is as Islam describes it, and I commit to God in a Christian way, then I suffer eternal misery (on the version of Islam now under consideration). The point is that once we've added other religions into the mix, committing to God in a Christian way no longer weakly dominates (or even close) all the other possible strategies. If Islam is true, one loses greatly by being Christian. And the same conclusion will hold if we substitute for Islam any other religion promising eternal misery for Christians, or even if we take into account any other religion that teaches that the chance of gaining eternal happiness is significantly lower for those who commit to Christianity than for those who take some other course of action.

In academic literature on Pascal's wager this line of reasoning is called the "many gods objection," and it's taken by some to be the most serious objection to the wager. In fact, however, it's easy enough to adapt the basic argument of chapter two so that it is immune to the many gods objection. Nothing in the objection so far challenges the conclusion that it is better to commit to God in a Christian way than to not be religious at all. If the conclusions of chapter two were correct, then committing to God in a Christian way still weakly dominates (or close enough) the strategy of not committing to any religion. (To see this, compare outcome 1 to outcome 7, outcome 2 to outcome 8, and outcome 3 to outcome 9, in the 3x3 matrix above.) All the objection has shown is that the reasoning of previous chapters gives us no way to choose between Islam and Christianity. That's true enough. But it hardly follows that there *is* no way to choose between Islam and Christianity. The way is clear: practice the religion that seems to you, on careful examination and reflection, to be most likely to be true. This policy reflects a proper love for the truth, and it is the policy that maximizes one's chance at eternal happiness with God.[3]

Let me elaborate on this solution to the many gods objection. Suppose our eccentric billionaire from chapter one appeared at your door and gave you a choice between two games of chance to play. Game A is for him to use a computer to randomly select a natural number (1, 2, 3 and so on) and then to give you $1 million if the number selected is even. Game B is for him to use a computer to randomly select a natural number and then to give you $1 million if the number selected is evenly divisible by ten. Which game would you pick?

The smart move is of course game A, since it gives you a 50 percent chance of winning, while game B only gives you a 10 percent chance of winning. Next, would your preference for game A over game B change if, instead of the eccentric billionaire offering you a chance at one million dollars, it was God offering you a chance at eternal happiness? The fact that eternal happiness is so much more valuable doesn't change anything because it's rational to maximize one's shot at something one cares about. Of course this is an outlandish example, but the point remains: even when we're considering incomparably valuable outcomes like eternal life, one's decision making should still be informed by some such principle as "other things being equal, take the action that is most likely to result in the desired outcome." This is a very good reason to practice the religion that seems to you most likely to be true.

Another very good reason, as mentioned above, is that we should care about the truth. If one thinks that the probability of Christianity is above 50 percent and the probability of Islam is quite low, then one's love for the truth and one's reasonable fear of being ensnared in a deception gives one an excellent reason to practice Christianity rather than Islam.

So the many gods objection poses no difficulty for the individual who thinks that both (a) Christianity is considerably more credible than any other religion and (b) the truth of Christianity is more probable than not. For such a person, committing to God in a Christian way is more reasonable than not committing to God in any way (for the reasons discussed in chapters two and three), and committing to God in a Christian way is more reasonable than committing to God via some other religion (for the two reasons mentioned above). Thus for such a person committing to God in a Christian way is more reasonable than each of the other available courses of action.

On what basis could one confidently conclude that one religion is considerably more credible than another? In brief: on the basis of the available evidence. Although it is relatively uncommon to submit the panoply of religions to rational criticism and scrutiny, it is something that the person interested in finding God should do. It is possible to consider available evidence and assess the credibility of Christianity, Islam, Hinduism, Scientology and so forth. Relevant questions to ask will include: Is the moral content of this religion consistent with the claim that the religion is revealed by God? (Or, in the case of nontheistic religions, is the moral content consistent with what one knows just from reason?) Does the religion speak convincingly to the human condition—can it explain both the heights and the depths of which humans are capable? Are there strong arguments (historical, scientific or philosophical) against the truth of this religion? If so, do proponents of the religion have convincing replies to such arguments? Is there positive evidence for the truth of this religion? While no one has the time to become an expert in all religions, it is possible to make some headway on such questions.

In part two I'll ask some of these questions with respect to Christianity. Due to length constraints, I won't take up a comparison between Christianity and other religions, but doing so won't be required for the aim of this book. For if the arguments of part two are successful, they will provide sufficient reason to place a 50 percent or higher level of confidence in Christianity. But one thing at a time . . . for now, suffice it to say that the many gods objection poses no difficulty for the wagerer who has made adequate investigation and comes away judging that the probability of Christianity is 50 percent or more and thinks Christianity is also considerably more likely than any of its religious rivals.[4]

IS THE WAGER UNCHRISTIAN?

Despite being an argument in support of Christianity, Pascal's wager is sometimes viewed as unchristian, that is, opposed in some way to the doctrines of Christianity itself. The common Christian belief that God should be loved for his own sake, for example, might be taken to imply that Pascalian wagering is wrong. But for reasons mentioned in chapter three, I think this rests on a misunderstanding. The goods that motivate the wagerer need not be limited to goods of self-interest. And even if initially the wagerer were motivated by self-interest, it's more likely that he or she will eventually develop a purer love for God if a commitment is made than if not.

On this point it's worth noting that the founder of Christianity was not adverse to mentioning the good things in store for those who follow him:

> Peter began to say to him, "Look, we have left everything and followed you."
> Jesus said, "Truly I tell you, there is no one who has left house or brothers or
> sisters or mother or father or children or fields, for my sake and for the sake
> of the good news, who will not receive a hundredfold now in this age—houses,
> brothers and sisters, mothers and children, and fields, with persecutions—
> and in the age to come eternal life." (Mk 10:28-30)

Jesus mentions both "this age" and "the age to come," and benefits during earthly life as well as in the afterlife. A Christian life requires transformation and sacrifice, and for some it involves real persecution, but this does not mean that the follower of Jesus will have nothing but loss on earth. Balanced against the trials are a number of benefits already enjoyed in this life, including the goods that come from personal relationships within the Christian community. The sense of the text quoted seems to be that, even taking into account the tribulations, those who sacrifice for the sake of Jesus come out ahead in this world as well as in the next. So the mere fact that the wager draws our attention to benefits doesn't make it unchristian. But there are other objections that can be made against the wager on the basis of certain interpretations of Christian doctrine. In the rest of this chapter, I'll consider three: the first concerns the interplay between God's grace and human free choice; the second focuses on predestination; and the third relates to Paul's statement that if there is no resurrection, Christians are of all human beings the most to be pitied (1 Cor 15:19).

GRACE AND FREE WILL

Who will be saved? Who will enjoy eternal communion with God in the next life? Numerous passages in the New Testament assert that whether a human being attains salvation depends on his or her actions, for example:

> For all of us must appear before the judgment seat of Christ, so that each may receive recompense for what has been done in the body, whether good or evil. (2 Cor 5:10)

> If you invoke as Father the one who judges all people impartially according to their deeds, live in reverent fear during the time of your exile. (1 Pet 1:17)

A natural conclusion to draw from such passages is that your eternal destiny depends at least in part on how you choose to act.[5] But other texts of Scripture seem to imply that salvation depends on God and not human beings, for example:

> No one can come to me unless drawn by the Father who sent me; and I will raise that person up on the last day. (Jn 6:44)

> Apart from me you can do nothing. (Jn 15:5)

> So it depends not on human will or exertion, but on God who shows mercy. (Rom 9:16)

The question of how these two sets of statements fit together has exercised Christian thinkers throughout the centuries. Some interpreters have tended to emphasize human free will at the risk of denying the necessity of God's gratuitous gift of grace, while others have tended to emphasize God's initiative at the risk of denying human freedom. Those in the latter group might object to the wager's fundamental assumption that a human being's choice to commit to God can raise the chances of that human being's salvation. This objection can be formulated as an argument in five steps:

(1) If Christianity is true, then one's salvation depends on God's will and is in no way within one's own control.

(2) If one's salvation depends on God's will and is in no way within one's own control, then it's false that one's choices can have an effect on whether one attains salvation.

(3) If it's false that one's choices can have an effect on whether one attains salvation, then the choice to commit to God can't raise the chance that one will enjoy eternal life with God.

(4) But a key premise of the wager was the claim that committing to God would raise the chance that one will enjoy eternal life with God.

(5) So, if Christianity is true, then a key premise of the wager is false.

In my view, this objection fails because premise (1) is false. While salvation does depend on God's will, it *also* depends on human will, because a human being can freely reject God's offer of salvation. And besides this, even those who would accept (1), like John Calvin, have a reason to deny premise (2).[6] I'll expand on each of these claims below.

Taking into account verses like John 15:5, Christian thinkers through the ages have denied that a human being can without God's grace perform an action that merits salvation. At the same time, early Christian thinkers up to the time of Augustine were nearly unanimous in holding that there is a key role for human responsibility when it comes to salvation. Thus Irenaeus of Lyon (c. 130–200) writes: "If . . . you give Him what is yours, that is, faith in Him, and obedience . . . you will be a perfect work of God. But if you do not believe Him, and run from His hand, the cause of the imperfection will be in you who did not obey, and not in Him who called you."[7] John Chrysostom (c. 347–407):

God never compels anyone by necessity and force, but He wills that all be saved, yet does not force anyone. . . . How then are not all saved if He wills all to be saved? Because not everyone's will follows His will. He compels no one. But even to Jerusalem He says: "Jerusalem, Jerusalem! How often would I have gathered your children together, but you were unwilling."[8]

And Jerome (died 420): "No one is saved without his own will (for we have free will)."[9]

From these and many other passages, we can conclude that the standard view of the early church was that[10]

(6) A human being's salvation depends in part on how that human being responds to God's assistance.

But early Christian writers also insisted that

(7) Human beings cannot do anything good without grace.[11]

What is difficult is to see how these two claims can both be true. The acceptance of God's offer of salvation is itself a good thing, which implies by (7) that humans cannot accept God's offer without first being moved by God's grace. But if God's grace is needed for human acceptance of God's call, then how can a person's salvation depend on that person, as (6) states? A possible answer is that, while God's grace is necessary for salvation, it is not enough all by itself—the human person must contribute something of his or her own. But what can the human person contribute of his or her own, if humans can perform no good act on their own? Augustine (354–430) struggled mightily with this puzzle and could see no way to resolve it.[12]

Yet an important advance in the understanding of free will, found already in the work of Thomas Aquinas, allows for a solution.[13] This advance is the realization that the human will doesn't have just two possible positions (willing and unwilling); it has three (willing for, willing against, and omitting an act of will).[14] It's one thing to positively choose in favor of something and another to positively choose against it, but it's a third thing to simply refrain from making a choice about it. Eleonore Stump explains:

The will's motion is thus analogous to bodily motion, on Aquinas's views. I can walk east or walk west, but I can also simply cease walking east; and my ceasing to walk east is not by itself an instance of my walking west. Furthermore,

I can move from walking east to ceasing to walk east without having to walk west in order to do so. Finally, my ceasing to walk east is not a special kind of walking; it is simply the absence of walking, an inactivity or quiescence in those particular bodily parts that function to produce walking.[15]

Simply refraining from walking east is analogous to simply refraining from willing a certain thing; refraining, then, is not strictly speaking an act but the absence of an act. It is sometimes within human power to either choose or refrain from choosing. Of course one can choose, positively, to not make a choice about some matter, but it's also possible to omit a choice C1 without any prior, positive choice C2 to omit C1.

This complication in the understanding of the will opens a way to see how (6) and (7) are compatible. God can inspire a good act of will in a human being, but it is within the human being's power to resist or omit resistance. Herein lies a place for human responsibility.[16] Omitting resistance to God's grace is within one's control, which allows for (6) to be true. But (7) is not contradicted because omitting resistance is not itself a good act, for two reasons. First, it is not an act at all but the absence of an act. And second, merely omitting resistance to God is not particularly good or meritorious. Although omitting resistance is better than resisting, what would be really good here would be to positively will to turn away from sin and toward God—this human beings can't do on their own. But to resist or refrain from resisting is within our power.

Because human beings have the ability to resist grace, there is at least one important way in which one's salvation is within one's control. Aquinas explains:

> Although one is not able to merit or summon divine grace by a motion of one's free choice, nevertheless one can hinder oneself from receiving it. . . . And since it is within the power of free choice to either impede the reception of divine grace or not to impede it, the blame charged to one who puts up an obstacle to the reception of grace is not undeserved. For insofar as it lies in him himself, God is prepared to give grace to all, for "he wills all human beings to be saved and to come to the knowledge of the truth," as is said in 1 Tim 2:4. But indeed, the only ones deprived of grace are those who place within themselves an obstacle to grace.[17]

Given the views of early Christian writers that salvation depends in part on a human being's free response to God, and the subsequent development of a coherent account showing how this need not lead to a denial of the human need for grace, we can conclude that there are good grounds within the Christian tradition to reject (1).

Even so, a person who accepts (1) and denies that one's salvation is in any way within one's own control is not compelled to accept the five-step objection to the wager above, because such a person may hold that (2) is false. This is because (2) ignores the possibility that one's choice to commit to God could be inspired by God. A person who thinks (as I do not) that salvation is ultimately outside of human control can accept the wager as a sound argument because she can understand the choice to commit to God in whatever way she understands other good choices relevant to salvation (like a choice to have faith in God). If one holds that sometimes a human being chooses, albeit under the determining influence of grace, to place saving faith in God, then one should grant the possibility that sometimes a human being chooses, albeit under the determining influence of grace, to seek God in the way recommended by the wager. But then, contrary to (2), the human being's choice could have an effect on whether he attains salvation, without salvation being within human control.

Predestination and the Wager

Philosopher Jeff Jordan relates a joke about an old Calvinist in colonial America who travels with a loaded gun. His good neighbor says to him, "Brother why do you travel with a gun? No harm can befall you unless the Lord decides it is your time and permits the Indian arrow to find its mark. Trust the Lord." After a long and awkward pause, the old Calvinist replies, "Aye, I do trust the Lord. The gun is just in case it is the Indian's time."[18] Our old Calvinist might view the wager with suspicion.

The doctrines of predestination and reprobation have been understood differently by different Christian thinkers. The predestined are those whom God has chosen, from eternity, to be saved, while the reprobate are those whom God has not so chosen. The crucial interpretive question has to do with the reasons for God's choice. Some have held that God, who sincerely wills the salvation of all, chooses the predestined because he foresees that they will freely accept his offer of salvation.[19] Others have held that God passes over the reprobate because he foresees that they will persistently reject his grace and then out of love predestines everyone else to eternal life (so that predestination to eternal life is not on the basis of foreseen merits, although it is responsive to something within the scope of a human being's free choice).[20] And still others have held that God chooses the eternal destiny of each person without any regard to their future actions—call this a doctrine of unconditional election.[21] I consider unconditional election to be in grave contradiction with the goodness of God, but nonetheless it has been held by many. It's therefore worth addressing an objection to the wager on its basis.

How exactly does unconditional election suggest a problem for the wager? Let's consider the perspective of a person—call him John—who accepts unconditional election or at least believes that *if* Christianity is true, then the doctrine of unconditional election is correct. John might then reason as follows:

(8) If Christianity is true, then my destiny is fixed from eternity by God's decree and therefore is ultimately outside my control.

(9) If my eternal destiny is ultimately outside my control, then it's false that I'll maximize my chance of salvation by committing to God (rather than not).

(10) Thus, if Christianity is true, it's false that I'll maximize my chance of salvation by committing to God (rather than not).

(11) But the wager argument relies on the claim that if Christianity is true, then one maximizes one's chance of eternal salvation by committing to God (rather than not).

(12) So the wager relies on a false premise.

For reasons given in the previous section, I believe (8) is false. But even if one accepts (8), (9) should be rejected. Suppose we asked John whether there are any acts that raise the epistemic probability a given person will be saved. Presumably, John will hold that there are many: having faith in Jesus, loving God, forgiving one's enemies, obeying the moral law—if it were known of one person that at the time of her death she was doing all these things, and it were known of another person that at the time of his death he was doing none of these things, then it would be reasonable to be more confident that the former person was among the predestined than that the latter person was. So even John should grant that the chance (in the sense of epistemic probability) of salvation is raised by having faith, loving God and so on. Even if John denies that such actions are ultimately within one's control, he should grant that they raise the probability that a person is among the predestined and thus raise the probability of salvation. And John should think the same thing about the action of committing to God. Even if John thinks his eternal destiny is outside his control, he should think that the epistemic probability of his eventual salvation is higher if he commits to God than if not, and so he should reject (9).

Perhaps the real problem, from John's point of view, is that so long as he retains his interpretation of predestination, he must hold that if Christianity is true he isn't in the driver's seat and can't by himself freely do anything to affect whether he commits to God. When confronted with the wager, John's attitude would have to be something like "Sure hope I commit to God," that is, "Sure hope God causes me to commit to God." But this need not undercut the wager, which concludes that committing to God is rational and should therefore be done. John can agree that it should be done. The proponent of unconditional election will hold that propositions like "I should have faith" are true, and whatever account he gives for the truth of those propositions can also be applied to the wager's ultimate conclusion that one should commit to God.

ST. PAUL AGAINST THE WAGER?

A crucial premise in the basic argument of chapter two was the claim that

(13) Even if naturalism is true, choosing to live a devout Christian life (rather than not so choosing) wouldn't make one much worse off, all things considered.

I argued in chapter three that for the person who disputes this claim, a modified Pascalian argument can still succeed. Even if one thought one would lose much by committing to Christianity if Christianity were false, one should still commit to a Christian life because the risk of loss associated with Christian commitment is more than outweighed by the risk of loss associated with refraining from Christian commitment. However, if (13) is true, the basic argument stands. And since it seems to me both that (13) *is* true for most people (those in typical circumstances), and that the basic argument, if successful, is somewhat more compelling than the modified argument, I want to further defend (13). More particularly, I want to defend (13) against a certain objection—an objection apparently found, of all places, in the Bible itself.

In his first letter to the Corinthians, Paul takes up a report that some among the Christian community in Corinth were denying that there is a bodily resurrection of the dead. Paul then gives an extended argument in support of the resurrection. In the course of that argument he makes a number of *reductio ad absurdum* arguments. In other words, he supports the resurrection by pointing out the difficulties and falsehoods that would follow if there were no bodily resurrection: "If there is no resurrection of the dead, then Christ has not been raised; and if Christ has not been raised, then our proclamation has been in vain and your faith has been in vain. . . . If for this life only we have hoped in Christ, we are of all people most to be pitied" (1 Cor 15:13-14, 19). In that last sentence Paul clearly seems to imply that if there is no afterlife, then Christians have lost much. And that clearly seems to imply that if naturalism is true, those who live a devout Christian life lose much. It seems that St. Paul, then, would reject (13) and would therefore reject the basic argument of chapter two.

A careful consideration of the context of Paul's remarks casts doubt on this objection, however. The first thing to note is that in the context of the early church, harsh persecution was a real risk. Later in the passage, Paul asks, "And why are we putting ourselves in danger every hour?" (1 Cor 15:30), that is, why do I risk constant danger for the sake of Jesus' message if there is no resurrection to hope for? When Thomas Aquinas comments on Paul's claim that Christians are the most to be pitied, he interprets Paul's reasoning as follows:

> If there is no resurrection of the dead, it follows that nothing good is had by human beings except in this life only. And if this is true, then those who experience much suffering and many tribulations in this life are more miserable than others. Since, therefore, the apostles and Christians suffer many tribulations, it follows that they are more miserable than other humans, who at least enjoy the goods of this world.[22]

Paul, his fellow missionaries, the apostles and no doubt many of the initial recipients of his letter to the Corinthians faced severe this-worldly costs because of their religious commitments. They are thus in circumstances atypical for the average person living today in a country with religious freedom. If Paul and his original audience would have lost much because of their Christian commitments if naturalism is true, it doesn't necessarily follow that a given person today will lose much because of her Christian commitment if naturalism is true.

But there is a much more important way in which the objection we're considering goes wrong. It has to do with the alternative Paul has in mind when he writes the conditional statement "if there is no resurrection of the dead . . . we are of all people most to be pitied." If someone today began a sentence, "If the Allies hadn't won World War II," it would be natural for the listener to assume that the speaker means "If the Allied powers had lost World War II and the Axis powers had won." But it's also possible for the speaker to have in mind something like "If the Allied powers hadn't won, and the war ended in stalemate." Similarly, it's easy for a modern reader to assume that when Paul says "if there is no resurrection of the dead," he means "If there is no resurrection of the dead, and God does not exist, and all this supernatural religion stuff is false, then . . ." But that is probably not the alternative Paul had in mind, as 1 Corinthians 15:15 indicates: "If Christ has not been raised, then our proclamation has been in vain and your faith has been in vain. *We are even found to be misrepresenting God,* because we testified of God that he raised Christ—*whom he did not raise* if it is true that the dead are not raised" (1 Cor 15:14-15). Paul asserts here that if Christ has not been raised, then God did not raise Christ, and Paul is misrepresenting God. The contrast to resurrection and Christianity that Paul seems to be imagining is not naturalism but the view that, while God exists, Christianity is a departure from the true religion. And this makes sense once we recall Paul's context: the view that there was a resurrection of the body was contested among Jews of Paul's time, but the existence of God was not. So from Paul's perspective the situation would probably have looked like this:

> If Christ has not been raised, and if, therefore, Christianity is a hoax and God (who definitely exists) is not pleased with it, then we should have remained traditional believing Jews (or, for the Gentile Christians, should become

Jews), and we've given up the law and violated the covenant, and we are of all men the most to be pitied, suffering danger from man and incurring anger from God.

Paul's thought is not "if *naturalism* is true, then Christians are of all human beings the most to be pitied," but something more like "If we apostles and believers of the apostolic preaching are wrong and are therefore committing sacrilege and blasphemy against God, then we are both outside the true religion and suffering much in this life. We are therefore in a very bad situation." And if this is what Paul had in mind, then nothing in what he says implies that if *no* religion is true, then Christians today are in a very bad situation and have lost much by their religious commitments.

TAKING STOCK

We've now considered the strongest objections to the wager. None appears successful. We're left with the conclusion, then, that if Christianity has at least a 50 percent chance of being true, then it's rational to commit to living a devout Christian life. So, *does* Christianity have at least a 50 percent chance of being true? It's time to examine the evidence.

Part Two

EVIDENCE

5

WHERE DID PHYSICAL THINGS COME FROM?

IMAGINE THAT YOU ARE STANDING ON THE MOON, looking at a vibrant blue sphere with white swirls. It floats in the blackness of space. Such a gigantic object, the Earth, and yet from your vantage point it appears small, contained and even vulnerable in the vast dark void. Exactly twelve human beings (all American astronauts) have enjoyed this view in person, but now imagine something that no human being has experienced. Picture yourself being rapidly transported away from Earth, to the edges of the solar system. There you rest, watching the Earth make its long, slow curve around the sun. With a powerful telescope, you see that the Earth and the moon now appear very close together, a mere 240,000 miles or so, while the sun flares in its place over 91,000,000 miles away from the pair. Jupiter, Mars, Venus and the other planets glide on their silent journeys through what appears to your eyes as mere emptiness. As you know, however, even "empty" space is filled with objects and activity—tiny particles of dust, protons streaming out of the sun, photons traveling from distant stars. There it is, the solar system, a whole collection of fascinating objects, hanging in space like fish in a fishbowl.

And now suppose you are transported yet farther away, beyond the edges of our galaxy, the Milky Way. The sun is lost amid billions of other stars, but you can make out clearly the spiral-shaped structure of the Milky Way, resembling some fantastic starfish careening through the darkness.

Move farther and farther back, forget now about vision and telescopes, and simply picture in your mind's eye the entire group of all the physical objects in existence. Perhaps physical reality is finite, or perhaps it goes on forever. But with the power of thought we can consider the collection of all the physical objects that exist, finite or infinite as the case may be. Electrons, protons, hydrogen atoms, helium atoms, planets, stars, black holes and things we as yet know nothing about. And in at least one place, plants, animals and particular human beings, some of them thinking thoughts about the cosmos. It is a strange and mysterious collection. Why is it here? Where did it come from? Why is there anything at all? That is, why isn't there just nothing?

If I surprised you by pulling a rabbit out of an apparently empty hat, you'd be curious to know how I did it. Suppose I said, "No trick—it just popped into existence, and I pulled it out." You would not believe me. Why? Because physical things have causes. What if I lifted a whole group of rabbits out of an apparently empty box? Same reaction. Now consider the group of all the physical things that have *ever* existed (both those that exist now and those that have existed in the past). Whether this group is finite in number or infinite, we can still ask, "Why has there been *that* particular group of things, rather than something else, or nothing at all?"

This question, and the accompanying sense that there must be some explanation for the existence of physical reality, have prompted thinkers though the ages to construct arguments for God. Aristotle, Moses Maimonides, Thomas Aquinas and many others (including many contemporary philosophers) have presented arguments that start from some simple fact about the objects in the world (e.g., the fact that these objects exist but might not have) and move to the conclusion that some sort of transcendent being exists, which explains the existence of the ordinary, physical objects that surround us.[1] Taking their name from the Greek word for the whole world or the universe (*kosmos*), these arguments are called cosmological arguments, because they often focus on the whole of physical reality.[2] In this chapter we'll examine a powerful contemporary cosmological argument inspired by the work of two great thinkers of the past: philosopher, mathematician and scientist Gottfried Wilhelm Leibniz (best known, with Isaac Newton, as one of the two discoverers of calculus) and Francisco Suarez, the last great medieval philosopher.

POSSIBILITY AND NECESSITY

Some philosophical background is required in order to understand the cosmological argument. Specifically, one needs to understand what is meant by a "necessary being" and a "contingent being," and one must have a grasp of the concepts of possibility and necessity. In brief: anything whatsoever that exists is a "being," and a *contingent* being is a being that exists but does not absolutely have to exist. It could have been absent from reality. You, me, the tree outside my window, the moon and the sun are all contingent beings. In contrast, a necessary being, if there is one, would be a being that exists, and *has* to exist, in the strongest sense of "*has* to." If there is a necessary being, the fact that it exists is as necessary as it is necessary that $1 + 1 = 2$. But this is getting ahead of ourselves a bit.

To ease into things more slowly, consider the following two sets of propositions (or claims):

(1) You are now alive.

(2) The capital of the United States of America is located on a river.

(3) Mount Everest is the highest mountain on earth.

(4) Nobody is taller than himself.

(5) All bachelors are unmarried.

(6) If some things are made of carbon and some are not, then not everything is made of carbon.

What makes these two lists different? All six statements are true. But the first three could have been false. A tragic car accident could have ended your life yesterday. The early leaders of the US could have chosen a different site for the capital. And while Mount Everest is the highest mountain on earth now, someone could blow the top thousand feet off the summit and it would fall to number two. (Don't try that at home, kids.) So while true, propositions (1) through (3) could have been false. They are true, but only *contingently* true.

In contrast, propositions (4) through (6) could not have been false. As philosophers say, they are *necessarily* true. There's just no alternative way reality could be in which there would be a person who is (now) taller than he is (now). Similarly, it's impossible for there to be a situation in which some things are made of carbon and some aren't, and yet, somehow, every-thing is made of carbon. And although the word *bachelor* could have meant something else, once we agree on the meaning of our language, it is guar-anteed that all bachelors are unmarried.

How about the proposition "The Allies won World War II"? It's true, and because it's about the past, there is nothing anyone can do now to make it false. But that is not enough to make it *necessarily true*. It counts as contin-gently true because there is a possible way the world could have gone that would have made "The Allies won World War II" false. A proposition is necessarily true if and only if it is true and could not have been false, in the strongest sense of "could not have been."

To say that a proposition is necessarily true is not to say that it is certain. I'm certain that I'm now sitting, but the proposition that I'm now sitting is not a necessary truth. Necessity is about the way things have to be, not about our knowledge of them.

Next, consider two further sets of propositions:

(7) You are now wearing purple shoes.

(8) Mount Whitney is the tallest mountain in the continental US.

(9) $1 + 1 = 2$.

(10) Sarah is taller than herself.

(11) Jupiter is larger than Mars, and it's false that Jupiter is larger than Mars.

(12) $1 + 1 = 5$.

How are these two groups different? The last three are all necessarily false. As philosophers say, they are *metaphysically impossible*. There is no way things could have gone, and no way things could ever go, that would make (10), (11) or (12) true. Statements (7) through (9), by contrast, are not neces-sarily false. They are not metaphysically impossible; thus (7), (8) and (9) each count as *metaphysically possible*. (7) is false, I assume, but it could have been true (if you had made different shopping choices in the past). Statement (8) is true, although it could be made false. And (9) is necessarily true. A proposition is metaphysically possible if and only if it is either true, or it at least could have been true. A proposition is metaphysically impossible (i.e., necessarily false) if and only if it is not true and could not have been true.

NECESSARY AND CONTINGENT BEINGS

With these ideas in mind, we can now state the following definitions:

Something counts as a *contingent being* if and only if it exists but does not *have* to exist (in the strongest sense of "have to"). That is, its nonexistence is metaphysically possible.

Something counts as a *necessary being* if and only if it exists and has to exist (in the strongest sense of "has to"). If there is such a being, its nonexistence is metaphysically impossible. Equivalently, the existence of a necessary being, if there is one, is metaphysically necessary.

My pen, the Golden Gate Bridge and the tree outside my window are all contingent beings, as is the earth itself. Reality didn't have to include them in the way that 1 + 1 has to equal 2.

Note that anything that did not always exist is contingent, since if there was a time when a thing did not exist, then that thing apparently does not *have to* exist in the strongest sense. For example, take any given electron—it didn't always exist. According to current physics, electrons and other particles were formed soon after the Big Bang, approximately fourteen billion years ago. So no electron is a necessary being. The same can be said about any of the physical objects that we know about.

A necessary being, if there is one, is not your ordinary, garden-variety object. What could possibly qualify as a necessary being? God, who according to traditional Western philosophy doesn't just happen to exist but exists necessarily. There are other possibilities—more on this at the end of the chapter—but for now the question to ask is this: are all existing things contingent? As we'll see, the cosmological argument gives us good reason to answer no. From the fact that there are contingent beings we can show that there must be at least one necessary being, which explains the existence of contingent beings.

CAUSAL EXPLANATIONS

A causal explanation of something is an explanation that explains why that thing exists (rather than not) by citing its cause or causes. The causal explanation of an acorn would involve the oak tree that produced it.

Imagine again that I pull a rabbit out of a hat. Everyone has the insight that there has to be some trick—it can't have been that the rabbit just popped into existence. And we can generalize this insight: no contingent being can just pop into existence. No contingent thing exists without having had some source or cause. In other words, every contingent being has a causal explanation.

There are several reasons to believe this. For one thing, every single one of the contingent beings in our experience has a cause. If all the crows anyone has ever seen are black, that's a good reason to think all crows are black. Not a proof, but still a good reason. Now, in discussions of popular science, one does sometimes hear talk of particles popping into existence out of nothing.[3] But this is a misleading way of speaking; in such cases there is, on inspection of the details, always some preexisting entity out of which the particles are supposed to emerge, an underlying field for example. So these aren't really cases of contingent beings coming into existence without any cause. All our empirical evidence indicates that every contingent being has a cause.

Second, if contingent beings could come to be without a cause, we would expect to occasionally see stuff popping into existence from literally no cause at all. We'd see the odd elephant just showing up . . . why not? It's no harder for a big thing to pop into existence than a small thing, if things can just pop into existence without any sort of cause. What sort of physical laws could govern what *nothing* can produce or how often *nothing* can produce something?

But most fundamental is the third reason to think that no contingent being exists without having had some cause. Take any contingent being you like. By definition it is something that exists but does not *have* to exist. So both its existence and its nonexistence were real possibilities. And yet only one of those two possibilities was realized—the thing exists. So there must be *some* explanation of why the one possibility was realized rather than the other—of why the contingent being exists rather than not.

Let me elaborate on this third point. For many of the things we believe, we believe them on the basis of other things we believe. For example, I believe that when the water heater is set right and working properly, I can get hot water out of the faucet in the kitchen. Suppose that one morning I cannot get hot water out of the faucet in the kitchen. I then form the belief "something must be wrong with the hot water heater." This belief is based on two of my other beliefs, "I can't get hot water" and "when my water heater is set right and working properly, I can get hot water."

Very many beliefs are like this. But as Aristotle pointed out long ago, it can't be that *all* of our beliefs are like this. Suppose I believe A and you ask me why. I reply that I believe A because if B is true, then A is true, and B *is* true. You then ask me why I believe B is true. "Easy!" I say, B is true because C is true, and C implies B. You then ask me why I believe C is true. Clearly, this can't go on forever. There must be some point at which one can just see that something is true, without having to rely on other things one believes as evidence. A proposition that you simply see to be true (and don't believe just because other beliefs you have are evidence for it) is called a foundational belief, or a basic belief. Examples include perceptual beliefs like "there is something red in front of me," beliefs about logic or mathematics like "a statement cannot be true and false at the same time" or "1 + 1 = 2," and memory beliefs like "I had oatmeal for breakfast this morning."

And we have basic beliefs about contingency and explanation, too. On October 23, 1947, the people of Marksville, Louisiana, experienced some unusual weather: hundreds of fish raining from the sky. A. D. Bajkov, a biologist with the Louisiana Department of Wildlife and Fisheries, happened to be present. He collected specimens and wrote up a report published in the journal *Science*.[4] The fish ranged in length from two to nine inches and were of various kinds, including largemouth bass, two species of sunfish and several species of minnows. Hard to believe, but such reports of "fish falls" (and toad falls too) are surprisingly common in the records of history. Although the weather was calm on the day of the fish fall, Bajkov and a colleague had observed several small tornadoes on the previous day. The tornadoes, he speculated, could have lifted the fish high into the atmosphere. Whether that's the true explanation or not, one thing is abundantly clear: there must have been *some* explanation of how the fish got up into the air—they didn't just spring into existence up there from nothing. This intuition is so deep and so natural that we would rarely even think to mention it. When Bajkov was wondering how the fish had gotten into the air, if a bystander had suggested the possibility that they just came into existence there without a cause, Bajkov would not have taken the suggestion seriously. Rightly so. Science progresses because we accept the idea that contingent beings have causes, and then we search for those causes.

The third and most foundational reason, then, to accept the claim that every contingent being has a cause is that this claim expresses a basic insight about contingent beings. Take any given contingent being you like. By definition, it is something that exists but did not have to exist. So there must be *some* explanation of why it exists, rather than not. And that explanation will have to include, at some point, at least one cause.

GROUPS OF CONTINGENT BEINGS

We can apply this same reasoning to a group of things. If you have a heap of rabbits, there must be some causal explanation of where that pile came from. It's no easier to pull a heap of rabbits out of an empty box than to pull a single rabbit out of an empty hat.

And we can apply this same reasoning to the group of all the contingent beings that have ever existed. Imagine every single contingent being that has ever existed in the history of reality. Let's represent them with this figure (where the rectangles represent things, and the arrows represent causation):

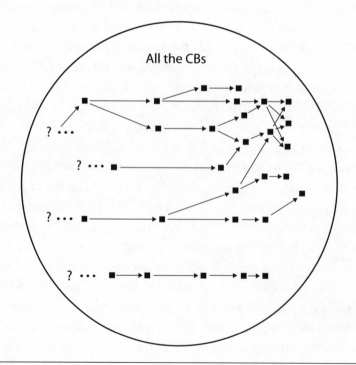

Figure 5.1

History has included a vast number of contingent things, some causing others, stretching back into the past. Is there an infinite past? Have there been an infinite number of contingent beings in the history of the world or only a finite number? For our purposes here, we don't need to know—because the whole group (the group of all the contingent beings that have ever existed) is itself *contingent*, whether it's finite or infinite. It could have been that none of those things existed. And since the whole group is contingent, there must have been some cause that explains why the whole group has existed, rather than not at all.

Let's slow down. Why think the whole group is contingent? Because every member of the group is a contingent thing, and there is nothing about contingent things that makes a larger group of them any less contingent than a smaller group. For example, a pen is contingent, and a piece of paper is contingent, and when we consider the group of the two of them together, they don't suddenly became necessary. It might have been that neither the pen nor the paper ever existed.

To see the point here, consider an interesting fact about female boas. Female boas, or at least some of them, have a special talent. They can reproduce healthy female offspring without any involvement from a male.[5] Now, imagine that the universe had always been here, and that there had always been boas, stretching back into the infinite past.

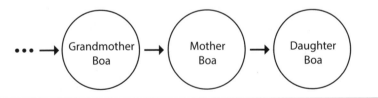

Figure 5.2

If there had really been such an infinite group of boas, we could ask whether that whole group is itself contingent. That is, did reality have to include this infinite group of boas?

It did not. Consider a single boa. It's contingent; it doesn't have to exist. Now consider the group of that boa and its mother. That group of two members is just as contingent. It's not as if reality without those two boas is impossible. Now consider the group of the boa, its mother and its grand-mother. That group of three members is just as contingent as the first boa. A world lacking all three of those boas is also a possible way the world could have been. As we keep adding members to the series, there's not the slightest suggestion that the larger and larger series that result are less contingent then the single boa with which we started. The general point is that there is nothing about contingent beings that makes it true that a larger group of contingent beings is more necessary than a smaller group. Contingency is not like weight. If you take a light thing, add another light thing, add a third light thing and so on, you will eventually have a group of things that, all together, is heavy. Not all properties are like lightness in this respect. If you have many red bricks, and you stack them on top of each other to make a wall, the wall is red, just like the individual bricks. Contingency is like redness, not like lightness. To go back to the case of the infinite series of boas, the mere fact that the snakes are unlimited in number wouldn't magically make a reality without boas an impossible reality.

So return to the group of all the contingent beings that ever were. Since every member of the group is contingent, and larger groups of contingent beings are no less contingent than smaller groups, it follows that the whole group is con-tingent. It could have been that the history of reality lacked all those contingent beings (all the contingent beings that have ever actually existed).

But this means that there were at least two possibilities for how reality might have been—both the existence and the nonexistence of that whole group were real possibilities. There were other possibilities too; maybe half the beings might have existed. But we can still consider and reason about these two of the many possibilities: (1) the possibility that all of the members of the group exist and (2) the possibility that none of the members of the group exist. And we can note that only one of those two possibilities was realized: the whole group has been part of the history of the world. So there must be some explanation of why the one possibility was realized rather than the other—of why all those contingent beings have existed, rather than none of them at all. Since both options were possible, there must be *some* explanation of why the whole group has been a part of reality, rather than not. And that explanation will have to include, at some point, at least one cause.[6] That is,

(A) The entire group of all the contingent beings that have ever existed has a causal explanation.

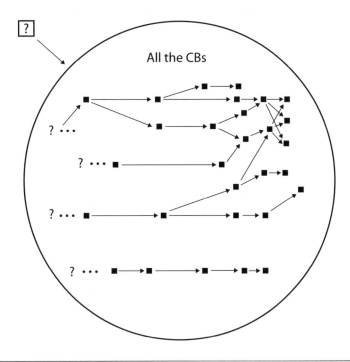

Figure 5.3

To sum up the argument thus far: we are considering all the contingent things there are and ever have been, and asking why this whole group of things has existed rather than not at all. Either it has some causal explanation, or the whole group has existed without any cause. But it is implausible that the whole group has existed without having had any cause to explain why the group has been there rather than not. Therefore the whole group has some sort of causal explanation. If we can't believe that a single rabbit can exist without a causal explanation, why would we believe that a group of trillions and trillions of contingent things can exist without a causal explanation?

We can make the next step in the argument by asking, "What would the causal explanation of the whole group of contingent beings have to involve?" A difficult question, but this much is clear: the cause of all contingent beings can't itself be a contingent being, for the group we're considering contains all the contingent beings that ever were. If the cause were a contingent being, then it would be inside the very group that needs an explanation.

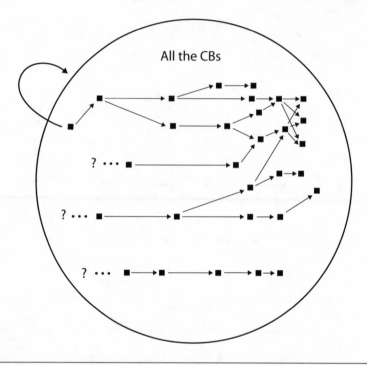

Figure 5.4

That would mean that it would have to cause itself (whether directly, or indirectly by causing something else that causes itself). But this is impossible; nothing can cause itself to exist, whether directly or indirectly. In order for something to cause itself to exist, it would have to be able to cause things, but in order to be able to cause things, it would have to exist. So to cause itself to exist, it would have to already exist to do the causing.

Next, if the cause of the whole group of contingent beings is not a contingent being, then it must be a necessary being (or several necessary beings). We can now state our cosmological argument:

(A) The entire group of all the contingent beings that have ever existed has a causal explanation.

But,

> (B) That causal explanation must involve the existence of a necessary being (or more than one).

So

> (C) There is at least one necessary being that provided, or played a crucial part in, the causal explanation of the entire group of all the contingent beings that have ever existed.

OBJECTIONS

Nothing I've said so far has shown that there is only one such necessary being. And even if there is only one, we haven't yet seen a reason to think that it has intelligence or is a personal being. But we have shown that there's reason to believe in more than just the contingent physical objects with which we are familiar. You won't find anything in a physics textbook about a necessary being, but there is absolutely excellent reason to think that there is at least one of them and that it is a cause of all the physical objects with which we are familiar (and any other contingent beings there may be).

Wait a second, though; how can we be sure that this necessary being referred to in (B) is still around? Maybe it started everything off but has since ceased to exist.

This objection would apply to a contingent being that created other things but doesn't apply to a necessary being. Recall that a necessary being is a being that *has* to exist, in the strongest sense. Proposition (B) shows that at one time there must have been such a being. But if there was ever such a being, it must still exist. If it was once true, in the past, that a necessary being exists, then it was true back then that a being exists which is absolutely necessary and so can't later cease to exist. So we can be sure the necessary being mentioned in (B) is still around.

A common response to cosmological arguments is to wonder, "Who made God?" Or, adapted to the argument of this chapter, "What caused this necessary being (or these necessary beings, if there are more than one)?" Sometimes this question is thought to form the basis of a potent objection to cosmological arguments, as when philosopher Daniel Dennett asks, "What caused God? The reply that God is self-caused (somehow) then raises the rebuttal: If something can be self-caused, why can't the universe as a whole be the thing that is self-caused?"[7] This "rebuttal" misses the mark; viable versions of the cosmological argument simply do not claim that God is self-caused. God is uncaused, not self-caused. In Aquinas's second argument for the existence of God, just to take one of the most well-known cosmological arguments, the conclusion is that there is an *uncaused* First Cause. As Aquinas is well aware, "It is neither observed nor is it possible that something be the efficient cause of itself; for thus it would be prior to itself, which is impossible."[8]

More to the point, the cosmological argument given in this chapter didn't proceed by arguing that everything needs a cause and didn't assert that the necessary being (or beings) mentioned in the argument are self-caused. Rather, the idea was that everything *contingent* needs a cause. There's a principled reason to think that contingent beings always need causes, while necessary beings don't. Contingent beings always need causes because both their existence and nonexistence were real possibilities. Since they exist *but might not have*, we rightly think there must have been some cause of their existence that explains why that one possibility (existence) was realized rather than the other (nonexistence). But in the case of a necessary being, there were never two possibilities in the first place. A necessary being exists, but it wasn't even possible for it not to. So we needn't seek some reason or cause that explains why it exists rather than not. What caused the necessary being (or necessary beings) mentioned in our cosmological argument? Nothing did. Why then does such a necessary being exist? Because it's impossible for it not to.

Once one has reason to believe that a necessary being does in fact exist, the explanation of *why* that being exists is a lot like the explanation of why there aren't any square circles. There aren't any square circles not because no one has bothered to make one, but because it is absolutely impossible for such a thing to exist. In the case of a necessary being, it is absolutely impossible for it *not* to exist. That's all the explanation there is, but it's just as good of an explanation in the case of the necessary being as it is in the case of the square circle. Well, maybe not *just* as good—in the case of square circles we can see the impossibility by reflecting on the nature of squares and circles. By contrast, we don't have the sort of access to the nature of a necessary being that would allow us to see why it *must* exist. But our lack of insight about what a necessary being would be like is no argument against the existence of one—especially when we have a very strong argument for the existence of one.

At this point in the argument Dennett might respond, "Okay, God is not supposed to be self-caused. But he's supposed to be uncaused. And if God can be uncaused, why can't the whole collection of physical things be un-caused?" The answer is that the only way the whole collection of physical things could be uncaused would be for it to be necessary. But that would mean that everything in the universe *had* to exist, which just isn't true. If your parents had made different choices and never met, for example, you would not exist.

WHAT DOES THE COSMOLOGICAL ARGUMENT SHOW?

Still, as noted above, the cosmological argument does not show that there is only *one* necessary being. And supposing there is only one, the cosmological argument by itself does not show that that necessary being is God. For all the cosmological argument proves, the explanation of contingent beings might simply be that there is a necessarily existing nonpersonal object (something like what physicists call a "field," perhaps) that gives rise to con-tingent beings. Or, for all the cosmological argument proves, the explanation of contingent beings might be this: there is a vast or even infinite number of necessarily existing "bits" of energy, which at any given time must compose or make up some number of contingent beings. Why do contingent beings exist? Because these necessarily existing bits of energy must at any time make up some set of things, and they just happen to have made up the con-tingent beings that have existed.

Now, there are some rather abstract considerations that favor the idea that there is just one necessary being responsible for the existence of con-tingent beings, rather than many. For one thing, the hypothesis that there is just one is simpler than the hypothesis that there are many. It's usually a good idea to refrain from postulating a large number of additional unob-served entities when the observed facts can be sufficiently well explained by just one unobserved entity.

And if the explanation of the contingent beings that have existed is simply that there are one or more nonintelligent necessary beings that have produced or composed the contingent beings, then we are left with the unexplained fact that the necessary beings gave rise to *this* particular group of contingent beings, rather than any of the other possible groups of contingent beings that reality could have contained. By contrast, we do have an explanation of this fact if there is an intelligent necessary being. If an intelligent necessary being is causally responsible for the group of all the contingent beings that have existed, then there is an explanation ready to hand for why there has been this particular group rather than another: namely, the choice of that intelligent being. To suppose there is a creator who has made a free choice about what to create provides more of an explanation than to suppose that there has just been one set of contingent beings rather than another for no reason at all.

Still, these considerations are far from compelling. We get a much stronger reason to believe in an intelligent creator when we consider some additional evidence—the fine-tuning of the universe for life. In the next three chapters, we'll take a close look at an amazing fact about our universe, a fact uncovered by physicists and astronomers only within the last several decades.

6

WHY IS THE UNIVERSE JUST RIGHT FOR LIFE?

THE 2011 NOBEL PRIZE IN PHYSICS went to Saul Perlmutter, Brian Schmidt and Adam Riess for an observational discovery relating to the expansion of the universe. This was not the first recognition of their work; in 1998, when their results were originally published, *Science* magazine called the findings the top scientific breakthrough of the year. Physicist Brian Greene of Columbia University relates that many researchers found this discovery to be "the single most surprising observational result to have emerged in their lifetimes."[1] What was the discovery, and why exactly was it so surprising?

THE COSMOLOGICAL CONSTANT

To find an answer, we need to go back a century or so, to the time when Albert Einstein had recently put forward his general theory of relativity.[2] Einstein's theory is about gravity, space and time, and one of its insights is that space is not pure nothingness but has properties of its own. Space, for example, can have a shape. This is hard to visualize in the case of three-dimensional space, but one can get the idea by considering a two-dimensional surface: imagine a flat piece of spandex, shaped like a piece of paper. If you had a basketball at hand and were crafty enough, you could stretch the spandex so that it completely covered the surface of the ball. You'd have to stretch more in some places than in others, and maybe hold it in place with some very special glue, but supposing you did all that, the surface of the spandex would then have a different shape and different geometrical properties.

When the spandex was flat, if a tiny two-dimensional creature living on the surface of the spandex had walked in one direction, it would have eventually reached an edge. But once the spandex is shaped like a sphere, the creature could walk in one direction and eventually return to the same spot, coming from the opposite direction. It turns out that something similar can be true of three-dimensional space. It's possible for space itself to be curved in various ways, even in such a way that if you shone a beam of light in one direction (and space wasn't infinitely large), then eventually the light would come back to the same spot, from the opposite direction.

Besides mere curvature, it is also possible for space to expand or contract. For space to expand isn't just a matter of things in space (like stars) moving farther apart from each other *through* space. Rather, the idea is that space itself can expand. Imagine that you drew two dots on the surface of a balloon and then inflated the balloon so it got bigger. As the surface of the balloon stretched, those two dots would get farther and farther away from each other, even though the dots wouldn't be moving *across* the surface in the way we imagined our two-dimensional creature was in the previous example.

Now, not only can space expand, it *is* expanding, as scientists have known since the early twentieth century.[3] It was thought that, ever since a time very soon after the Big Bang, space was expanding at a slower and slower rate as time went on; that is, it was thought that the expansion of space was decelerating. Perlmutter, heading one research team, and Schmidt, heading another, independently set out to measure how much the expansion of space was slowing down. To their surprise they discovered that it was not slowing down at all—it was speeding up. And this in turn implied something surprising about the nature of what we would ordinarily think of as empty space. "Empty" space, it turns out, experiences a repulsive force (a sort of opposite to gravity). Or perhaps the way to describe it is that a number of fields that permeate space generate that repulsive force.[4] However we describe it, something is causing an acceleration in the expansion of space. The rate of this acceleration is related to a parameter (a number) that scientists refer to as the effective cosmological constant. If the effective cosmological constant is a positive number, space tends to expand at an accelerating rate, and the larger the positive number the more rapid the acceleration. If the effective cosmological constant were a negative number, the expansion of

space would decelerate, and then space would begin to contract; the larger the negative number the sooner the contraction would begin. Crucially, the observations of Perlmutter, Schmidt and their research teams allowed for a precise calculation of the value of the effective cosmological constant. Measured in Planck units, it turns out to be an extremely small positive number, almost but not quite zero.[5] Taking account of recent data, it's this:
.000000000000000000000000000000000000000000000000000000000000 000000000000000000000000000000000000000000000000000000000000 0000135.

That's 1.35×10^{-123} of the relevant units.[6]

Interesting, you might be thinking, but what's the big deal? Well, the value of the effective cosmological constant isn't a mere piece of trivia. As Nobel Prize–winning physicist Steven Weinberg convincingly argued in the late 1980s, the precise value of the cosmological constant is fundamentally important as far as life is concerned. If the effective cosmological constant were about one thousand times bigger than it is (bigger than about 1 over 10 to the 120th Planck units), the universe would have expanded too rapidly in its earlier stages, and galaxies, stars and planets would never have formed. This would have made it very unlikely that life could have evolved anywhere in the universe, since all the chemical elements except the three simplest (hydrogen, helium and lithium) are only produced within stars, and it's very hard to see how there could be living beings made only out of these elements and/or subatomic particles. If the effective cosmological constant were bigger still, the universe would have expanded so rapidly that, very soon, those simplest atoms would not be near enough to each other to interact at all. Next, if the effective cosmological constant had been negative but a bit less than about negative 1 over 10 to the 120th Planck units, the universe would have collapsed far too soon, before any life could have evolved.[7]

And now we get to the punch line: given what we know about physics today, there is no reason at all to have expected the value of the effective cosmological constant to lie within the narrow life-permitting range, between about negative 1 divided by 10^{120} and about positive 1 divided by 10^{120} of the relevant units. It appears that the cosmological constant could have been anywhere in a *very* large range ("large" relative to the size of the narrow life-permitting band). If it hadn't been just right, we would not exist.

Let's look at this issue more closely. The underlying physical reason or reasons why the value of the effective cosmological constant is what it is are not fully known. That is, it's not fully understood why "empty" space experiences the repulsive force to the degree that it does. Still, at least part of the reason has to do with the energy of various fields that permeate space (the fields that are associated with the fundamental particles, such as the electron or the various quarks). Some fields contribute a positive quantity to the effective cosmological constant, some contribute a negative quantity. But when physicists make their best attempt at estimating the energy that the several known fields should contribute all together, they get a result that is much, much bigger than the observed value. Indeed, that's putting it mildly— what's expected is a value about 10 to the 123rd bigger than the observed value![8] What's going on here? A natural conclusion to draw is that, in addition to the known contributors to the effective cosmological constant, there are also one or more other contributors, as yet unknown. And whatever these other contributors are, they *almost* exactly cancel out the contributions from the fields mentioned above, so that the effective cosmological constant is almost zero.

What is amazing to physicists is that, even though each of the individual contributions to the cosmological constant could have taken any of a huge range of values, it somehow turned out that all of the various individual contributions conspire to almost cancel each other out, *almost but not quite.* A cancellation to exactly zero would suggest the presence of some relatively simple underlying mechanism by which various pairs necessarily cancel each other. But when Perlmutter, Schmidt and Riess discovered that the effective cosmological constant is not exactly zero, this simple explanation was ruled out—and this is why the discovery was so surprising to the researchers mentioned by Brian Greene in the quotation at the beginning of this chapter. With the prospects exceedingly dim for a simple, elegant solution showing why the cosmological constant has to be zero, we're left with what appears to be an enormous coincidence.

An analogy will be helpful here: suppose that we have twenty gigantic silos containing numbered Ping-Pong balls. Ten of the silos contain balls each labeled with a different positive whole number (1, 2, 3 and so on), so that inside each of these silos there is exactly one ball labeled with "1," exactly one ball labeled with "2" and so on up to a very high number. The other ten silos contain balls labeled with negative whole numbers (-1, -2, -3, etc.), so that inside each of these silos there is exactly one ball labeled "-1," exactly one ball labeled "-2" and so on. And the silos contain *a lot* of Ping-Pong balls—the largest silo contains 10^{120} balls, the smallest 10^{60}. One billion is 10^9, or 1,000,000,000. One trillion is 10^{12}, or 1,000,000,000,000. So 10^{120} is an unimaginably large number. The balls have all been jostled around—the "deck" has been shuffled, so to speak. Now, suppose you are told to select (without looking) one Ping-Pong ball from each silo, and that the numbers on the balls you've picked will then be added up. You are further told that if the sum is anything other than -1, 0 or 1, you'll be shot. You realize that this means almost certain death, given all the possible sums you might end up with. But, with no other choice, you nervously pick your twenty balls. The sum is calculated, you wince, and . . . it's the number 1! This would be an unbelievable coincidence.

In this analogy the different silos represent the different contributions to the effective cosmological constant (known and unknown). The large number of Ping-Pong balls in each silo represents the fact that each individual contribution could have been any of a very large range of values. With this in mind, we can understand why physicists were so amazed by the discovery that the cosmological constant is a tiny, positive number. The different contributions to the effective cosmological constant appear to have balanced almost perfectly, for no apparent reason. Stanford University physicist Leonard Susskind explains:

> When the laws of elementary particles meet the laws of gravity, the result is a potential catastrophe: a world of such violence that astronomical bodies, as well as elementary particles, would be torn asunder by the most destructive force imaginable. The only way out is for one particular constant of nature— Einstein's *cosmological constant*—to be so incredibly finely tuned that no one could possibly think it accidental.[9]

Now, neither Susskind nor Weinberg concludes from this enormous coincidence that the universe has been designed for life. They adopt an alternative explanation, which we'll examine in detail in chapter eight. For now the point is this: according to the majority view among experts, only the tiniest fraction of the possible values of the effective cosmological constant would allow for life to develop in our universe. This apparent coincidence calls out for an explanation.

Fine-Tuning

It's time to introduce a key term: fine-tuning. To say that the effective cosmological constant is "fine-tuned for life" is to say that if it had been slightly different than what it in fact is, then the evolution of life would have been impossible, or at least vastly more unlikely. To speak of "fine-tuning" here does not automatically imply belief in the existence of a Fine-Tuner; it's simply an expressive way of saying that some physical feature has to be "just right" if living material beings are going to be able to emerge. If a given physical feature (e.g., the value of the cosmological constant) has a range of possible values, but only a narrow subset of that range is life permitting, and that physical feature does fall within that narrow range, then the feature is said to be fine-tuned for life.

Although the cosmological constant is the most impressive case of fine-tuning, it's not the only one. As Brian Greene notes:

> For many of nature's constants, even modest variations would render life as we know it impossible. Make the gravitational constant stronger, and stars burn up too quickly for life on nearby planets to evolve. Make it weaker and galaxies don't hold together. Make the electromagnetic force stronger, and hydrogen atoms repel each other too strongly to fuse and supply power to stars.[10]

This is just the beginning. There are strong arguments that each of the following physical parameters is fine-tuned: the strength of gravity, the strength of the strong force (which holds protons and neutrons together in atomic nuclei), the strength of the electromagnetic force (responsible for the fact that opposite charges attract), the strength of the weak force (which is involved in the decay of certain unstable subatomic particles, like a freestanding neutron), and the difference between the mass of the neutron and the mass of the proton.[11] Scientists who accept the claim that our universe is fine-tuned for life (or at least, life "as we know it") include John Barrow, Bernard Carr, Brandon Carter, Paul Davies, George Ellis, Brian Greene,

Alan Guth, Edward Harrison, Stephen Hawking, Andrei Linde, Don Page, Roger Penrose, John Polkinghorne, Martin Rees, Lee Smolin, Leonard Susskind, Max Tegmark, Frank Tipler, Alexander Vilenkin, Steven Weinberg, John Wheeler and Frank Wilczek—all eminent scholars.[12] While it can't be said that the evidence for fine-tuning is beyond all doubt, the claim that our universe is fine-tuned for life (i.e., that it has at least one fine-tuned feature) is well supported and widely accepted among experts.

The fine-tuning argument. The strong scientific evidence for fine-tuning provides the key premise in an argument for the existence of God known as the fine-tuning argument. As you'll recall from chapter five, one of the possibilities that emerged from a consideration of the cosmological argument is that there is a single necessarily existing being that is the cause of the existence of contingent beings. The hypothesis that this necessary being has a mind provides a satisfying explanation for the apparent coincidences involved in fine-tuning. If the cause of our universe is an intelligent being capable of deliberately designing and producing a universe, then the fact that our universe permits life is not particularly surprising. An intelligent being would be able to see that the existence of embodied beings who could think, choose and interact would be a great good, and so would have a reason to create a life-permitting universe rather than a universe containing only, say, mindless particles and fields. If the universe were designed, it would not be at all unexpected for it to be life permitting. If, however, the universe is not designed but is merely the product of some unguided physical process, then it is immensely unlikely that it would be life permitting, because the proportion of life-permitting universes within the entire range of possible universes is so small. And when I say "immensely unlikely," I'm talking about probabilities like one in 10^{120}, or one in 10^{53} if we err on the side of skepticism about fine-tuning. These are estimates for the degree of fine-tuning just for the cosmological constant.[13] When other cases of fine-tuning are taken into account, the degree of fine-tuning becomes even more amazing. Since a coincidence so large is extremely unlikely, the fact that the universe is fine-tuned for life is strong evidence for the hypothesis that it was designed by an intelligent agent.

Well then, are all the astrophysicists rushing off to church? No. There are several objections to the fine-tuning argument, as well as certain sociological factors at play. In the rest of this chapter and the next, we'll look at four initial objections. Then in chapter eight we'll turn to the most powerful objection to the fine-tuning argument, which concerns the possibility that our universe is just one of a vast number of separate universes.

The Star Trek Objection

Life as we know it is carbon based. Carbon is a constituent of a huge number of molecules found inside living things; most crucially, a large proportion of the atoms in a strand of DNA are carbon. The important role this element plays for living beings is related to its unique properties—carbon is special in its ability to combine with other atoms in a huge number of different ways. Astronomers Geraint Lewis and Luke Barnes of the University of Sydney give just one example:

> Consider carbon's siblings on the first row of the periodic table of elements: Lithium (Li), Beryllium (Be), Boron (B), Nitrogen (N), Oxygen (O), Fluorine (F) and Neon (Ne). Now ask: how many compounds can be made using each element and hydrogen, the simplest element of them all?

Li	Be	B	C	N	O	F	Ne
3	5	41	28,827	72	23	5	0

> Hopefully, one of those numbers strikes you as unusually large. You can make an awful lot of things with carbon. It is versatile and flexible in a way that is unmatched by any other element.[14]

As noted above, carbon is only produced within the superheated interior of stars. Part of the case for the claim that our universe is fine-tuned comes from the observation that if various physical parameters were different, then there would have been no stars, and hence no carbon, and hence no carbon-based life. But what if there could be different forms of life, not based on carbon at all? Perhaps there could be a form of life in which silicon takes the place of carbon. Or maybe there could be a friendly, emotionally sensitive cloud made just out of hydrogen gas. Call this the Star Trek objection: the fine-tuning argument is unpersuasive because life forms very different from our own might be able to emerge even in universes that wouldn't permit carbon-based life. By focusing just on the form of life with which we are familiar, we've been led to think that only a universe of a very special sort could be life permitting, but maybe this isn't so.

A consideration of the fine-tuning of the cosmological constant uncovers a decisive reply. When discussing the life-permitting range of the cosmological constant, above, we noted Steven Weinberg's estimate of a life-permitting range between about negative $\frac{1}{10^{120}}$ and positive $\frac{1}{10^{120}}$ Planck units. If the cosmological constant were positive and bigger than $\frac{1}{10^{120}}$ Planck units, the formation of galaxies, stars and planets would be precluded, and that would be enough to rule out life as we know it. But what about highly conjectural forms of life, like that good-natured hydrogen gas cloud? Even such wildly speculative forms of life as these would be ruled out if the cosmological constant were bigger still, say one trillion times bigger than Weinberg's limit of $\frac{1}{10^{120}}$, which comes to $\frac{1}{10^{108}}$ Planck units. What would happen if the cosmological constant had a value greater than that? In that case, Lewis and Barnes write: "The universe would be a *very* thin soup of hydrogen and helium. The most that these particles would do would be to bounce off each other, and head back out into space for another trillion years of lonely isolation."[15] No remotely plausible form of life could exist with so little interaction between atoms.

Turning to the case of a negative cosmological constant, a value below negative $\frac{1}{10^{108}}$ would result in a universe that would collapse in on itself so quickly as to rule out the emergence of life of any conceivable sort. An effective cosmological constant of $-\frac{1}{10^{108}}$ Planck units would result in a universe that lasted only fifteen thousand years.[16] Evolution may be impressive, but that's asking a bit much. So even if we concede to the objector that the possibility of non-carbon-based life forms should be taken into account, we are still left with a life-permitting range no bigger than $-\frac{1}{10^{108}}$ to $\frac{1}{10^{108}}$ Planck units, a span that is minuscule compared to the total possible range for the cosmological constant. Well-understood physics predicts that the effective cosmological constant could have been (for all we can tell, *should* have been) as high as roughly 1 Planck unit, or as low as around -1 Planck unit. This would mean that the range of possible values for the cosmological constant is about 10^{108} times larger than our new life-permitting range. Alternatively, if physicists err on the side of skepticism and perform the key calculation differently, the total possible range is 10^{53} times wider than Weinberg's life-permitting range, which translates to 10^{41} times wider than the new life-permitting range we are conceding to the Star Trek objector.[17]

So it turns out that we can do an end run around the Star Trek objection by widening our estimate of the life-permitting region for the cosmological constant. Instead of an apparent coincidence involving, say, a one in 10^{120} chance (or a one in 10^{53} chance), we'll be left with an apparent coincidence involving a one in 10^{108} chance (or a one in 10^{41} chance) . . . still an unimaginably huge coincidence. Henceforth I'll assume that the life-permitting region is one trillion times wider than ordinarily thought, that is, between negative $\frac{1}{10^{108}}$ and positive $\frac{1}{10^{108}}$ Planck units. As we'll see in chapter seven, the fine-tuning argument remains more than sufficiently strong even with this handicap.

THE MERCHANT'S THUMB

The effective cosmological constant could have been any of a huge range of values, but it just happened to fall within the narrow, life-permitting range. On the assumption that there was no intelligent being involved, this was a very improbable outcome. But wait a moment, wouldn't *any* particular value of the cosmological constant be equally improbable? Imagine you are going to draw at random a Ping-Pong ball out of one of those silos, say, one with 10^{60} balls. Yes, it's very unlikely that you'll draw the ball labeled "1." But it's equally unlikely that you'll draw the ball labeled 1,587,397,289,086,421 or any other particular ball. And the ball you draw has to have some number written on it. One knee-jerk response to the fine-tuning argument proceeds along these lines, suggesting that facts about fine-tuning aren't in any special need of explanation.

The philosopher John Leslie nicely explains where this objection goes wrong.[18] Suppose a clever merchant is selling you a fancy piece of silk. You're about to buy it, but then you notice that as he has been displaying the cloth to you, his thumb has been covering a significant hole in the fabric. Getting a little angry, you point this out. "No need to get excited," he replies, "I had to put my thumb somewhere!"

Why does the merchant's excuse leave one suspicious? In certain situations, we are happy to accept a very improbable event as the outcome of chance. Consider case one: you're playing poker and in three successive hands your opponent gets {Q♣, 10♦, 6♦, 3♥, 9♠}, {J♠, 2♣, 4♦, 3♥, 10♠} and {A♦, A♣, 10♣, 9♣, 2♥}. In this case there is every reason to suppose that your opponent's hands are simply the result of chance and no reason to think they stand in special need of explanation. And this is true even though it's immensely improbable that your opponent would get precisely those three hands. By contrast, consider case two: your opponent gets a royal flush three times in a row.[19] In this second case, you would suspect your opponent of cheating, even though getting three royal flushes is no more improbable than getting the three hands of case one. Why the different reaction? Because in case two, there is a plausible explanation (cheating) that, if true, would explain the three royal flushes by showing that they weren't so improbable after all. Three successive royal flushes are much less unlikely given the hypothesis of cheating than given the hypothesis that the hands were a result of chance. By contrast, there is no antecedently plausible hypothesis that would raise the probability of the three hands involved in case one. In Leslie's words: "A chief (or the only?) reason for thinking that something stands in [special need of explanation], i.e. for justifiable reluctance to dismiss it as how things just happen to be, is that one in fact glimpses some tidy way in which it might be explained."[20] In the case of the merchant, one glimpses that a desire for dishonest gain would provide a tidy, probability-raising explanation of the otherwise unlikely coincidence that the merchant's thumb was over the hole, and this is why one would be right to remain suspicious. Similarly, one can glimpse a tidy explanation for the enormous apparent coincidences involved in fine-tuning: an intelligence behind the universe. If the cause of the universe was an intelligent, necessary being, this would raise the probability that it would be life permitting. Because this probability-raising explanation is on the table as a plausible option, it's irrational to dismiss fine-tuning as mere chance. Just as it'd be irrational for you to continue to say "No special need for explanation here; all hands equally unlikely!" if your opponent kept getting royal flush after royal flush for dozens of times in a row.

THE OBJECTION THAT PROVED TOO MUCH

A third objection contends that the fine-tuning of the universe for life is sufficiently explained by one simple fact: since we (as living beings within the universe) can only exist in a life-permitting universe, of course we observe a life-permitting universe! We couldn't very well expect to observe a universe without life. And so we have no reason to think there's a deeper explanation of the apparent coincidences of fine-tuning.[21] This objection is typically elaborated with the help of a term from statistics: "selection effect." A selection effect occurs when something about the conditions required for collecting data or making an observation turns out to bias the kinds of observations that can be made. For example, suppose you're trying a new way to fish; instead of bothering with a single line, you're dragging a large net through Lake Superior. At the end of the day you examine your catch and discover that all 1,027 fish in your net are over eight inches long.[22] You then start to wonder about the population of fish in Lake Superior. If the lake contained small fish as well as big fish, then it would take an extraordinary coincidence not to have caught any small ones. Your observation (that all the fish in your net are over eight inches in length) looks to be good evidence that the overall population of fish in Lake Superior contains no more than a tiny proportion of fish under that size. But then you realize your mistake: the gaps in your netting are big enough to let small fish out. What had appeared to be evidence for the hypothesis that Lake Superior contains mainly big fish can now be recognized as the inevitable result of the way your data was gathered. Initially it might have appeared improbable that you would observe no small fish in your net, on the hypothesis that the lake contains both big and small fish. But you must not forget that, because of the physical features of your net, it's guaranteed that you won't observe any small fish even if there are small fish in the lake. From this it follows that your observation (of no small fish in your net) was not improbable at all, even on the hypothesis that the lake is teeming with small fish.

Applying considerations of a selection effect to the case of fine-tuning, the objector's contention is this: Initially it might have appeared improbable that our universe would permit life on the hypothesis that it is just the result of some blind physical process. But we must not forget that because we are living beings produced within our universe we *cannot* observe our universe to be non–life permitting. From this it follows that our observation of a life-permitting universe was not improbable at all, even on the hypothesis that our universe was the result of a blind physical process.

This objection has been called the anthropic objection, but I like to refer to it as the objection that proved too much, because exactly parallel reasoning would have us reject some obviously correct probabilistic arguments. Suppose you sit before a firing squad, about to be fired on.[23] You aren't hopeless, though, because you have some reason to believe that your cousin, who is on the firing squad, may have convinced the others to intentionally miss you. The signal is given, shots ring out, and you find that all the bullets have missed. Intuitively, it's clear that you've just gained evidence for the hypothesis that the shooters were intending to miss. It is very improbable that they would all miss given the hypothesis that they were trying to hit you, while it is not at all improbable (indeed it's very probable) that they would all miss on the hypothesis that they were trying to miss. In other words, your evidence (which is the proposition that you survived) is much more to be expected on the trying-to-miss theory than on the trying-to-hit theory. Notice, however, that the anthropic objection gives the wrong answer here. The anthropic objection would have us wrongly conclude that the trying-to-miss hypothesis is given no support at all by your observation that you survived. You must not forget, it will be urged, that because you must be alive in order to observe anything at all, you cannot observe a situation in which you didn't survive, and so your observation of a firing-squad survival is not improbable at all, even on the hypothesis that the firing squad was trying to hit you.

To see that something has gone wrong here, imagine that the firing squad keeps firing, volley after volley for hours, and they miss you every time. Surely you would eventually have evidence that they are not a normal firing squad intending to hit you.[24]

It's one thing to cast doubt on an objection by showing that it proves too much; it's another thing to understand exactly where it goes wrong. The short version (of where it goes wrong) is that the anthropic objection asks us to focus on an irrelevant probability: the probability that the universe is life-permitting given that the universe is the result of a blind physical process *and* we're here to observe it.[25] True, *if* we're here to observe it, it must be life-permitting. But we might very well have never been here to observe anything! Without a Fine-Tuner in the picture, what is likely is that we would never have been here at all. Since we are here, we have evidence for a universe designer.

The general idea of the fine-tuning argument has now been introduced and some initial objections cleared away. To make the argument more rigorous we need to dig deeper into the theory of probabilistic reasoning. This will get complicated, but take heart; it's the last bit of technical background material we'll need for the argument of this book.

7

A PRIMER ON PROBABILITY

IF YOU EXAMINE A TEXTBOOK on the theory of probability, you'll see expressions like P(A), P(B|C) and P(E|H&K). I'll follow a standard convention according to which the capital letters inside the parentheses (A, B, etc.) always stand for propositions (e.g., *the coin will land heads* or *the theory of continental drift is true*). The "P" stands for "probability," and the expression "P(A)" is just a quick way to write "the probability of A." P(B|C) is an abbreviation for the probability of B, assuming C is true, and is commonly read "the probability of B given C." So P(E|H&K) would be read "the probability of E, given H and K." But what is meant by *probability*?

In different contexts this term has different meanings. We should distinguish three. If a statistician said, "there is a 50 percent probability that an American male living in the twenty-first century will die before age seventy-eight," he might mean only this: of all the American males who have died in the twenty-first century so far, half have been age seventy-seven or younger. That is, he might be using the term *probability* to express claims about a *group* of similar occurrences (American male deaths in the twenty-first century) and the proportion or frequency of occurrences in that group that were of a specified sort (deaths under age seventy-eight). Alternatively, if a physicist said that the probability that a certain plutonium atom will decay in the next twenty minutes is ½, she might be making a statement about that particular atom, asserting that *it* has an objective tendency or disposition to decay in the next twenty minutes and that that tendency has a strength or measure of ½. Finally, if a detective said that the probability that Mr. Rogers committed the theft is very high, she would be making a statement about how confident we should be that Mr. Rogers committed the theft. She would not be saying that of all the many Mr. Rogers in the world, most of them committed thefts. And she would not be saying that Mr. Rogers has now a high objective tendency to have committed the theft in the past. The detective would be making a claim about the level of confidence it is reasonable to have in the proposition "Mr. Rogers committed the theft." Since this meaning of *probability* concerns human beliefs, it is often called *epistemic probability* (from *episteme*, the Greek word for "knowledge"). The epistemic probability of a proposition A given another proposition B, written $P(A|B)$, is a measure of how plausible A is, if B is taken as certain.[1]

The symbols in probability theory, then, can be given different interpretations, and the theory accordingly has different applications. Just as we can apply the formal symbols of algebra to different sorts of problems (here the variables refer to dollars, there they refer to distances), so we can use probability theory to approach different sorts of questions. Most relevant for our purposes is epistemic probability, because we want to use probability theory to address questions of this sort: how should we draw conclusions based on evidence? How do we tell when some fact (like the evidence for fine-tuning) provides a reason to have confidence in some hypothesis or theory? And *how much* of a reason does it provide?

Sometimes a piece of evidence will be decisive. If you're considering the hypothesis that there are no prickly pear cacti on Catalina Island and then accidentally sit on one while visiting there, you will be unfortunate in one respect (I speak from experience). But you will at least be fortunate in this sense: you have acquired the best sort of evidence regarding your hypothesis. Your evidence, the proposition "I am sitting on a prickly pear cactus on Catalina Island," necessarily implies, "It's false that there are no prickly pear cacti on Catalina Island." But much of the time we don't have and can't get evidence that guarantees the truth or falsity of some proposition we're interested in. That's when epistemic probabilities come into play.

Let's look closely at a situation in which the available evidence supports a hypothesis without guaranteeing it. Suppose you are ushered into a room with two tables. On each table is an urn. You are told that one of the urns contains ninety red marbles and ten white marbles, and the other contains ten red marbles and ninety white marbles. But you aren't told which urn is which. You're then asked to select one of the urns and, without looking, to draw from it a marble. You take a marble from the urn on the left, open your eyes and see that the marble is red. So your evidence (E) is that you drew a red marble. Now you are asked, how likely is it that the urn you drew from is the urn with mostly red marbles?

Your evidence E clearly counts in favor of the hypothesis that the urn from which you drew is the one with ninety red marbles (call this hypothesis H_R), and it counts against the hypothesis that it is the one with ninety white marbles (H_W). But precisely how much does E favor H_R over H_W? And at the end of the day, how confident should you be that you drew from the urn with ninety red marbles?

The first step toward answering these questions is to figure out how much E was to be expected if H_R is true. A good way to do this is to imagine a hypothetical thinker who is certain that H_R is true and knows you have selected a marble but who hasn't yet learned what color your marble turned out to be. How strongly would such a person expect that you have drawn a red marble? Since our hypothetical thinker believes with certainty that you were drawing from the urn with ninety red marbles (out of one hundred total), he should judge that there is a ninety out of one hundred chance you drew a red marble. Thus the epistemic probability of E given H_R is $\frac{9}{10}$. Symbolically, $P(E|H_R) = 0.9$. Similarly, $P(E|H_W) = 0.1$.

Actually, I've left something out. We can come up with these numbers because we have in mind some specific background information: you selected without looking. It's also important that nothing in our background knowledge provides a reason to think that any one ball was more likely to be selected than any other ball. (If your hand were a red ball magnet, we'd be wrong to judge that $P(E|H_R) = 0.9$; that would be too low.) Background knowledge is always essential when estimating a probability, and we should make room for this in our symbolism. This is done by including a term (commonly, K) that is meant to be a list of all the relevant background knowledge. So, the point is, a third party who believed with certainty that you drew from the urn with ninety red and ten white marbles, and who also knew about your process of drawing a marble but who hadn't learned of the outcome of the "experiment"—that third party would rightly have a 0.9 level of confidence that you drew a red marble. Abbreviate this as $P(E|H_R\&K) = 0.9$. Similarly, $P(E|H_W\&K) = 0.1$.

All this only gets us halfway to where we want to be; we want to know how confident you should be that you drew a marble from the urn with ninety red marbles, given the background knowledge and the evidence that you drew a red marble. That is, we want to know

$$P(H_R|E\&K) = ?$$

And for this we can turn to a famous rule known as Bayes' theorem, which relates the probability of the hypothesis given the evidence (which is what we want to know) to what we calculated earlier (the probability of the evidence given the hypothesis). Continuing to use H_R to abbreviate the hypothesis that you drew from the urn with ninety red marbles, Bayes' theorem implies:

$$P(H_R|E\&K) = \frac{P(H_R|K) \cdot P(E|H_R\&K)}{P(E|K)}$$

The meaning of $P(E|H_R\&K)$ and $P(H_R|E\&K)$ have been explored above. $P(H_R|K)$, for its part, is known as the prior probability of the hypothesis. It represents the proper level of confidence to have in H_R given the background knowledge K but without the additional information of your evidence (E) that you drew a red marble. Here it's ½.

To see why, it's helpful to again think from the perspective of a third party, this time one who isn't sure which urn you drew from but who, as before, knows what you know about the setup and who hasn't yet observed the outcome of the experiment (your draw). $P(H_R|K)$ is the level of confidence such a person should have in H_R. That level of confidence is ½ because our third party would know you had to select one of the two urns to draw from but would have no information at all that would favor H_R over H_W, or vice versa. So it would be arbitrary for him or her to place a higher confidence in one hypothesis than the other; thus, both hypotheses should be assigned a prior probability of ½.

We've now got this far:

$$P(HR|E\&K) = \frac{(½) \cdot (\%_{10})}{P(E|K)}$$

To get an answer to our question, all that remains is to calculate $P(E|K)$, which represents the level of confidence that should be placed in the proposition "you will draw a red marble" by a third party who has the relevant background knowledge but who has not observed what you have drawn and who does not know which hypothesis is true. It turns out that P(E|K) must equal the sum of two quantities: (a) the prior probability that you would pick the mostly red urn (½) multiplied by the probability that you would draw a red marble supposing you picked the mostly red urn (%₁₀), and (b) the prior probability that you would pick the mostly white urn (½) multiplied by the probability that you would draw a red marble supposing you picked the mostly white urn (¹⁄₁₀). Thus,

$$P(E|K) = (½) \cdot (\%_{10}) \cdot (½) \cdot (\frac{1}{10}) = ½$$

So

$$P(H_R|E\&K) = \frac{(½) \cdot (\%_{10})}{(½)} = (\%_{10})$$

Intuitively, it was clear that drawing a red marble gave you reason to think you probably drew from the urn with ninety red marbles. But now we can be more precise: you should have a 90 percent level of confidence that you drew from the urn with mostly red marbles. When evidence doesn't guarantee a conclusion, probability theory can be a powerful aid toward reasoning well.

For the sake of clarity I've picked an example where we can come up with particular numbers for the various probabilities involved. Ordinary life isn't usually like that, but even in situations where we lack precise numbers, working with Bayes' theorem can often be surprisingly helpful. As we'll see below, Bayes' theorem will shed considerable light on the case of fine-tuning.

A MISTAKE TO AVOID

Imagine that someone reacted as follows to our analysis of the two urns problem:

> At one point we needed to calculate P(E|H_R&K), the epistemic probability of E ("you drew a red marble") given H_R and K. But the epistemic probability of "you drew a red marble" is about the rational level of confidence you should have in the proposition "you drew a red marble." And since you have seen with your own eyes that you drew a red marble, by the time you're asked to calculate P(E|H_R&K), you should be 100 percent confident that you drew a

red marble. So $P(E|H_R\&K) = 1$, not 0.9 as was said above. If you had been asked to calculate $P(E|H_R\&K)$ before drawing a marble, the right answer would be 0.9, but now that you've drawn the marble there is no probability involved; E is certain.

There is an error here, somewhat subtle but very important. The error is a misunderstanding of the meaning of the symbol $P(E|H_R\&K)$. The purpose of applying Bayes' theorem is to estimate the plausibility of a hypothesis given everything we know, but this is done by separating the problem into two subproblems: (1) how plausible is the hypothesis given everything we know *except* some piece of evidence E, and (2) how much do things change when we bring E back into account. As we calculate the various probabilities needed to answer these questions, we have to put aside certain information at certain points. The point of the "given such-and-such" language is to keep track of what we're setting aside when. The background knowledge is "background" relative to the acquisition of the evidence E, and so the background knowledge K is specifically meant to exclude E. Thus $P(E|H_R\&K)$ is the level of confidence we should have in E if K and H_R are believed with certainty but E has been set aside. And so it is 0.9, not 1. The device of the imaginary third party was introduced partly because it helps in keeping all this straight.[2]

FORMULATING THE FINE-TUNING ARGUMENT
WITH THE HELP OF BAYES' THEOREM

We now have the logical tools to see just how powerful the fine-tuning argument is. As discussed in the previous chapter, several features of the universe are fine-tuned for life. For the sake of conceptual clarity, though, I'll focus on just one: the effective cosmological constant. Let

E = The effective cosmological constant falls within the life-permitting range.

H_D = An intelligent being was involved in the production of our universe.

$H_{\sim D}$ = It is not the case that an intelligent being was involved in the production of our universe.

Our relevant background knowledge K includes the proposition that the cosmological constant could have fallen within a very wide range of values—a range at least 10^{41} wider than the life-permitting range.[3] What we are interested in is $P(H_D|E\&K)$, the rational level of confidence to place in the hypothesis of intentional design, given everything relevant we know. Bayes' theorem tells us:

$$(1)\ P(H_D|E\&K) = \frac{P(H_D|K) \cdot P(E|H_D\&K)}{P(E|K)}$$

The strength of the fine-tuning argument comes from the premise that a life-permitting cosmological constant is much more to be expected if there is a designer than if there is not. In symbols, this is the premise that $P(E|H_D\&K) \gg P(E|H_{\sim D}\&K)$, where the symbol ">>" stands for "is much, much greater than."

We'll err on the side of skepticism with regard to fine-tuning and work with the view that the relevant possible range of the cosmological constant is 10^{41} wider than our extra-generous life-permitting range. We can then say that $P(E|H_{\sim D}\&K)$ is about $1/10^{41}$, since apart from our knowledge of E we have no information that would lead us to think any one value of the cosmological constant in its possible range is more likely than any other. Next, how much should E be expected given the designer hypothesis and K? The existence of embodied persons like ourselves is a great good—rational material beings are objectively valuable. And a life-permitting universe is a prerequisite for rational material beings. So the designer of a universe would have a good reason to make that universe life permitting. This reason could be overridden, no doubt; it's not as if nothing could possibly trump it, and it's not as if the universe designer would be doing something wrong by creating a universe that wasn't life permitting. But, given that there would be a good reason to make the universe life permitting and no easily identifiable, strong reason to make it lifeless, we can conclude that it's not unlikely that an intelligent being creating a universe would deliberately select a life-permitting universe rather than a non-life-permitting one.

At the end of the day, how likely is it that an intelligent designer of the universe would design a life-permitting universe rather than a lifeless one? If I had to guess, I'd say over ½. But let's concede as much as possible to the person who will say that we know very little about what a universe designer might want. Very well, shall we estimate $P(E|H_D\&K)$ at 1 in 10? 1 in 100? How about 1 in a million? The smaller the number, the weaker the fine-tuning argument will be.

In order to rely only on a premise that even a skeptic could agree to, let's be generous and assume $P(E|H_D\&K) = 1$ in a billion, i.e., $\frac{1}{10^9}$. The reader may be surprised to learn that, even so, the fine-tuning argument will be exceedingly strong. Starting with equation (1), a little calculation[4] shows that

$$(2)\ P(H_D|E\&K) = \frac{10^{32} \cdot P(H_D|K)}{1 + (10^{32}-1) \cdot P(H_D|K)}$$

This equation relates the rational level of confidence to have in the designer hypothesis given everything relevant we know except for E—this is the so-called prior probability, $P(H_D|K)$—to the rational level of confidence to have in the designer hypothesis given everything relevant we know including E—this is the so-called posterior probability $P(H_D|E\&K)$. Different people will have different estimates of the prior probability of a universe designer. If you have a strong intuitive sense of the existence of God and you don't think the evidence against God is very strong, you'll think $P(H_D|K)$ is relatively high. Although it's impossible to put a definite numerical value on it, you might still judge the prior probability of the designer hypothesis to be "very likely" or "quite likely" or "more likely than not." On the other hand, if you lack an intuitive sense of the existence of God and you think the arguments against the existence of God are very strong, you will probably judge $P(H_D|K)$ to be very low. The usefulness of equation (2) is that it shows that it is reasonable to accept the designer hypothesis as *nearly certain*, even if one started out thinking it was quite unlikely that our universe was produced by an intelligent being. Suppose you start out thinking that the prior probability of the designer hypothesis is ½. Then equation (2) implies you should think, after taking the evidence about the cosmological constant into account, that the probability of the design hypothesis is a virtual certainty, well over 0.999999. If instead you think $P(H_D|K)$ is $\frac{1}{10}$, $P(H_D|E\&K)$ is still over 0.999999. If $P(H_D|K)$ is $\frac{1}{10000}$, $P(H_D|E\&K)$ is *still* over 0.999999. Even if one began by thinking that $P(H_D|K)$ is only 1 in 10^{28} (which is one in ten thousand trillion trillion), $P(H_D|E\&K)$ would still be a bit over 0.999900. One's prior probability for the designer hypothesis would have to be all the way down at 1 over 10^{32} in order for the posterior probability $P(H_D|E\&K)$ to be ½. Taking a moment to think about these numbers will reveal how much the evidence of fine-tuning raises the plausibility of the designer hypothesis.

COULD THE UNIVERSE REALLY HAVE BEEN DIFFERENT?

Thus far I've been assuming that the various fine-tuned features of the universe could have been different than what they in fact are. I've said things like "the cosmological constant could have taken on any of a very wide range of values." A fourth objection to the fine-tuning argument challenges this assumption. For all we know, it is argued, the deepest laws of reality require that the cosmological constant be exactly what it is. Perhaps the physics of the universe *had to* be the way it is, in the strongest sense of "had to." If so, then even if there were a universe designer, there would be no scope for it to do any designing: there would be only one possible blueprint to work with. Thus the existence of a designer wouldn't raise the probability of our universe's being life permitting. Thus, for all we know, the fact that our universe is life permitting isn't evidence for a designer. Call this the necessity objection.

In the previous section, when presenting the fine-tuning argument with the help of Bayes' theorem, I relied on the premise that the probability of the cosmological constant falling within the life-permitting range, given a Fine-Tuner and our background information, is much greater than the probability of the cosmological constant falling within the life-permitting range given no designer and our background information. That is, $P(E|H_D\&K) \gg P(E|H_{\sim D}\&K)$. The necessity objection challenges this premise, noting that if the value of the cosmological constant is fixed by necessity, then the supposition that a universe designer exists won't raise the probability that the cosmological constant will be life permitting. The cosmological constant will either necessarily be life permitting, or it will necessarily be non–life permitting, but no designer would be able to affect whether it is the one or the other. This suggests the following argument:

(a) If the cosmological constant can't have a different value than whatever value it actually has, then $P(E|H_D\&K) = P(E|H_{\sim D}\&K)$.

(b) For all we know, the cosmological constant can't have a different value than whatever value it actually has.

Thus,

(c) For all we know, $P(E|H_D\&K) = P(E|H_{\sim D}\&K)$.

And so,

(d) The fine-tuning argument relies on a doubtful premise.

It should be acknowledged that if we did know with certainty that the relevant features of the universe couldn't have been different, the necessity objection would indeed derail the fine-tuning argument.[5] As it stands, though, we know no such thing. The necessity objection is concerned with metaphysical or absolute impossibility, impossibility in the strongest sense. And there is little reason to think that it was absolutely impossible for the relevant parameters of physics to have been different. What's more, there is actually some positive reason to think that they could have been different. The main reason to think something is metaphysically impossible is that we can see that it involves a contradiction (like a square circle). Yet physicists can describe many models of the physical universe with the same laws as ours but with different parameters, and on close and detailed inspection these models appear to be free of contradictions and hence metaphysically possible. The apparent consistency of mathematical models of different sorts of universes is evidence that there is no contradiction involved in a universe with different parameter values. Granted, it's not completely out of the question that physicists aren't seeing an inconsistency that's really there, but this seems unlikely.

Still, it should be granted that we don't know for sure that the following proposition is false (call it "N" for "necessity"):

N = For whatever value the cosmological constant has, it is metaphysically necessary that the cosmological constant have that value.

So we should grant to the objector that N *might* be true. Even so, the necessity objection still poses no difficulty for the fine-tuning argument. An analogy will help show why.

Imagine that one day you check your bank account balance and instead of the usual $500 or so you find that you have a balance of about $1,000,500. (Call this discovery your evidence E.) You instantly think of your great uncle Abe, the sausage king of Chicago. Uncle Abe has been at death's door for some time. Rumor has it that his will contains instructions to deposit $1 million, on his death, into the bank accounts of each of his few surviving relatives. You don't know of any other remotely plausible reason why you would suddenly have $1 million of mystery money in your account, so you form the belief that

H_U: Uncle Abe died, and his will contained instructions that $1 million from his estate should be deposited into the accounts of each of his surviving relatives.

Your background knowledge K includes the information that you are a surviving relative and that there are no other plausible sources of such a windfall for you. Your strong emotions of grief over the apparent death of dear old Abe—that sweet, sweet man—are clouding your thinking somewhat, but you have just enough presence of mind to explain to a friend why you have come to believe H_U. Letting $H_{\sim U}$ stand for the hypothesis that H_U is false, you explain to your friend that $P(E|H_U\&K) \gg P(E|H_{\sim U}\&K)$. That is, your evidence that you have an extra million dollars in your bank account was much more to be expected given the hypothesis that your uncle died and left this money to his relatives than it was to be expected given the hypothesis that your uncle didn't die or didn't include in his will directions to leave those million-dollar gifts to his relatives. This reasoning seems entirely correct. So far the analogy is straightforward: the evidence about the money in your bank account has taken the place of the evidence for fine-tuning, and the hypothesis about your uncle has taken the place of the universe designer hypothesis.

But now your friend calls your attention to the fact that your uncle might have owed large amounts of money to the government or other creditors. Indeed, for all you know your once-wealthy uncle had incurred so many debts that on his death there would be nothing left for his relatives. Let N (now for "no money") be the proposition that your uncle had no money to leave to his relatives. Your friend presses the point: if N is true, then even if your uncle died and his will contained *instructions* about those $1 million gifts, his relatives would never see any money from his estate because the creditors would get it all first. So $P(E|H_U\&N\&K) = P(E|H_{\sim U}\&K)$. Since you don't know whether N is true, how can you be confident that $P(E|H_U\&K) \gg P(E|H_{\sim U}\&K)$?

A careful application of probabilistic reasoning shows that you do in fact have good evidence that the money in your account is from your uncle, so long as you thought H_U was a real possibility to start with. Essentially, the money in your account becomes powerful evidence that your uncle didn't have great debts. You can split your original hypothesis H_U into two: (1) your uncle died and his will included his relatives, but he had great debts ($H_U\&N$);

and (2) your uncle died and his will included his relatives, and he had no great debts—so he had plenty of money to fund the instructions in his will (H_U&~N). Your evidence E is not to be expected on the first of these two hypotheses, but it is very much to be expected on the second. While $P(E|(H_U\&N)\&K) = P(E|(H_{\sim U}\&K)$, it is also true that $P(E|(H_U\&\sim N)\&K) \gg P(E|(H_{\sim U}\&K)$. So your evidence E is powerful evidence for the second hypothesis, that your uncle died and left money to his relatives and didn't have great debts (H_U&~N). The analogous claim is true in the case of fine-tuning. The evidence that the cosmological constant falls within the life-permitting range is powerful evidence for the hypothesis that *there was a designer involved and the value of the constant is contingent.* (For the mathematically inclined, a formal argument is included in the notes.)[6]

We've now examined the basic fine-tuning argument and considered four common objections: (1) the claim that life could have arisen in very different ways (the Star Trek objection), (2) the objection that a life-permitting universe is no more surprising than any other (the merchant's thumb), (3) the contention that nothing about fine-tuning is surprising because we couldn't exist in a non-life-permitting universe (the anthropic objection), and (4) the possibility that the parameters of physics might be necessary (the necessity objection). In each case, the fine-tuning argument has come out smelling like a finely tuned artificial rose fragrance. But there is another objection to consider, the most potent one of all.

8

GOD AND THE MULTIVERSE

WE'VE NOW LOOKED CAREFULLY at the argument from fine-tuning to Fine-Tuner. If a necessarily existing cause of the universe were also a being with a mind, that would provide an explanation of the apparent coincidences involved in fine-tuning. But is a personal creator the only viable explanation here? Many scientists and philosophers answer with an emphatic "No!" If you were at a physics or astronomy conference discussing fine-tuning with the scholars there, you wouldn't hear much about God or design, but you would hear the term "multiverse." Whereas we're accustomed to thinking of the observable universe as the entirety of physical reality, this may be a mistake. Perhaps there is a vast number, possibly an infinite number, of separate universes. These different universes might exhibit a huge array of different physical features: in some the force of gravity being stronger, in others weaker; in some space expanding more rapidly, in others less rapidly; etc. Considered all together, the different universes would make up *the multiverse*, which would be the whole of physical reality. Within the multiverse, the proportion of universes capable of supporting life would indeed be very, very small, but because there would be so many universes in total, there would be many that do support life. If this were the case, we would be wrong to be surprised by the fact that we have found ourselves in a life-permitting universe. Since only the life-permitting universes will contain beings able to observe their own existence, all the observers throughout the vast multiverse will find themselves in life-permitting universes. Each observer will find himself in a universe that appears designed. And since the separate universes are not visible to one another, each observer will be tempted to think, mistakenly, that he is in the only universe. This is the multiverse explanation of fine-tuning, and it is the preferred explanation of Weinberg, Susskind and many (though not all) of the other physicists mentioned earlier.

There is no direct observational evidence of these other universes. But the potential of the multiverse to explain the apparent coincidences of fine-tuning has rightly made it the subject of much important speculative research among physicists and astronomers. The existence and popularity of multiverse hypotheses raises two distinct problems for the argument of the last two chapters. First, the fine-tuning argument makes much ado about certain pieces of scientific evidence, but if the scientists themselves don't think that that evidence provides a good reason to believe in a universe designer, then isn't it likely that there's some mistake in the fine-tuning argument? Second, even if the mere authority of people like Weinberg and Susskind doesn't settle the issue, there's still the question of why anyone should prefer the designer explanation to the multiverse explanation, given that we now have two apparently viable explanations of the coincidences of fine-tuning.

Regarding the first problem, it's worth asking why there is more talk about multiverse theory than God at an astrophysics conference. One possible reason is that the astrophysicists all have convincing evidence and cogent arguments that there is no such being as God or any other sort of designer. But there is another far more plausible reason, one relating to the methodology of science. The major goal of natural science is the understanding of physical reality. How far would scientists get at that goal if they appealed to God every time they came across a puzzling phenomenon? Can't figure out how lightning works? God is angry. Done! If scientists carried on like that, there would be much less progress in the goal of uncovering the mysteries of nature. Faced with a puzzle about the empirical world, there is almost always nothing to be lost and much to be gained by assuming the existence of a natural explanation as opposed to a supernatural explanation. For this reason and perhaps for other reasons too, there are powerful social pressures within the various scientific disciplines to resist any foray outside the realm of natural explanation. The view of Leonard Susskind is thus fairly typical: "I thoroughly believe that real science requires explanations that do not involve supernatural agents."[1]

Two things should be kept in mind at this point. First, while it may be best for scientists in their work as scientists to always assume the existence of a natural explanation for any given puzzling phenomenon, it must not be forgotten that this is a pragmatic *assumption*, not a reason to think there is no God. And when the puzzle involves not just a question about some phenomenon within physical reality but a question about the very production or source of physical reality, the appropriateness of the assumption that we must never turn to a supernatural explanation is far less apparent. Second, and more crucially, we can grant to Susskind that invoking God to explain something isn't "science." But it still could be "reasoning," and perfectly valid reasoning at that. Suppose Susskind looked up at the night sky one evening to see the stars rearrange themselves to spell "I most certainly exist, Leonard." Perhaps this would not provide a "scientific" reason to believe in God, but it'd be a pretty good reason all the same. The takeaway: while the philosophical argument from fine-tuning to the existence of a universe designer doesn't get much discussion at physics conferences, this is no indication that it's an unsuccessful argument. Let's turn, then, to the second of the two problems mentioned above: the fine-tuning argument fails because the multiverse hypothesis is at least as good of an explanation of fine-tuning as the designer hypothesis. Call this the multiverse objection.

THE THEISTIC MULTIVERSE

Logicians use the term *constructive dilemma* to refer to a form of argument recognized and loved since the days of Socrates. Suppose the zookeeper explains why you need to cut short your visit to the zoo: "Either the lions have escaped or the snakes are loose. If the lions have escaped, we have a serious problem. If the snakes are loose, we also have a serious problem. So either way, we have a serious problem."[2] I, for one, would be convinced. The form of the argument is

A or B

If A, then C

If B, then C

So C

An argument in this same form can show that the multiverse objection fails. No one knows for sure whether there are many universes, but we do know this: either ours is the only universe or there is a multiverse. On the one hand, if ours is the only universe, it is much more likely that the universe was designed than that it just happened to be life permitting by chance. (The last two chapters support that claim.) So if there is only one universe, the evidence of fine-tuning favors the view that our universe was designed. On the other hand, our universe may exist within a multiverse. But even then, either theism or atheism may be true. (God may have wanted to create many universes.) If we exist in an atheistic multiverse, then the proportion of life-permitting universes will be *very* small. But if we exist in a multiverse created by God, we should expect the proportion of life-permitting universes to be not nearly so small. (Since life is a good, any intelligent being has a reason to value it, and thus God would have some reason to create more of it.) So the proportion of life-permitting universes will be much higher in a theistic multiverse than in an atheistic multiverse. This in turn implies that the epistemic probability that our universe would be life permitting is much higher on a theistic version of the multiverse hypothesis than on an atheistic version. So if there are many universes, the evidence of fine-tuning favors theism over atheism. Either way, considerations of fine-tuning strongly favor the existence of a universe designer.

The key step in this argument is the claim that if we are in a multiverse, then the fine-tuning of our universe is strong evidence that we are in a theistic multiverse rather than an atheistic multiverse. Three main ideas lend support to this claim. First, God might very well want to create many universes. Second, the reasons to create many universes that God would have are also reasons to think that a significant proportion of universes created by God would be life-permitting universes. Third, this fact about proportions implies that it is much more likely that the universe we are in fact in would have a life-permitting cosmological constant given a theistic multiverse hypothesis than given an atheistic multiverse hypothesis. Let's look at each of these three ideas in turn.

The thought that God might create many universes may seem odd and unfamiliar. On reflection, though, nothing about the notion of God implies that God would make only a small number of living beings or a small number of different kinds of living beings. According to Christian tradition, God has not only brought about the existence of large numbers of individual living physical beings and a large number of *kinds* of living physical beings, but he has also created a vast number of intelligent living nonphysical beings (the angels). So the idea that God's creation of life was vast is not a new idea. The main difference introduced with a theistic multiverse is the great spatial separation between the various products of God's creative activity—these other universes are so distant (or otherwise separated from us) that there's no chance of travel between them. But if God wanted to create very many more physical living things than, say, can exist on Earth, then it seems likely that at some point so much space would have to be provided that any given set of physical beings would have to be separated from most of the others. There's only so many elephants you can fit in one place.

So God and the multiverse aren't incompatible. But would God have any reason to create many universes? The existence of more individual living beings would be a good thing for those individuals, and hence there is always some reason for God to make more individuals. Furthermore, the existence of different kinds of creatures adds value to creation, and the number of *possible* kinds of creatures is so large that the existence of many universes would be a suitable way to allow for their realization.[3] Finally, consider this argument: for any single universe God creates, there's probably a better single universe God could've created. So if God creates only a single universe, he must necessarily forgo creating a vast, possibly infinite number of better universes he could have created. A theistic multiverse would allow him fuller scope to share the goodness of existence.[4]

These considerations aren't by any stretch decisive; God could very well have other, stronger reasons not to create many universes. But it would be hasty to hold a firm opinion that God definitely would not create more than one universe. If one knew God existed but didn't know how many universes God had created, the proper attitude about the number of universes would be to have an open mind. Proceeding to the second idea listed above, all the reasons just mentioned that God would have for creating many universes are also reasons to create many universes with many and diverse forms of life. Let's say one learned that God had created many universes, and one was then asked to guess what proportion were life permitting. For each given physical universe that God creates, that universe would exhibit more value if it contained living beings (especially living rational beings) than if it contained no life at all. So God would have some reason to make an appreciable proportion of the universes life permitting. On the other side, there doesn't seem to be any very strong reason God would have to create many lifeless universes. So the expected proportion of life-permitting universes should not be very low. No particular number is obviously correct as the number to guess, but certainly one would think the proportion was nonnegligible. Shall we say one in two? One in ten? The lower the proportion, the weaker the argument for a theistic multiverse will be. In keeping with the procedure of conceding as much as possible to the skeptic, let's assume that only one in a billion would be life permitting. This will still be more than enough to secure the fine-tuning argument against the multiverse objection, because what is crucial is the difference between the proportion of life-permitting universes to be expected in a theistic multiverse and the proportion to be expected in a multiverse that is the unguided product of a mindless cause (or causes). If there is no Mind behind the multiverse, we would expect the proportion of life-permitting universes to be miniscule, one in 10^{41} or smaller. Surely the proportion would be much, much higher if the cause of the multiverse were a purposive being likely to value life. Compare: suppose one learned of the existence of a thousand oil "paintings" all produced by the same cause, and suppose one was told that that cause was either a blind, chance process or an artist believed to value paintings of flowers. One should surely expect many, many more paintings of flowers on the artist hypothesis than on the chance hypothesis.

And now for the third and final idea: this fact about proportions means our evidence E (that the cosmological constant in our universe is life permitting) is much more to be expected on a theistic multiverse than on an atheistic multiverse. And this in turn means that, even if the existence of a multiverse is assumed, the fine-tuning argument still succeeds. In order to see why, take the background knowledge we had before (K) and add the claim (M) that there is a vast number of universes. D now stands for the proposition that there was an intelligent being involved in the production of these universes, and ~D stands for the proposition that there wasn't. What made the fine-tuning argument successful in the case where we were assuming just a single universe was the premise that $P(E|D\&K) \gg P(E|{\sim}D\&K)$. Now that we're assuming a multiverse, the analogous premise is still true: $P(E|D\&M\&K) \gg P(E|{\sim}D\&M\&K)$, since $P(E|{\sim}D\&M\&K)$ will equal $\frac{1}{10^{41}}$ or smaller. An analogy will help to illustrate the reasoning here. Let's take a break from all these universes and talk a bit about widgets.

THE DEADLY BLUE WIDGET

Suppose that John has ordered a single widget, but he can't remember which company he ordered it from.[5] It might have been Redd's Widget World, which makes mostly red widgets. For every hundred widgets Redd's makes, ninety-nine are red, and only one is blue. Or it could have been the Blue Velvet Smooth Widget Company, which makes ninety-nine blue widgets for every one red. John does remember that he didn't order a specific color, and he knows this means that the widget company will simply grab any widget at hand when they pack his box. Later that afternoon John's box arrives, and he opens it to find a red widget. Whom did he probably order from?

The evidence is

E = The widget in the box sent to John's house is red.

The two hypotheses being considered are

H_R = The box was sent by Redd's Widget World.

H_B = The box was sent by the Blue Velvet Smooth Widget Company.

Relevant background knowledge K includes the information that when John's order was filled, no attention was paid to color. Given the information about the relative proportions of red widgets at the two companies, $P(E|H_R\&K) = 0.99$, while $P(E|H_B\&K) = 0.01$, and so E strongly favors H_R over H_B. If we suppose that prior to learning E, John had no information to favor one hypothesis over the other, then Bayes' theorem tells us that after taking E into account, John should think it 99 percent likely that he ordered from Redd's.

Next, let's complicate this example so that it more closely parallels our situation vis-à-vis fine-tuning. In the case of fine-tuning, if the cosmological constant in our universe hadn't been in the life-permitting range, we would not have been able to observe that it hadn't. But in John's case as described above, John would have been able to observe a blue widget if the box sent to his house had contained one. This disanalogy can be removed by adding a piece of information to the background knowledge: both Redd's and Blue Velvet are actually fronts for the mafia, specializing in assassinations. When either company sends blue, they send an assassin, too. The assassins are flawless, and they always eliminate their target before anyone has had a chance to open the box sent to the target's residence. Both companies maintain an Internet presence for tax purposes, and unsuspecting folks like John sometimes end up being "collateral damage." Let's suppose John learns all this only after he's opened his box. Question: should John alter his judgment that he almost certainly ordered from Redd's?

He should not. A red widget was much more likely on H_R than on H_B. If H_B were true, John would almost certainly be dead and not observing anything. But he is not dead. His survival and the fact that he received a red widget are equally evidence for H_R.[6]

We can apply this analogy to the case of fine-tuning. Instead of the relevant background knowledge including the claim that both widget companies make many widgets, now the relevant background knowledge includes the claim that there are a vast number of universes. Since we used K to refer to the relevant background before, when we weren't thinking about many universes, let's use K* to refer to our old background knowledge K plus the additional proposition that there are a vast number of universes. Next, in place of "the widget in the box sent to John's house is red" we once again have

E = the cosmological constant in our universe is within the life-permitting range.

In place of the hypothesis that John's widget was from Blue Velvet, we have

~D = No intelligent being was involved in the production of the universes.

And in place of the hypothesis that John ordered from Redd's, we have

D = An intelligent being was involved in the production of the universes.

Importantly, $P(E|\sim D\&K^*)$ will be extremely low, $1/10^{41}$ or smaller. To see this, consider the perspective of an imaginary third party who is in ignorance about E but who believes with certainty that the multiverse exists and was not produced or influenced by any intelligent designer. $P(E|\sim D\&K^*)$ is the rational level of confidence for such a person to place in the proposition (E) that the cosmological constant in our universe will turn out to be life permitting. Since the third party is in ignorance of E, from his perspective our universe is just one particular universe in the multiverse—he has no information that would lead him to think it's more likely than any other to be life permitting. So the rational level of confidence for him to place in E can be no greater than the estimated proportion of universes with life-permitting cosmological constants within the multiverse as a whole, which on his information should be 1 in 10^{41}.[7]

$P(E|D\&K^*)$, on the other hand, will be thousands and thousands of times higher than $P(E|{\sim}D\&K^*)$. Imagine a third party who is in ignorance of E but who believes with certainty that there is a multiverse that *was* produced by an intelligent designer. $P(E|D\&K^*)$ is the rational level of confidence for such a person to place in the proposition (E) that the cosmological constant in our universe will turn out to be life permitting. Again, this level of confidence will track his estimate of the proportion of universes with life-permitting cosmological constants. If this was 1 in 10^{41}, above, when no designer was believed to be in the picture, then now, when a designer is assumed to be involved, it will be thousands of times higher—on our previous assumptions not less than 1 in 10^9. Thus $P(E|D\&K^*) \gg P(E|{\sim}D\&K^*)$, and the fine-tuning argument will be as strong as it was in the case when we were assuming the existence of only a single universe.

SUMMING UP

Though the multiverse objection is the strongest objection to the fine-tuning argument around, it overlooks an important point: God might well have created a multiverse. So there are really two multiverse hypotheses we need to consider: an atheistic multiverse hypothesis and a theistic multiverse hypothesis. And when we compare these two, the evidence for fine-tuning favors the theistic version, because a theistic (or designed) multiverse should be expected to contain a much higher proportion of life-permitting universes. If the atheistic multiverse hypothesis were true, some rational beings in some universe would likely exist to observe a life-permitting universe, but it's very unlikely that we would be among them. Since we can only exist if *our* universe (the universe we are in fact in) is life permitting, and since the existence of many universes (without a designer) leaves it very unlikely that any given universe will be life permitting, it's very unlikely that we would exist at all if there is a multiverse but no designer. Yet we do exist, and thus if we are in a multiverse, it's very probably a multiverse designed by an intelligent being. On the other hand, if there's just a single universe, the strength of the fine-tuning argument is even more evident. Either way, atheism has a serious problem.

If the arguments of the last four chapters are sound, there is strong, publicly available evidence for the existence of an intelligent cause of physical reality, a Mind behind all this matter. Given the endless disagreement about such issues, perhaps we should take such arguments with a grain of salt. But this much certainly seems true: it is not at all unlikely that there exists a necessarily existing intelligent creator, perhaps the omnipotent, omniscient, perfectly good God of traditional Christian thought. Still, there's more evidence to consider. On the one hand, there's counterevidence—maybe some things we know count strongly against the idea of an intelligent creator. This is an important point, and we'll examine it in chapter ten. But first, there's another place to look for evidence for God. If the universe was produced for a reason, and if the universe designer values rational living beings like ourselves, then we might expect that designer to reach out to us in some way, to communicate some message that would help us. If God existed, we might well expect him to reveal himself.[8] Has he?

9

THE BEAUTY AND EXISTENTIAL
RESONANCE OF CHRISTIANITY

WRITING ABOUT FOUR HUNDRED YEARS before the time of Jesus, Greek philosopher Plato depicts a conversation between Socrates and several friends during the final hours before Socrates's execution. The topic fits the scene: What happens to a human being after death? Does our existence continue, or do we simply cease to be? One of Socrates's friends remarks on the difficulty of attaining certainty about such questions. Still, he continues, if a person is unable to definitively uncover the truth, he should "select the best and most dependable theory which human intelligence can supply, and use it as a raft to ride the seas of life—that is, assuming that we cannot make our journey with greater confidence and security by the surer means of a divine revelation."[1] Unaided human reason is powerful, but a divine revelation would indeed carry us more surely and safely through life. So it's worth inquiring into whether God has made such a revelation, and how we would recognize it if he had. If God did have a word to send us, what would it—or he—be like?

In the preface, I mentioned that I was raised Catholic but started in my early teens to have questions about the existence of God and the truth of Christianity. Later I began to experience a firm intuitive sense of the presence of God, and I've also since become acquainted with various strong arguments for the existence of God and the truth of Christianity. But that was all later. What happened first was that I began reading the Gospels, and I was struck by the moral character of Jesus. Reading the Sermon on the Mount, in which Jesus says such things as "love your enemies," I remember thinking "*This* is the way to live . . . and yet no one actually lives this way. There is something important here, something to learn." To my mind, the moral beauty of Christian doctrine is some evidence of its truth—not overwhelming, decisive evidence, but still an important clue. In this chapter I'll try to explain why I see things this way. I'll also consider two other aspects of Christian teaching that possess a noteworthy ring of truth: (1) the teachings of Jesus explain both the greatness and the depravity of human beings, and (2) according to Christianity, human life is no mere accidental result of meaningless forces but a meaningful drama with an objective purpose. Insofar as the content of Christian revelation is evidence of its divine origin, this content is at the same time evidence for the existence of God and for Christianity, in particular.[2]

LOVE AS THE KEY TO LIFE

If someone wanted to know what you believe in, what you value, how you think human beings should act and what you think is most worth pursuing in life, she could ask you and then listen to what you have to say. But there is something else she could do: she could observe what you do. Often our actions reveal our deepest convictions more accurately than our words. If I say that I value my family over my career, but I spend little time with my children and use all my spare moments to get ahead at this or that office task, perhaps I'm deceiving myself about what I really value. If I say I care about morality but spend more of my money on entertainment then on sharing with the poor, perhaps my words don't tell the full story. Suppose we try to take an objective perspective and look at human beings from the outside, so to speak. What should we conclude about what people value? Clearly, much of what people do is aimed at maximizing pleasure and comfort. And much of what people do is aimed at success or achievement and at gaining the approval of others (social status, popularity, prestige, recognition). These are all good things, but if one values only one's own pleasure, success and social status, one has neglected something. How about . . . other people? It's possible to view one's relationships with others as, at the end of the day, mere means to the end of promoting one's own personal satisfaction. But this is an impoverished view of human relationships. How much nobler to care about the well-being of another person for his or her own sake and to consider the well-being of the other as an end in itself. One's own pleasure, success and social status are goods worth desiring, but the objective well-being of others as well as oneself should rank higher on one's scale of values. And what about moral goodness? Where does that fit in?

There is a distinction sometimes made between two approaches to ethics: an ethics of minimal obligation and an ethics of moral excellence. The ethics of minimal obligation asks, "What must I do to satisfy my moral obligations?" And one answer to this question is that I must never violate the human rights of other people, but other than that I can pretty much do as I please. Taking this as a starting point, it's easy to think that the goal of my life is my own personal satisfaction, and the requirements of moral goodness are a sort of constraint on how I can pursue my personal satisfaction. By contrast, an ethics of excellence has a very different flavor, because it starts with a very different question: "What can I do to become a morally excellent person?" The teachings of Jesus exhibit this second approach to ethics. "Be perfect, therefore, as your heavenly Father is perfect" (Mt 5:48). And at the root of Jesus' teaching about moral excellence are two precepts: love God and love one's neighbor as oneself. Let's examine these precepts more closely.

Several of the Gospels relate a conversation between Jesus and a scholar of the Jewish law:

> When the Pharisees heard that he had silenced the Sadducees, they gathered together, and one of them, a lawyer, asked him a question to test him. "Teacher, which commandment in the law is the greatest?" He said to him, "'You shall love the Lord your God with all your heart, and with all your soul, and with all your mind.' This is the greatest and first commandment. And a second is like it: 'You shall love your neighbor as yourself.' On these two commandments hang all the law and the prophets." (Mt 22:34-40)

To love God involves valuing him, caring about what he cares about and desiring to be united with him. To love one's neighbor involves the intention that one's neighbor flourish and, depending on the circumstances, the desire to be united with one's neighbor in the way appropriate to the nature of the relationship. Who is one's neighbor? Anyone whom one can help (Lk 10:29-37). As commentators have noted, this passage also implies a duty to love oneself.

If one did not love oneself well, then loving one's neighbor *as oneself* would not amount to much. So we are to love God, love others and love ourselves.

As a philosopher, the last line in the quotation above intrigues me. Jesus appears to be making a statement about the *structure* of ethics: there are many precepts we should follow, but these two are in some sense the source, the pegs on which the rest depend. There's a certain simple logic here. We should treat things according to their value; persons are the most valuable beings in all reality; and love is the proper response to a person. So of course the key precept of ethics is that we should love persons. Yet despite its simplicity, Jesus' teaching is revolutionary. If everyone in the world loved others as much as we love ourselves, the world would be a very different place. Politics, economics, the organization of society, personal relationships—everything would be different. And Jesus' teaching is revolutionary in another way. With all its myriad implications for self-sacrifice on behalf of the poor, the marginalized and the powerless, Jesus' teaching stands in tension with so much of natural human inclination. Following the way of Jesus requires an internal revolution, a conversion of the heart. This internal revolution involves sacrifice, but there's something deeply attractive about the person of Jesus and the prospect of following him.

Jesus' invitation to orient one's life around love comes with specific, practical instructions: Feed the hungry. Welcome the stranger. Take care of the sick. Visit the imprisoned (Mt 25:31-46). It includes inner thoughts and acts of will as well as external actions (Mt 5:21-32). Love requires not only that we act with justice but that we show mercy and forgiveness. This is a high bar! But if God were going to give us a revelation, wouldn't we expect it to be something like this?

There are many deep and insightful moral truths to be found in the New Testament, though here is not the place for an exhaustive exposition. Better for the reader unfamiliar with the New Testament to explore it in an unhurried way, with the help of suitable commentaries. It should be acknowledged, too, that there are biblical passages that raise serious moral difficulties. But a consideration of each of the difficult texts in the Bible is also far beyond the scope of this chapter, and there are numerous thought-provoking resources already written on such topics.[3] My point here is just this: the moral teachings of Jesus have a sublime character that is suggestive of a divine origin.

THE GRANDEUR AND THE WRETCHEDNESS OF HUMANITY

Human beings have a certain majesty about them.[4] Though limited in time and place, our thoughts can range over all times and places. With our senses we grasp particular bits of information, but with our minds we engage in abstract thought. We are capable of uncovering unseen mysteries of nature, eternal laws of logic and mathematics, and universal truths of morality. Though our bodies are composed of atoms blindingly following the laws of physics, we somehow are able to make free choices, rising above chance and necessity to affect the course of the future, as true causes, not just responders to stimuli. We are persons, not just bags of atoms. We can grasp the moral good and choose accordingly. We can make promises and sacrifice our own interests out of love for others. We create works of art and music of amazing beauty.

Yet in other ways we are so weak. We are subject to illness, injury and death. We are prone to error, easily distracted and suffering from numerous cognitive biases. We are even capable of deceiving ourselves when some truth is unpleasant to us. We have the ability to ignore blindingly obvious moral truths (think, for example, of the long persistence through history of slavery as an accepted institution, or of the disregard for the equal rights of men and women). And while we have a capacity for love and goodness, we show a remarkable tendency for moral wrongdoing. When our perceived self-interest clashes with morality, things can get ugly fast.

So humans are a bit of a puzzle. Though finite, we long for the infinite. We have a natural desire for perfect knowledge and complete understanding, but on our own we can't discover the answers to the most basic of questions. How did we get here? Why are we here? Where are we going? Our origin, purpose and destiny remain obscure. We recognize lofty moral ideals yet continually fail to live up to them. We desire an unending life of perfect happiness, but death is inescapable, and in our short time on earth happiness so often eludes us. What a mismatch between our desires and the reality around us! Though the earth is the place of our birth, we long for something more.

Humans are at the same time both exalted and lowly. Pascal reflects at length on this "dual nature" of ours, these strange contradictions of human nature. "Man's greatness and wretchedness are so evident that the true religion must necessarily teach us both that there is a great principle of greatness and a great principle of wretchedness in man."[5] Pascal goes on to argue that Christianity does teach us both: humans were created in a state of right-eousness and connection with God, but through their own free will they rebelled against God. We, the descendants of the first humans, have in-herited a nature that is great but wounded. We are like kings who have been deposed.[6] Or like a beautiful painting that has been damaged.[7] The ultimate source of our greatness is that we are created in the image and likeness of God. The source of our wretchedness is that we are fallen.

And there's more: the teachings of Jesus don't just explain our unique combination of grandeur and misery, they offer a solution, a way back to God and happiness. In the words of Augustine, "our hearts are restless till they rest in Thee."[8] Pascal writes that man tries "vainly to fill [his emptiness] with everything around him, seeking from things absent the help he does not receive from things present. But they are all inadequate, because only an infinite and immutable object—that is, God himself—can fill this in-finite abyss."[9]

So here we have another clue: Christian doctrine about human beings makes sense of our existential situation.

A Meaningful Life

From the perspective of atheism, it can be difficult to view one's life story as a meaningful narrative, with an objective, big-picture purpose and a tran-scendentally valuable goal. If individual atoms have no purpose, can a human-shaped bag of atoms have one? It may be possible to give an atheistic account of the meaningfulness of human life, but it is difficult, as is indicated by the large number of secular philosophers who have felt forced to accept a grim view of reality. Thus, Bertrand Russell:

> Even more purposeless, more void of meaning, is the world which Science presents for our belief. . . . That Man is the product of causes which had no prevision of the end they were achieving; that his origin, his growth, his hopes and fears, his love and beliefs, are but the outcome of accidental collocations of atoms; that no fire, no heroism, no intensity of thought and feeling, can preserve an individual life beyond the grave; that all the labours of the ages, all the devotion, all the inspiration, all the noonday brightness of human

genius, are destined to extinction in the vast death of the solar system, and that the whole temple of Man's achievement must inevitably be buried beneath the debris of a universe in ruins—all these things, if not quite beyond dispute, are yet so nearly certain that no philosophy which rejects them can hope to stand. Only within the scaffolding of these truths, only on the firm foundation of unyielding despair, can the soul's habitation henceforth be safely built.[10]

And similarly, the contemporary philosopher Simon Blackburn:

> Science teaches that the cosmos is some fifteen billion years old, almost unimaginably huge, and governed by natural laws that will compel its extinction in some billions more years, although long before that the Earth and the solar system will have been destroyed by the heat death of the sun. Human beings occupy an infinitesimally small fraction of space and time, on the edge of one galaxy among a hundred thousand million or so galaxies. We evolved only because of a number of cosmic accidents, including the extinction of the dinosaurs some sixty-five million years ago. Nature shows us no particular favors: we get parasites and diseases and we die, and we are not all that nice to each other. True, we are moderately clever, but our efforts to use our intelligence to make things better for ourselves quite often backfire, and they may do so spectacularly in the near future, from some combination of manmade military, environmental, or genetic disasters. That, more or less, is the scientific picture of the world.[11]

From a secular perspective, it's natural to think that there's no such thing as "the purpose" of one's life. We can give ourselves purposes to follow, and our lives can be meaningful in the sense of being significant to ourselves and others, but if humans are just an accidental result of chance processes, it's hard to avoid the conclusions that there simply is no such thing as "the meaning" of life and that we have no objective purpose standing above our own desires. Physicist Steven Weinberg, himself an atheist, writes, "The more the universe seems comprehensible, the more it also seems pointless."[12]

According to Christianity, by contrast, our lives each have an objective, transcendent purpose: to enjoy forever the love of God and other, created persons. Your life is a particular story within a larger story. And the particular story of your own life does not end at death. You are the deliberate creation of a loving God, who made you for a reason, and who has both a powerful desire for your eternal fulfillment and a plan to help you attain it. You have been given free will, and over the course of your life you will help to form your own character through your free choices. Above all, you must make a fundamental choice between being open to relationship with God or remaining closed. It is not certain that you will make the right choice and reach your goal. But God's help is not lacking, and the only way to lose the battle is by saying no to God's love and mercy.

I wonder whether you've had an experience I sometimes have—a vague, inchoate sense, deep down, that my life has a purpose. That there is some thing or things that I am meant to do. This thought naturally suggests an argument: If humans are the accidental result of blind physical forces, then my life doesn't have a purpose. But my life does have a purpose! So it must be false that humans are the accidental result of blind physical forces. Of course this doesn't settle the issue; the sense that our lives have a purpose could be misleading. Human intuition is far from infallible. Yet there's still a valuable clue here. The Christian doctrine that our lives have transcendent meaning and an objective purpose resonates with something deep within the human heart.

I've argued in this chapter that Jesus' teachings have the ring of truth. But is there more solid evidence available? I think there is. In chapters eleven and twelve we'll examine some of the best recent research on the question of whether there is good historical evidence for the truth of Christianity. First, however, we need to turn to a different topic: counterevidence.

10

COUNTEREVIDENCE

Divine Hiddenness and Evil

THERE WAS ONCE A YOUTHFUL KING who fell in love with a beautiful maiden in his kingdom . . . before he had even met her. He had seen her from afar while on royal business near her village. After inquiring and hearing at length of her good character, nimble mind and sparkling personality, he was irrevocably smitten. But she had no knowledge of any of this. She was a lowly peasant, and her impoverished family had no connections to high society. The king realized that if he approached the maiden in all his regal splendor, it would be easy to gain her hand in marriage. Too easy, and this very fact put him in a difficult position. He was a virtuous man and wanted her choice to be one of complete freedom. And he didn't want a trophy wife; he wanted a real marriage, and he wanted a wife who loved him for who he was as a person, not for his power or wealth. He knew that if he came to her as the king, he would make it difficult for her to freely choose him for the right reasons. What was he to do?

After some thought, he settled on a course of action, although it involved great risk. He disguised himself. Posing as a traveling laborer, he moved to her village and sought her acquaintance in the ordinary way.[1]

One of the strongest obstacles to belief in God is what philosophers and theologians call the problem of divine hiddenness. If God loves us, why does he remain hidden? Why doesn't God make his existence obvious, to everyone, as obvious as the existence of trees and rocks? An all-powerful God surely could do this, and since belief in God would be a good thing, it seems that a God who loved us would want to do this. So why hasn't he? The

foregoing parable suggests an answer. God does not want our belief or obedience per se; he wants our freely given love. And if he made his existence
undeniably obvious to everyone, he would jeopardize something very
valuable: the possibility we have (in this ambiguous world) to love God
freely and for the right reasons. If God's existence were obvious to all, it
would be hard for people to refrain from viewing God in a Machiavellian
manner, making the Ultimate End into a mere means to power and pleasure
for the self. I am no critic of cost-benefit analysis, as a reader of part one of
this book will know. But, psychologically, there is a world of difference between a situation in which all know with certainty that the only way to happiness is with God, and our actual situation, where God remains hidden, at
least for most people much of the time. Knowledge of God is easily resistible,
and so the choice to seek God remains free and capable of being readily
motivated by moral considerations as well as considerations of self-interest
narrowly construed.[2]

In chapters five through eight, we considered evidence for the existence
of God. The cosmological argument shows that there must be at least one
necessary being that is part of the explanation for the existence of contingent
beings, and the fine-tuning argument gives us a good reason to think that
the cause of contingent beings is (or at least includes) a being with intelligence as well as great power. The beauty of Christian teaching (chapter nine)
carries an evidence all its own. Now it's time to consider some counterevidence. The two most forceful arguments against the existence of God are
the argument from divine hiddenness and the argument from evil (or suffering). They can be encapsulated in just a few lines:

> If God existed, then he would make his existence obvious to everyone.
> But he hasn't made his existence obvious to everyone.
> Thus God does not exist.

> If God existed, then there wouldn't be a vast amount of suffering in the world.
> But there is a vast amount of suffering in the world.
> So God does not exist.

As indicated above, in my view the argument from divine hiddenness
can be answered by attending to considerations about the value of a free
and virtuous human response to God.[3] The argument from suffering is

more challenging. In this chapter I want to briefly summarize what I take to be the two most insightful examinations of this argument to have yet been elaborated.[4]

THE ARGUMENT FROM SUFFERING

When one is young it's easy not to realize how much pain there is in the world. As one gets older, it's hard to ignore. In all probability, during this very hour someone somewhere will be murdered, someone will be raped, someone will be betrayed and someone will be tortured. It's a horrible thought. It's a horrible fact. And in addition to the suffering humans cause each other, there is the suffering caused by disease, accidents and natural disasters. If God existed, surely there wouldn't be all of this suffering—this is the first premise of the argument from suffering, and on the face of it, it is a very plausible premise indeed. If there is a God (as traditionally conceived), then he is both good and powerful, and so he would want to prevent suffering and would be able to. But if he wants to prevent suffering and is able to, then he would prevent it. And if he prevented it, it wouldn't exist. So if God existed, suffering wouldn't exist.

One reaction to this argument is to reject the traditional understanding of God: perhaps God exists but isn't all-powerful or isn't all-good. This reaction is overly hasty. Notice that the justification for the first premise of the argument from suffering (in the preceding paragraph) includes the general claim that if God both desires and is able to prevent some instance of suffering, then he *would* prevent that instance of suffering. This claim is false. Imagine that you have a five-year-old daughter with bone cancer. Chemotherapy causes her great suffering; it makes her sick, feel terrible and lose her hair. You desire that she not suffer like that, and you are perfectly able to prevent it—just put a stop to her chemotherapy treatments. Yet you don't prevent it. Why? Because there is a greater good involved, the possibility of her being cured of cancer, and chemotherapy is the only way available to you to achieve that greater good. Generalizing: it's not always true that if a good person is able to prevent some instance of suffering, then he or she will do so. This observation raises the possibility that God could have a reason for allowing suffering: doing so may be necessary to achieve one or more greater goods or ward off one or more greater evils.

While helpful as far as it goes, this reply to the problem of evil still leaves us wondering what this greater good (or goods) might be. What could possibly be so good as to be worth all the suffering humans experience?

THE BASIC FREE-WILL DEFENSE

The place to start is with the concept of free will. It might well be that God needs to allow suffering in order to give humans a significant say in what happens in the world. Here's the idea: God caused many good things to be— stars and planets, plants and animals. But he also wanted to create even greater beings, beings who, like himself, could understand and freely choose among alternatives. And so he created beings with free will, including us. The main value of free will is that it makes a certain sort of love possible. Freely given love is worth more than the love of, say, a robot determined by its programmer to act benevolently.

And God didn't just want to give his creatures free choice about unimportant things, like what color shirts to wear. He wanted to give us significant free choice, free choice about decisions that really matter. He didn't want to reserve all the important decisions for himself, because there is a great value in letting his creatures have a real say in how they will live their lives, in who they will become, in what or whom they will love.

Unfortunately there's a risk here, and a cost. If God really does give us significant free will, then he must allow the possibility that we will use our freedom wrongly and introduce evil and suffering into the world. And that is exactly what has happened. So, according to the basic free-will defense (as the foregoing line of thought has been called), suffering has entered the world because God's creatures have misused their free will.

VAN INWAGEN'S EXPANDED FREE-WILL DEFENSE

Though thought provoking, the basic free-will defense suffers from two major problems. First, God might allow *some* suffering for the sake of giving humans free will, but why allow *so much*? Just to take one example, God could have easily stopped the Nazi rise to power before it went very far, without completely taking away anyone's free will. It's one thing to take away a person's ability to freely choose this or that; it's another thing to allow evil plan after evil plan to be successful. Second, the basic free-will defense suggests that all evil is the result of free creaturely decisions, but shark attacks and earthquakes, pain and death, seem to be part of the natural world God has (allegedly) created. It's hard to see how *all* suffering can be traced back to the misuse of creaturely free will.

With these objections in mind, the philosopher Peter van Inwagen has offered a response to the argument from evil that expands on the basic free-will defense. The logic of van Inwagen's response is somewhat subtle, and to understand it we should begin by considering a lengthy story he develops. Take a moment and simply imagine the following scenario: Over the course of millions of years, God brought it about that very clever primates evolved on earth and then miraculously raised a small group of them to rationality. These were the first humans. God gave them free will and put them in a paradisal state, exempting them from age and death and protecting them from physical danger. "But, somehow, in some way that must be mysterious to us, they were not content with this paradisal state. They abused the gift of free will and separated themselves from their union with God."[5] The result was horrific. Humans were now subject to disease and death and began to mistreat each other. Their descendants went from bad to worse:

> A certain frame of mind had become dominant among them, a frame of mind latent in the genes they had inherited from a million or more generations of ancestors. I mean the frame of mind that places one's own desires and perceived welfare above everything else, and which accords to the welfare of one's immediate relatives a subordinate privileged status, and assigns no status at all to the welfare of anyone else. And this frame of mind was now married to rationality, to the power of abstract thought; the progeny of this marriage were continuing resentment against those whose actions interfere with the fulfillment of one's desires, hatreds cherished in the heart, and the desire for revenge. The inherited genes that produced these baleful effects had been harmless as long as human beings had still had constantly before their minds a representation of perfect love [because of their union with God]. In the state of separation from God, and conjoined with rationality, they formed the genetic substrate of what is called original or birth sin: an inborn tendency to do evil against which all human efforts are vain.[6]

The first human beings, then, had freely chosen to reject God, and as a natural consequence humans had been left with disordered wills in a

dangerous and capricious world. But all was not lost. Out of love, God
formed a rescue plan, a plan of atonement. His goal: for humans to freely
choose to be reunited with him. Since we cannot reliably will what is right
on our own, and God cannot *unilaterally* bring it about that we *freely* choose
to be reunited with him, God's rescue plan necessarily requires cooperation.
Yet human beings will not cooperate with God in this rescue plan unless
they realize that they need to be rescued. And for them to realize that, God
needs to allow much terrible suffering. If he did not, too many people would
be content in their state of separation from God: "If God simply 'canceled'
all the horrors of this world by an endless series of miracles, he would
thereby frustrate his own plan of reconciliation. If he did that, we should be
content with our lot and should see no reason to cooperate with him."[7] Thus
ends the story.

Van Inwagen will be the first to admit that he has no proof that this story
is true. But a careful attention to the logic of the argument reveals, somewhat
surprisingly, that the burden of proof is actually on the proponent of the
argument from evil at this point. Let me explain. The first premise of the
argument from evil is "If God existed, then there wouldn't be a vast amount
of suffering in the world." A helpful way to assess a claim of the form "If A
were true, then B would be true" is to imagine that A *is* true, and then see
whether (once we've accepted A just for the sake of argument) we should
also be confident that B is true. You imagine that a certain man is a bachelor.
You realize that, supposing him to be a bachelor, he couldn't have a mother-
in-law. You thereby know to be true the claim "If this man is a bachelor, then
he doesn't have a mother-in-law." Imagine now that this certain man is
married. Supposing he is married, you can't be confident he *does* have a
mother-in-law. For all you know, the mother of his wife might have passed
away. Thus you should consider unreliable the claim "If this man is married,
then he has a mother-in-law." Applying all this to the case at hand, van Inwagen's point is that if we suppose God exists, we should admit that for all
we know he might allow a vast amount of suffering, because if God exists,
the preceding story is a real possibility. If God exists, then the rest of the
story, or something like it, may very well be true. And this implies that we
should consider doubtful the claim "If God existed, then there wouldn't be
a vast amount of suffering in the world." Since an argument with a doubtful

premise doesn't provide a good reason to accept its conclusion, the argument from evil doesn't provide a good reason to reject the existence of God.

And now we can return to the two main objections to the basic free-will defense. Why does God allow humans to do so much damage to each other? Because if a vast amount of suffering weren't allowed, something even worse would follow: too many humans would not realize they need to be rescued and would show no interest in cooperating with God in their own moral regeneration and reunion with him. Why does God allow the suffering of earthquakes and cancer? The same reason.

VAGUENESS AND CHANCE

We've yet to explore a key feature of van Inwagen's views on God and evil. When faced with a particularly terrible evil (the rape of a child, for example), it's natural for a theist to wonder, "Why on earth did God allow that?" To understand van Inwagen's suggested answer, we'll need to take a slight detour into the subject of vagueness. A concept is vague, in the philosophical sense, if there is no clear dividing line between situations in which the concept applies and situations in which it doesn't. The concept "bald" is like this. If you have a full head of hair, you're not bald; if you have no hair at all, you are bald. But if you start out with a full head of hair, and we pluck hairs from your head one by one, it's not at all clear that we'll reach a last single hair the removal of which will transform you from not being bald to being bald.

Certain facts about vagueness have an implication for what God's providence might involve. Suppose God wants to make France an agriculturally fertile country in the year 1952, and so God sends a good amount of rain that year. How many drops should he send? He has to draw the line somewhere—the number of drops that fall must be some particular number. But notice that however many drops of rain God sends (so as to make France a fertile country), it will be true that he could have allowed one less drop of rain to fall without jeopardizing the overall goal of making France fertile. If he sends 1,844,259,207,548 drops, and that is enough to make France fertile, then surely France would also have been fertile with 1,844,259,207,547 drops. There are deep logical puzzles here, and we could spend the rest of this book exploring the paradoxes of vagueness. But for our purposes it's sufficient to grasp the general idea that clear dividing lines may sometimes not exist.

What does this have to do with the question of why God allows a given particular evil? According to van Inwagen, even an agnostic about God should grant that it is a very real possibility that if God did exist, God would have a reason for allowing terrible suffering. The reason is that unless he allows a large amount of suffering, a greater good will be lost, namely, the good of helping people realize they need to be rescued by and reunited with God. But when it comes to the question of how much suffering God should prevent and how much he should allow, God has to draw a line somewhere. And no matter where he draws it, it will be true that he could have prevented one more instance of suffering without making a difference to his overall goal of helping us realize that we need to be rescued. So it's simply not logically possible for God to avoid a situation in which he allows some particular evils which he could have prevented without jeopardizing the overall reason for allowing suffering. Thus, although God has a reason for allowing much suffering, he doesn't have a different specific reason for allowing each different particular suffering that occurs. And so the answer to our question "Why did God allow *that* particular instance of terrible suffering?" may be that there was no particular reason. To live in a world separated from God is to be a "plaything of chance."[8] On this score, van Inwagen's views differ markedly from those of the second thinker we'll here discuss—philosopher Eleonore Stump.

A METICULOUS PROVIDENCE

Recall the story of Cain and Abel (Gen 4:1-16). Cain murders his brother out of jealousy, right under God's nose. If God is good and Abel is just, as the story presupposes, why doesn't God protect him? Or if protection is too much to ask, how hard could it have been for God to give Abel a simple warning about Cain's intentions? Stump points out that these questions make an easily unnoticed assumption, the assumption that it is Abel rather than Cain who is most in danger and most in need of God's help.[9] But this assumption is mistaken. If Christianity is true, it is Cain who is most in danger, for he is in danger of eternal separation from God. For Abel, what is at stake is bodily death, which though in itself a bad thing, will be for Abel a transition into fuller union with God. For Cain, what is at stake is his relationship with God and his eternal destiny. And so it is Cain, not Abel, who receives a warning, in the form of encouragement from God to refrain from the murder he is contemplating. Yet God leaves Cain free.

Like van Inwagen, Stump thinks that the argument from evil does not provide a good reason to disbelieve in God and that human freedom plays an important role in understanding why. And like van Inwagen, Stump attempts to undercut the claim that if God existed, there wouldn't be so much suffering. But she does so in her own way—by explaining, expanding and defending Thomas Aquinas's views on the place of evil in God's providential plan.

These views (of Aquinas, as interpreted by Stump) can be summarized as follows. First, the life of a human being is divided into two unequal segments: a short earthly life and an everlasting afterlife. The best thing for a human being is unending participation in a close, personal relationship with God and other, created persons (this is heaven). The worst thing for humans is the everlasting absence of that personal relationship (this is the essential component of hell). Those in hell have through their own choices become permanently alienated from themselves and others, including God. Ultimately, every human being will end up in one of these two states, heaven or hell. Although every human being will eventually either be in heaven or not, for those in heaven, union with God can come in degrees. It's possible for a person to be closer or less close to God in the afterlife, even though everyone in heaven will have as much union with God as they desire.

Second, one's openness to God's love at the time of death is the crucial determinant of one's eternal destiny—God will draw to himself all those who are not unwilling. But after one's first vision of God in the afterlife, change in the level of one's openness to God is no longer possible. And so the state of one's soul at death is immensely important.

Third,

> the primary obstacle to any person's flourishing in union with God comes from dispositions in that person's will[10] that incline him to prefer his own short-term pleasure and power over greater goods. On Aquinas's understanding of the doctrine of original sin, all human beings have this disposition, which is a sort of cancer of the will, a proneness to evil that eventuates in moral wrongdoing sooner or later and that can blow up into moral monstrosity.[11]

Fourth and finally, God allows suffering as a sort of medicine, in order to provide an opportunity for the healing of this moral and spiritual cancer within all of us. In Aquinas's words:

> As water extinguishes a burning fire, so tribulations extinguish the force of concupiscent desires, so that human beings don't follow them at will. . . . Therefore, [the church] is not destroyed [by tribulations] but lifted up by them, and in the first place by the lifting up of the mind to God, as Gregory says: the evils that bear us down here drive us to go to God.[12]

And more generally: "pains purge sins, bring evildoers to humility, and stimulate good people to love of God."[13] It's important to note that here Stump is trying only to identify a plausible possible reason for God to allow the suffering of fully functional adult human beings, not the suffering of children (or animals, for that matter). But at least in the case of adults, I think we can see how God could use suffering to break open a closed psyche, to reach a person who has become attached to his or her own pleasure or power. In some cases God permits suffering in order to provide the sufferer with an opportunity to let go of the lesser goods he or she clings to in place of moral goodness and God, an opportunity to become open to a new ordering of priorities and, ultimately, to become open to God. In these cases, the primary goal of allowing suffering is to ward off the worst thing for that sufferer—the unending loneliness that will result if he or she remains closed to God. In other cases, cases in which a person is already open to God, suffering can provide an opportunity for the sufferer to grow morally and spiritually in ways that will allow the sufferer to enjoy greater closeness with God and others in the next life. Needless to say, Aquinas is well aware that during earthly life we humans are often ignorant of how a particular suffering is intended by God to benefit the sufferer; but on his view the connection to a benefit for the sufferer is always there.

One might get the idea that, according to Aquinas, those who are further from God will suffer more. In fact, the opposite is the case. In his commentary on the book of Job, Aquinas explains:

> It is plain that the general of an army does not spare [his] more active soldiers dangers or exertions, but as the plan of battle requires, he sometimes lays them open to greater dangers and greater exertions. But after the attainment of victory,

he bestows greater honor on the more active soldiers. So also the head of a household assigns greater exertions to his better servants, but when it is time to reward them, he lavishes greater gifts on them. And so neither is it characteristic of divine providence that it should exempt good people more from the adversities and exertions of the present life, but rather that it reward them more at the end.[14]

Van Inwagen's and Stump's Views as Complementary

In order to keep this chapter within reasonable bounds, I've had to leave to the side much of van Inwagen's and Stump's rich analyses of the problem of suffering. But enough has been said to allow us to see how Stump's account is both similar to and different from van Inwagen's. The major difference is that, according to Stump, the suggested possible reason why God allows suffering includes the claim that, for every instance of suffering, God's justifying reason for allowing that suffering has to do with a benefit to the particular person suffering. God thus has a specific reason for allowing each particular suffering he allows. According to van Inwagen, by contrast, God does not necessarily have a particular reason to allow each particular suffering he allows, although he does have a reason to allow suffering in general, and a reason (having to do with vagueness) *for not having a reason* for allowing some particular evils. So van Inwagen and Stump offer different possible accounts of why God allows suffering. But recall that they are each merely pointing out that their accounts of why God allows suffering are *real possibilities*, because this is all that is required to show that the argument from evil does not provide a compelling case against the existence of God. And so they could both be right—both of their accounts *are* quite possible. So, for more than one reason, we should be very skeptical of the first premise of the argument from evil, the claim that if God existed there wouldn't be so much suffering. Thus while the suffering of the world may provide some evidence against God, it is not strong evidence against God.

We've now examined arguments for the existence of a necessarily existing, intelligent creator of the universe and discussed some ways in which Christian doctrine resonates with human experience. We've also explored arguments against the existence of God from divine hiddenness and evil, and I've argued that they aren't compelling. It's time to turn to the question of whether there is solid evidence for the truth of Christianity.

11

HISTORICAL EVIDENCE FOR CHRISTIANITY
The Resurrection

Is there good historical evidence that Jesus literally rose from the dead? This question provokes a surprising variety of responses from scholars, ranging from emphatic denials to confident affirmations. According to Matthew McCormick: "the case for Christ is orders of magnitude weaker than it should be to justify believing."[1] According to William Lane Craig: "Once one gives up the prejudice against miracles, it's hard to deny that the resurrection of Jesus is the best explanation of the facts."[2] Let's take a look at the controversy.

A Common Argument

A common argument for the truth of Christianity focuses on the resurrection. The apostles claimed they saw and conversed with a gloriously resurrected Jesus after his death. Either (1) they were *deceivers* (knowing they hadn't had any such experiences but saying they had for some ulterior motive), or (2) they were *deceived* (thinking they had really seen Jesus when in fact they hadn't, perhaps experiencing vivid hallucinations, for example) or (3) Jesus *really was* resurrected. But the apostles had too little to gain and too much to lose by such a deception—so they weren't deceivers. And the experiences they had of Jesus aren't the sort of thing a group of sane people can be deceived about; multiple, utterly convincing group hallucinations are too improbable. So they weren't deceived. The best explanation, then, is that Jesus really did rise from the dead and appear to the apostles. And given that, we can trust that the teachings of Jesus are true.

This argument has been criticized at many points and in numerous ways by learned, contemporary scholars; it has also been carefully reformulated and powerfully defended by other learned, contemporary scholars.[3] In this chapter and the next, I'll present an updated version of this argument and assess the three strongest objections made against it.

OBJECTION: NOT ENOUGH EVIDENCE

Arguments for the resurrection rely on various assertions about what the earliest Christians experienced (an empty tomb, extended conversations with the resurrected Jesus, a shared meal with the resurrected Jesus and so forth). These assertions are typically supported by reference to the four Gospels. But, as many critics have noted, most biblical scholars today think that even the earliest of the four Gospels was written about thirty-five years after Jesus' death. That's a long time for inaccuracies to creep in or legends to develop. It's also noted that we don't possess any original copies of the books of the New Testament; we have only copies of copies of copies. The oldest actual manuscripts we possess date mainly from around AD 200 and after. Thus we must acknowledge the possibility that our version of the New Testament today is importantly different from what the original authors wrote. Moreover, besides the four Gospels accepted today, there were other early Christian writings (e.g., the Gospel of Thomas) that were rejected by early Christian bishops. Perhaps the four Gospels give us a skewed portrait of Jesus, having been selected by Christian leaders for reasons unconnected with historical accuracy or truth.

And even if we just focus on Matthew, Mark, Luke and John, there are inconsistencies in the Gospel narratives about the resurrection. For example, when the women went to Jesus' tomb on Sunday morning, did they find two men in dazzling apparel (as in Lk 24), or one angel sitting on the stone (as in Mt 28), or a young man sitting *in the tomb* (as apparently implied in Mk 16)?

Finally, there are now available very few documents containing information about Jesus that were written by non-Christians in the first hundred years after Jesus' death. So the worry is that we don't have reliable, nonbiased information about Jesus. Given all this, the objection goes, the amount and quality of the evidence is just too poor for us to believe in something as unusual as the resurrection of a dead man. As the late Carl Sagan observed, extraordinary claims require extraordinary evidence.

The Minimal Facts Approach

Faced with the objection that arguments for the resurrection rest on shaky ground, philosopher Gary Habermas and theologian Michael Licona have developed and utilized an approach to the issue termed *the minimal facts approach*. The goal of the approach is to identify and rely only on those historical facts that are agreed on by all or almost all scholars who study the topic—theists, agnostics and atheists alike. Licona settles on three facts, which are strongly supported by evidence and which "are regarded as historical by a nearly unanimous consensus of modern scholars":

1. Jesus died by crucifixion.

2. Very shortly after Jesus' death, the disciples had experiences that led them to believe and proclaim that Jesus had been resurrected.

3. Within a few years after Jesus' death, Paul converted after experiencing what he interpreted as a postresurrection appearance of Jesus to him.[4]

Note that all three of these facts, as described, are noncommittal with respect to the *truth* of the early disciples' belief in Jesus' resurrection. The minimal facts approach starts merely with statements about what the early Christians claimed and believed.

So what is the evidence that these three statements are indeed solidly established facts? Jesus' execution is attested to by Jewish historian Josephus (writing around AD 94), Roman historian Tacitus (writing around AD 115) and numerous early Christian sources. And it is presupposed in surviving ancient criticisms of Christianity (e.g., those of Celsus in the second century). As for the second and third facts, let's begin with two undisputed letters of Paul, 1 Corinthians and Galatians. In Galatians Paul claims that he had been a persecutor of the early Christian movement but that God had revealed his Son to him (or "in" him; Gal 1:16), and that Paul had joined the Christian movement. This would very probably have been two to three years after the death of Jesus.[5] Also in Galatians Paul says that he went to Jerusalem three years after his conversion experience, and while there met with Peter for fifteen days and saw "James the Lord's brother [or cousin]" (Gal 1:18-19). This would probably have been between five and six years after the death of Jesus. Paul goes on to say that after fourteen years he again went to Jerusalem, met with Peter, James and John (the leaders of the church in Jerusalem), and laid before them the gospel message he had been preaching (Gal 2:1-2). He says that he did this "in order to make sure that I was not running, or had not run, in vain"—that is, in order to make sure he hadn't been preaching the wrong thing (Gal 2:2). Paul says that Peter, James and John gave him "the right hand of fellowship," in other words, that they endorsed his message and ministry (Gal 2:9). There is thus good evidence that Paul, Peter, James and John were all preaching the same basic message about Jesus in the first two decades after Jesus's death.

And we don't have to simply take Paul's word here. The claim that Paul was teaching the same basic message as Peter and John is confirmed by Clement of Rome and by Polycarp.[6] Clement is thought to have died around AD 101; Polycarp was martyred at the age of eighty-six, sometime between AD 156 and 167. According to Irenaeus (c. AD 140–202) and others, Clement was an associate of Peter and the author of the letter we know as 1 Clement. But Clement holds Paul in great esteem, referring to him and Peter as "the greatest and most righteous pillars (of the Church)."[7] Clement would not have done this if Paul had taught a radically different message from Peter. Irenaeus also tells us how, when he was a youth, he met Polycarp and heard him teach about the sayings of the first disciples. Irenaeus says that Polycarp was instructed by several of the apostles, especially John. And Polycarp refers to Paul as one who taught "accurately and faithfully . . . the word of truth."[8] Polycarp would not have done this if Paul had taught an importantly different message from John. So there's excellent reason to conclude that Paul, Peter and John were all preaching the same basic gospel message.

So what was this gospel message? In 1 Corinthians, Paul tells us. Writing around AD 55, Paul reminds the Christians at Corinth of what he had said to them when he had previously been in Corinth in person:

> Now I would remind you, brothers and sisters, of the good news [gospel] that I proclaimed to you, which you in turn received, in which also you stand. . . . For I handed on to you as of first importance what I in turn had received: that Christ died for our sins in accordance with the scriptures, and

that he was buried, and that he was raised on the third day in accordance with the scriptures, and that he appeared to Cephas [Peter], then to the twelve. Then he appeared to more than five hundred brothers and sisters at one time, most of whom are still alive, though some have died. Then he appeared to James, then to all the apostles. Last of all, as to one untimely born, he appeared also to me. (1 Cor 15:1, 3-8)

Paul claims that a resurrected Jesus had appeared to Peter, to the apostles and to many other early Christians, and that all this had occurred before Jesus appeared to Paul himself. Since Paul's alleged encounter with the risen Jesus was itself not many years after Jesus' death, we have here evidence from Paul's testimony for both the second and third of Licona's three facts. But we have more than that. Paul could not have claimed that Jesus had appeared to Peter and the apostles if Peter and the apostles had never themselves claimed any such thing. If Peter and the apostles weren't themselves claiming that they had seen the resurrected Jesus, Clement, Polycarp, Irenaeus and other early Christian writers would have been quick to point out that Paul was an innovator who went far beyond the claims of Peter, James, John and so forth.

Based on these and other reasons, even most atheist and agnostic biblical scholars accept the three facts that comprise Licona's "historical bedrock." Well-known agnostic biblical scholar Bart Ehrman, for example, does not accept the resurrection but does accept the three facts in question:

1. "One of the most certain facts of history is that Jesus was crucified on orders of the Roman prefect of Judea, Pontius Pilate."[9]

2. "My own view is that the biblical authors thought Jesus was physically resurrected from the dead."[10]

3. "Why, then, did some of the disciples claim to see Jesus alive after his crucifixion? I don't doubt at all that some disciples claimed this. We don't have any of their written testimony, but Paul, writing about twenty-five years later, indicates that this is what they claimed, and I don't think he is making it up. And he knew at least a couple of them, whom he met just three years after the event (Galatians 1:18-19)."[11]

4. "[T]here is no doubt that [Paul] believed that he saw Jesus' real but glorified body raised from the dead."[12]

AN ARGUMENT FOR THE RESURRECTION

Paul, Peter, John and no doubt many others claimed that they had seen Jesus risen from the dead, despite the fact that they faced severe persecution and the danger of death on account of their proclamation of Jesus' resurrection and teachings. Why would they do this? What could have made them stake their whole lives on this claim?

One possibility is that Paul was simply lying about the resurrection, for some ulterior motive, and that Peter and the other apostles likewise lied when they claimed to have experienced postresurrection appearances.[13] But this is very unlikely—people lie when they have an incentive or reason to lie. And here the incentives are all wrong. Proclaiming the resurrection of Jesus exposed the early Christians to ridicule, abuse and mortal danger. Jesus' teachings had led to his torture and crucifixion, and the earliest disciples would have known that more of the same would likely be in store for them if they continued to proclaim his teachings, challenging as they were to existing religions and the power of Rome. Moreover, Paul, Peter and the other apostles appear to have benefited little, in worldly terms, from their leadership positions in the new religion of Christianity. This stands in stark contrast to the experiences of the founders of many other religions. Muhammad had ten or more wives and was the political and military leader of a new Muslim state in Medina.[14] Joseph Smith entered into clandestine marriages with upwards of twenty wives and exercised leadership over a local militia numbering in the thousands in Nauvoo, Illinois (then the center of the Mormon religion).[15] More recently, L. Ron Hubbard appears to have gained large financial profits through the Church of Scientology.[16] The self-abnegating, missionary life of Paul that emerges from our historical sources is of an entirely different character.

Second, if the resurrection story had been a lie, it would have involved the conspiracy of many people (including Paul, Peter, James, John and probably the hundreds of witnesses Paul mentions in 1 Cor 15). We would expect that when these early conspirators were later faced with the threat of imprisonment and death one or more of them would spill the beans, or at least abandon Christianity. Yet there is no evidence that this took place, despite the fact that those interested in opposing the new religion would have had a strong incentive to unearth and report such facts. Today we still have access to some early critiques of Christianity (e.g., those of Celsus, Porphyry and Julian), but they contain no claims that alleged witnesses of the resurrection recanted.

Third, if the resurrection stories were a deliberate lie, Paul, Peter and the others would have believed that they were spreading lies about God. What would they have to have believed about God in order to make this seem like a good idea? They would have to have been extremely confident atheists, in their heart of hearts, despite all their talk about God. But given their culture and their behavior, such a scenario is very unlikely. In the case of Paul, we can get a good sense of his character from the letters left to us. As Richard Swinburne observes:

> No one can read the more personal letters—Galatians, 2 Corinthians, and Philemon—without getting a very strong impression that Paul is a totally honest and generally very compassionate man (willing to rebuke those who he thinks have been deceitful or otherwise immoral, but keen for reconciliation with them; and keen not to get involved in matters which he thought relatively unimportant). What he says in his letters, above all what he gives his solemn word about, he means.[17]

Another possibility is that the early witnesses of the resurrection were sincerely deceived. They believed Jesus had appeared to them, although in actual fact Jesus was not resurrected; the appearances were just hallucinations. This hypothesis has been defended by several scholars in recent years.[18]

On inspection, though, the hallucination hypothesis suffers from three serious problems. First, while hallucinations among healthy people do sometimes occur in situations of bereavement (for example, when someone's spouse dies), these hallucinations don't lead to a firm belief that the deceased spouse has been *resurrected*. That is, they don't result in a conviction that the deceased, after a period of having been dead, is once again alive and embodied. When bereavement hallucinations are not simply recognized as hallucinations, they may naturally be interpreted (by the hallucinator) as brief visitations of the spirit of the deceased from "beyond the grave." The disciples interpreted their experiences very differently, which suggests that their total evidence must have gone far beyond the experience of a typical bereavement hallucination. This conclusion is confirmed by the fact that an individual resurrection such as that alleged of Jesus was contrary to expectations in the disciples' cultural context. Neither their cultural expectations nor a typical bereavement hallucination would have led the disciples to form a belief in the resurrection.[19]

Second, and to my mind most crucially, if the resurrection appearances were hallucinations, then the disciples experienced group hallucinations. For each of the three group appearances mentioned by Paul ("the twelve," the "more than five hundred" and "all the apostles"), those involved would have had to *each* experience a determinate, convincing hallucination with similar content at the same time. This is monumentally unlikely. A more probable occurrence would involve (for each of those three groups) one member of the group having a hallucination and the others saying that they had had the same hallucination, whether because of self-delusion or through outright deceit, perhaps born of a misguided desire to be included in a spectacular event. But it is very unlikely that the false or concocted claims (of those group members who did not really have hallucinations but said they did) would have survived the danger and social pressure faced by the early disciples. Furthermore, this suggestion does not explain the multitude of different appearances at different times (Paul mentions six, including individual and group appearances). Even if only one person had a convincing hallucination on each of these six occasions, we're still left with the improbable event of six hallucinations (to multiple individuals) of the same dead person, resulting in a firm conviction that the deceased had risen from the dead.

Third, what about Jesus' body? Suppose that the resurrection appearances were hallucinations. Then, once the apostles realized Jesus's body was still in the tomb, they would have concluded that they'd been mistaken in thinking Jesus had been raised and therefore would have not proclaimed the resurrection. Or even if the apostles would not have concluded this, the opponents of the Christian movement would have been quick to capitalize on the decisive counterevidence of Jesus' corpse. That the new Christian religion flourished in the very city where Jesus was crucified is evidence that this didn't happen. This line of reasoning suggests that for the hallucination hypothesis to work, we need to add the claim that the body was stolen, or lost, or never buried in the first place. Let's examine the plausibility of this further hypothesis.

After the crucifixion, Jesus was either buried or not. If Jesus was buried, he was buried either in a grave or tomb known by the disciples, or in a grave or tomb unknown to the disciples. If Jesus was not buried, then his body was likely consumed by wild animals (as appears to have been standard in cases of crucifixion). This gives us three possibilities to consider: (1) buried in a known location, (2) buried in an unknown location and (3) not buried.

If Jesus was buried in a known location, then the disciples would very likely have checked that location after they experienced what they took to be encounters with the risen Jesus. And surely at least some among the opponents of Christianity would have checked that location after the disciples publicly claimed that Jesus had been resurrected. But when this checking was done, the grave would have to have been found empty, or the disciples' belief in the resurrection would not have remained intact and any claims about the resurrection would not have been taken seriously. So, for the hallucination hypothesis to be credible (supposing Jesus was buried in a known location), the body of Jesus would have to have been stolen from the tomb. This reduces the probability of the hallucination hypothesis. A theft of Jesus' body would have been contrary to the interests of the Romans and the Jewish religious authorities, so they would not plausibly be behind such a theft (or if they were, they would have produced the body after the disciples began proclaiming the resurrection). A theft of the body by the disciples who were proclaiming the resurrection takes us away from the "deceived" hypothesis and back to the "deceiver" hypothesis, with the weaknesses mentioned above. This leaves the possibility that the body was stolen by a third party—grave robbers, for example. Yet grave robbers would have been interested in valuables buried with the body (e.g., the linen shroud) and would have had no reason not to leave the body in the tomb, once stripped of any valuables.[20]

Might Jesus have been buried in an unknown location, for example, a common grave for several crucified criminals, the location of which was unknown to the disciples? Four arguments reduce the probability of this suggestion. First, the location would likely have been known to the Roman authorities, who would therefore probably have been able to produce the body when the disciples began proclaiming the resurrection. Second, in a city as small as Jerusalem was in AD 30, it could not have been too difficult for an interested person to figure out where Jesus' body had been buried. After their apparent encounters with him, the disciples would have had strong reasons to discover this location and seek to verify his resurrection. Similarly, after the proclamation of the resurrection, the Jewish authorities would have had good reasons to discover this location in order to falsify that proclamation. Third, the earliest polemics regarding the resurrection presuppose that the tomb of Jesus was known but found empty—Matthew 28:11-15 indicates that the response of the Jewish authorities to claims about the resurrection was that the disciples had stolen the body. Finally, as Richard Swinburne has argued, the fact that the Christians celebrated the Eucharist on Sunday is relevant.[21] Very soon after Jesus' death, Christians were already celebrating the Eucharist weekly, on the first day of the week (Sunday). Why Sunday?

> There are other days on which it might have been more natural for Christians to celebrate the Eucharist (e.g. on the day of the original Last Supper—probably a Thursday and certainly not a Sunday—or annually rather than weekly). No such are known. There is no possible origin of the sacredness of Sunday from outside Christianity. There is only one simple explanation of this universal custom, which, I argued, must derive at the latest from the first two or three post-Resurrection years. The Eucharist was celebrated on a Sunday . . . because Christians believed that the central Christian event of the Resurrection occurred on a Sunday. Yet such early practice would have included that of the Eleven themselves, and so could only go with a belief of theirs that Christians had seen either the empty tomb or the risen Jesus on the first Easter Sunday. This shows that the visit to the tomb on Easter Sunday was not a late invention read back into history to make sense of the appearances but a separately authenticated incident.[22]

What of the possibility that Jesus was never buried at all? Bart Ehrman argues that "the common Roman practice was to allow the bodies of crucified people to decompose on the cross and be attacked by scavengers as part of the disincentive for crime."[23] We should therefore expect, other things being equal, that Jesus was not buried.

Three independent pieces of evidence count against this possibility, however. First, Paul's testimony in 1 Corinthians 15:4. The oral tradition Paul handed on to the Corinthians explicitly includes the claim "that he was buried." If Jesus was not in fact buried, we are either back to the "deceivers" hypothesis or the early disciples were somehow sincerely mistaken in their belief that Jesus was buried. But the latter seems unlikely for the following reason: Ironically, if Ehrman is right about the standard fate of the crucified, then the early disciples' default assumption would have been that Jesus was *not* buried, and they would only have (sincerely) come to the conclusion that Jesus *was* buried if they'd had good reason to think he was. So, if we set aside (for the reasons mentioned earlier) the hypothesis that the disciples were lying about the fate of Jesus, we should conclude that the disciples had access to good evidence of Jesus' burial.

Further, two of the reasons to doubt that Jesus was buried in an unknown location also count against the claim that he wasn't buried at all. It seems that the skeptical response to claims of the empty tomb (which are clearly present in Mark, within thirty-five or forty years after Jesus' death) was not "there was no empty tomb because he wasn't even buried" but was instead "His disciples came by night and stole him away" (Mt 28:13). And to the extent that the early Christian celebration of the Eucharist on Sundays is well explained by a visit to a known tomb on Easter Sunday, this early practice disconfirms the theory that Jesus was not buried at all.

To sum up: (a) the distinctive reaction of the disciples to their post-resurrection experiences of Jesus, (b) the improbability of group hallucinations and (c) the difficulties involved in supposing that Jesus' body was lost or not buried, taken all together, render the hallucination hypothesis very unlikely.

All this suggests a third explanation. If the eyewitnesses who claimed that Jesus had been resurrected weren't lying and weren't deceived, then the best explanation left is the traditional one: Jesus rose from the grave.

What are we to make of this hypothesis? On close inspection, the alternative explanations really do appear implausible. But can we, in today's modern world, accept a supernatural explanation invoking a literal *miracle*? At the outset of this chapter, I noted that there is a great disparity among people's reactions to the argument for the resurrection. As William Lane Craig and Richard Swinburne have suggested, this disparity may largely be a product of the different views people have about the plausibility of a divine miracle.[24] Let's turn to that issue.

12

MIRACLE OR MYTH?

AS WE SAW IN THE PREVIOUS CHAPTER, a common objection to arguments for the resurrection is that our evidence just isn't good enough. The minimal facts approach avoids this objection by utilizing only a small number of facts, all of which are historically very well evidenced. But there's a stronger objection to consider. I've argued that group hallucinations are very unlikely and that it is very, very unlikely that the apostles were lying. Still, isn't the resurrection of a dead man very, very, *very* unlikely? Many critics have argued that *no matter how improbable* the alternative naturalistic explanations are, we should conclude that one of them must be true, because the supernatural alternative is the most improbable of all.[1] Call this the improbability objection.

Clearly, if God exists and wanted Jesus to rise from the dead, God could make that happen. So whether we should accept the improbability objection all depends on how likely it is that God exists, and how likely it is that, if God does exist, Jesus would be resurrected. Consider an analogy: suppose the year is 1942, and you're an anthropologist studying a primitive tribe deep in the forests of Papua New Guinea. One day, one of the natives returns to camp and excitedly tells the rest of the tribe that he has just seen a gigantic stone bird descend from the sky and land on a lake. After the bird came to a stop, it floated on the lake, and a human being emerged from its head. Some members of the tribe believe the story, but others reject it out of hand—stones can't fly and don't float on water, and besides there are no such things as giant stone birds with humans in their heads! The tribe then begins arguing among themselves. Some point out that the witness is a trustworthy person, and it is very improbable that he would be sincerely deceived about whether a giant stone bird landed on a lake. Others reply that no matter how improbable deception or illusion is in this case, the alternative that there actually was a giant stone bird is the most improbable theory of all. Being a good anthropologist, you keep your mouth shut. But of course you know what to conclude. You know about airplanes and had heard that the US military was going to be doing reconnaissance in the area, and so you accept the witness's word, or the gist of it anyway. Because you know that airplanes exist, and that it is not unlikely that one equipped with pontoon landing gear would have landed in a nearby lake, it's not rational for you to be moved by the objection of the skeptically minded natives.

The lesson here is that background information is relevant to the assessment of evidence for Jesus' resurrection. If it were nearly certain that God does not exist, then it would be correct to reject the historical argument for Christianity on the grounds that the resurrection is simply too improbable to accept. But it's not nearly certain that God does not exist. Indeed, the cosmological and fine-tuning arguments render the existence of God quite plausible. So the crucial question becomes: If God does exist, is it plausible that Jesus would have been resurrected?[2]

To make some headway on this question, let's consider what God might do when faced with the problem of the human race gone wrong. It's hard to deny that human beings have a proclivity to engage in all sorts of harmful and morally wrong actions. For each of us, there is considerable distance between who are and who we should be. What could God do about this problem? Simply zapping us and compelling us to do right would be to turn us into robots, canceling our free will and with it our opportunity to freely love what is good for its own sake. Better to involve our cooperation in the process of our own healing. But how can we cooperate with God if we know very little about his plans and intentions? If God exists, then, he would have good reason to give us a definitive revelation, containing the information we need to be made right—although this revelation would likely be subject to the constraints concerning divine hiddenness discussed in chapter ten. If God makes his existence and desires too overwhelmingly obvious, that could render it difficult for us to choose to love him freely and for the right reasons. Still, some sort of revelation would be reasonable to expect.

Furthermore, God would have several good reasons to become incarnate (i.e., to take on a human nature). Although providing moral information is helpful, it would be even more helpful for God to provide us with a moral example—to show us, not just tell us, how a human life should be lived. And one excellent way to do this would be to become incarnate and live a perfect human life.

Second, humans are beset with suffering, some caused by other humans, some caused by natural forces. If God exists, he must have a good reason for allowing this situation, like the parent who allows her child to undergo the suffering caused by chemotherapy in order to avoid a greater evil (death because of cancer) and achieve a greater good (the goods that come with continued life for the child). We briefly examined the problem of suffering in chapter ten; now a point about suffering and the incarnation is in order. A good parent would not allow the suffering involved in chemotherapy without some reason, but the parent can do more than just *have* such a reason: a parent can voluntarily join in her child's suffering to demonstrate to the child her solidarity and love. Parents who shave their heads when their children go bald because of chemotherapy do precisely this. Similarly, God's becoming incarnate would give God the opportunity to share in our suffering. This constitutes a second reason for God to become incarnate.

Third, there is a long history of theological reflection on the atonement, including arguments that God's becoming incarnate was a necessary (Anselm) or fitting (Aquinas) way to bring about the reconciliation of God and human beings.[3] While we won't wade into these deep waters here, we can note that since the project of rescuing human beings will likely require more than just *information* from God, it is not implausible that God might want to become incarnate in order to bring about atonement through his work on earth.[4]

So, if God exists he might very well choose to become incarnate. If God did so choose, what would we expect the incarnate God to be like and do? We would expect him to live a holy life and provide powerful and sublime teaching about God and human beings, about how we can become good and how we can be united with God. And in order that this teaching might be passed on to future generations, we might well expect him to found a church, a community of people with the goal of living out and passing on his teachings. We would also expect him to share in our suffering and, very possibly, teach that our relationship to him was a crucial component in our salvation. Finally, it would not be at all unlikely that he would provide evidence that his teachings were true by means of one or more miracles. In a case where the incarnate God was put to death (something not terribly unlikely given the content of his teachings), the miracle of a resurrection would be a fitting divine signature on those teachings.

Having observed some reasons to become incarnate that God would have, and having noted their implications for how we would expect an incarnate God to act, we can now turn to specific evidence about Jesus. Does Jesus fit the profile? The evidence we have indicates that he does: It is beyond a reasonable doubt that Jesus lived a holy life, provided powerful teaching about God and humankind, founded a church (which has since grown to include vast numbers of people) and was put to death after experiencing great suffering. Somewhat less certainly but still very significantly, there is evidence that Jesus taught that our relationship with him is a crucial factor in our relationship with God (see, e.g., Mt 11:27) and that he taught a doctrine of atonement (that his life and death were a sacrifice for sin, which in some way enables humankind and God to be reunited). The claim that "Christ died for our sins" was present in the pre-Pauline tradition Paul cites in 1 Corinthians 15:3, and the natural interpretation of numerous New Testament texts is that Jesus understood his death as a sacrifice for sin.[5] Finally, even if we view the Gospels critically, a strong argument can be made that Jesus implied his own divinity, as Stephen Davis has shown.[6]

So Jesus matches the profile of what we'd expect from an incarnate God. It is equally important to note that no one else in history comes close to matching this profile. If any human being was God incarnate, Jesus was most likely that human being. And so, if God exists, we should not be surprised if it was Jesus (rather than someone else) who was resurrected.

In summary: if God exists, God would have reasons to become incarnate, and Jesus lived and died in a way that we would expect of the incarnate God. It is therefore not implausible that if God exists, Jesus would indeed be raised from the dead. And it is not unlikely that God *does* exist. Given all this, we should not approach the evidence for Jesus' resurrection with the background belief that such a resurrection is exceedingly improbable. It would therefore be a mistake to take the possibility of a miracle off the table and adopt the attitude that the resurrection hypothesis is simply too improbable to accept no matter how strong the arguments against the competing naturalistic hypotheses. The improbability objection therefore fails, and the argument for the resurrection remains in force.

THE MYTH OBJECTION

I've been assuming that when the early disciples claimed that Jesus was resurrected, they meant this literally. A third major objection to arguments for the resurrection challenges this assumption. According to this objection, the doctrine of an actual bodily resurrection of Jesus is a myth, a legend that grew in stages and only came to be accepted literally much later, by Christian communities long after Jesus's death. Thus Thomas Sheehan, professor of religious studies at Stanford University: "The gospel stories about Easter are not historical accounts but religious myths. . . . The New Testament does not in fact assert that Jesus came back to life on earth, or that he physically left his grave alive after he had died."[7] On Sheehan's view, language of "resurrection" was a metaphorical or mythical way for the earliest disciples to express the claim that after his death, Jesus was appointed by God to be "the absolute savior of the human race."[8] "Informed Christians," Sheehan tells us,

> who understand the New Testament rather than just parrot its words, know that the Easter narratives in the gospels are not literal accounts of historical events that supposedly took place during the six weeks after the crucifixion. They also know that the Easter victory did not happen on Easter Sunday or on any other day in time. . . . The Easter victory of Jesus was an eschatological occurrence, beyond space and time—a meta-historical act of God that took place "in heaven" when the crucified Jesus died on earth. . . . The theological meaning of Easter is not that Jesus "came back to life" in a spiritualized body, passed through graveclothes, and exited . . . from his tomb. . . . These are inspiring myths and legends that the gospel writers used to communicate the extra-historical, supernatural reality of God's "awakening" of Jesus from the dead and "exalting" him to heaven.[9]

Former Episcopal Bishop John Shelby Spong takes a similar line: "It is easy to identify the legendary elements of the resurrection narratives. Angels who descend in earthquakes, speak, and roll back stones; tombs that are empty; apparitions that appear and disappear; rich men who make graves available; thieves who comment from their crosses of pain—these are legends all."[10] So what happened to get all these legends going? How did the legend of bodily resurrection get started? Spong speculates that after Jesus' death, Simon Peter returned to Galilee and pondered the life of Jesus and the Scriptures for weeks and months. Eventually he came to believe that God *must* have vindicated Jesus, and then he had some sort of vision: "Simon saw. He really saw. Jesus had been lifted into the living God. It had nothing to do with empty tombs or feeling wounds. It had to do with understanding that Jesus made God real and that God had taken the life of Jesus into the divine nature."[11] The Gospel narratives of the resurrection were created later, according to Spong, as the disciples reflected on various elements in the Jewish Feast of Tabernacles.

Call the general idea here the *mythical view of the resurrection*: Christ was not raised bodily from the grave, and the earliest Christians did not intend to assert that he was. Rather, early Christian statements about "resurrection" were only intended as metaphors.

The mythical view can be supported in several ways. First, the earliest documents that contain Christian testimony to the resurrection are certain letters of Paul, but it is claimed that Paul did not assert that Jesus was physically resurrected, nor did he assert that Jesus' tomb was found empty. Second, it is noted that in its original form, the Gospel that most scholars believe was written first, Mark, ends before an account of the resurrection appearances are given, which in turn suggests that the detailed descriptions of Jesus' postresurrection appearances were inventions by later writers. Third, there are numerous inconsistencies between the different Gospel resurrection narratives, which might well be expected if the narratives were never meant to be literal histories.

REPLY TO THE MYTH OBJECTION

To assess the myth objection, we should distinguish two different questions: (1) *What* did the earliest Christians claim, regarding the resurrection of Jesus? and (2) Is there reason for us, today, to *believe* that claim? The myth objection is only about the first question, so while thus far we've been focusing on the second question, now let's focus on the first.

Resurrection in Paul. In his 738-page tome *The Resurrection of the Son of God*, N. T. Wright convincingly refutes the contention that Paul did not assert a bodily resurrection of Jesus.[12] While I can't do justice to Wright's lengthy argument here, several key points can be noted. First, Paul belongs to the tradition of the Pharisees, which very explicitly expected a future *bodily* resurrection for the members of God's people. But by the time he had become a Christian missionary, Paul had come to believe that Jesus' resurrection preceded and was the model for this future bodily resurrection, which was now the object of Christian hope. "God raised the Lord and will also raise us by his power" (1 Cor 6:14). And again:

> But in fact Christ has been raised from the dead, the first fruits of those who have died. For since death came through a human being, the resurrection of the dead has also come through a human being; for as all die in Adam, so all will be made alive in Christ. But each in his own order: Christ the first fruits, then at his coming those who belong to Christ. (1 Cor 15:20-23)

If Jesus' resurrection is the model for our future *bodily* resurrection, then it stands to reason that Jesus' resurrection was bodily too. And, indeed, Paul says in his letter to Philippians that Jesus "will transform the *body* of our humiliation that it may be conformed to the *body* of his glory" (Phil 3:21). And in Romans: "If the Spirit of him who raised Jesus from the dead dwells in you, he who raised Christ from the dead will give life to your mortal bodies also" (Rom 8:11). The clear suggestion is that there is a parallel between our future resurrection (which will involve the giving of life to our bodies) and the resurrection of Jesus (which by implication also involved the giving of life to Jesus' body).

Second, at Romans 1:4, Paul says that Jesus was marked out as the Son of God "by resurrection from the dead." But, Wright points out, it is hard to believe that Paul could have thought that the resurrection showed Jesus was the Son of God (and by implication the Messiah) if by "resurrection" Paul had merely meant that Jesus had been exalted to a place of honor by God after death, or that the soul of Jesus was now with God. Paul's claim makes much more sense if Paul is thinking that Jesus' resurrection involved the reversal and defeat of death.

Third, when in 1 Corinthians 15 Paul lists a number of individuals and groups to whom Jesus had appeared, he says that Jesus appeared to him

(Paul) "last of all" (1 Cor 15:8). A particular, finite number of Christians had had experiences of the risen Jesus, according to Paul. But this shows that having an experience of the risen Jesus, for Paul, can't have just been about sensing the presence or continued power of Jesus:

> This reference to seeing the risen Jesus cannot therefore, in Paul's mind at least, have anything to do with regular and normal, or even extraordinary, "Christian experience," with ongoing visions and revelations or a "spiritual" sense of the presence of Jesus. As is clear from 1 Corinthians 9.1, this "seeing" was something which constituted people as "apostles," the one-off witnesses to a one-off event. The Corinthians had had every kind of spiritual experience imaginable, as the previous chapters [in 1 Corinthians] have made clear; but they had not seen the risen Jesus, nor did they or Paul expect that they would do so.[13]

Fourth, Paul has much to say in 1 Corinthians 15 about what sort of bodies the people of God will have after their resurrection at the second coming. Because Paul says that we shall bear the image of the "man of heaven" (1 Cor 15:49), that is, Jesus, we can discern what Paul thinks about the body of the resurrected Jesus by attending to what he says about the bodies the people of God will have after their resurrection. And what he says is that the resurrected body will be incorruptible (not subject to decay), glorious and a *sōma pneumatikos*, a spiritual body. Drawing on the analogy of sowing a seed, he says that the body "is sown as a *sōma psychikon*, it is raised as a *sōma pneumatikon*" (1 Cor 15:44). The precise meaning of these Greek phrases is crucial.

This line, 1 Corinthians 15:44, is one of the main reasons why some scholars came to hold that Paul did not believe Jesus had been raised physically. The pair of phrases *sōma psychikon* and *sōma pneumatikon* have often been translated into English as "physical body" and "spiritual body." Some have therefore taken 1 Corinthians 15:44 to mean that, according to Paul, the resurrected body of a believer will be a spiritual, that is, nonphysical body, in contrast to our present physical bodies. By implication, the body of the resurrected Jesus must have been nonphysical too, according to Paul.

Wright shows that this is a misunderstanding of the passage.[14] Literally, *sōma psychikos* means a "soulish body," that is, a body animated by soul, while *sōma pneumatikos* means a "spiritual body," that is, a body animated by spirit. The contrast Paul is alluding to here is not the contrast between a physical body and a nonphysical body (whatever that would mean) but is rather related to the contrast he had already used in 1 Corinthians 2:13-16: the soulish person is a person who is animated by worldly values and moved by worldly (or "fleshly") things, while the spiritual person is the person who is animated by the Spirit of God and moved by godly things. Paul's point at 1 Corinthians 15:44 is that the resurrected body of the believer will be a body animated by the Spirit of God.

Similarly, when Paul says that "flesh and blood cannot inherit the kingdom of God" (1 Cor 15:50), he does not mean that bodily persons cannot exist in the next life but that humans will not exist in the next life with their present, ordinary, corruptible bodies (rather, they will possess transformed, glorious bodies).[15]

So Paul really did claim that Jesus, after having been dead, literally rose again in a new, glorious body. And if Paul had a literal, nonmythical understanding of Jesus' resurrection, then it is very unlikely that Peter and John had the radically different mythical understanding of the resurrection, given the argument from the previous chapter concerning the closeness between Paul's gospel message and that of Peter and John. To my mind, the mythical approach is sufficiently refuted by the facts that Paul asserts a bodily resurrection and that Paul's message was very likely the same, in this regard, as Peter's and John's.

It is sometimes noted, as part of an argument for a mythical view of the resurrection, that Paul never mentions the empty tomb. To move from "in the documents left to us by history, Paul never says X" to "Paul didn't believe X" is of course invalid. But a proponent of the mythical view might argue that if Paul believed in an empty tomb, he surely would have mentioned it when he speaks so much about the resurrection in 1 Corinthians. On the contrary, once it has become clear that Paul had a physical understanding of the resurrection, this argument loses its force. In 1 Corinthians, Paul asserts "that [Jesus] was buried, and that he was raised on the third day" (1 Cor 15:4). Given Paul's physical understanding of the resurrection, his statement that Jesus was raised *implies* an empty tomb: in Paul's thinking, if someone is raised, of course the tomb will be left empty! So Paul would not have felt any special need to highlight the empty tomb by mentioning it separately. If I tell you that my dad is in his office, I don't need to add that he's not at the pool.

The ending of the Gospel of Mark and inconsistencies among the Gospels. Some of the oldest and most authoritative manuscripts of the Gospel of Mark omit Mark 16:9-20 and instead terminate abruptly (apparently in midsentence in the Greek) at Mark 16:8, which reads, "So they [Mary Magdalene, Mary the mother of James, and Salome] went out and fled from the tomb, for terror and amazement had seized them; and they said nothing to anyone, for they were afraid." The resurrection appearances of Jesus are described in Mark 16:9-20 but not in the undisputed text of Mark to which we now have access. Noting this, an argument in support of the mythical view of the resurrection points out that the Gospel that appears oldest (Mark) doesn't contain resurrection appearances, while the Gospels written later do. This appears to be evidence of a development within Christianity, from an earlier time when the resurrection wasn't taught literally, to a later time when it was.

The crucial weakness in this argument is that the writings of Paul, earlier than Mark by far, contain the doctrine of a literal resurrection. What's more, even if the original ending of Mark did not contain narratives of any resurrection appearances, it is clear enough that the author of Mark believed such appearances had occurred: in the undisputed text of Mark the empty tomb is described, the young man at the tomb announces that Jesus has been raised (Mk 16:6), and the resurrection appearances of Jesus are predicted three separate times (Mk 8:31; 9:31; 10:34).[16]

A final motivation for the mythical view is yet to be addressed: inconsistencies in the Gospel resurrection narratives. On this score, it's helpful to realize that when several eyewitnesses see the same event, their subsequent accounts of what happened often differ in minor ways. Two people might both report that there was a car crash at a certain intersection, but one might think the crash involved a convertible and an SUV while the other might say that the vehicles involved were a convertible and a pickup truck. The mythical view suggests that the inconsistencies in the Gospels are evidence that they were intentionally fabricated (to express spiritual truths). But some level of minor inconsistencies is in fact exactly what we'd expect if the Gospels were intended as literal, factual accounts. So the presence of minor inconsistencies isn't good evidence for the mythical view.

Although the presence of inconsistencies in the Gospels does not support the mythical view, it does raise a problem for the main contention of the previous chapter, namely that the best explanation of the early disciples' claims was that Jesus was resurrected. Three points should be made concerning this problem. First, while the lack of perfect reliability should make us cautious about the *details* of an eyewitness account, it remains the case that when several witnesses agree on the major outlines of what happened, we can have good reason to be confident in those major outlines. Applying this to the Gospels: even if there are some inconsistencies when it comes to details, that fact alone need not remove one's confidence in the major outlines of the story. Indeed, as philosopher James Taylor points out, "the presence of discrepancies about peripheral details between [the Gospel accounts] is evidence that their sources are relatively independent of each other; agreement on essentials and disagreement on non-essentials would be expected of normal human eyewitnesses, and agreement on every detail would suggest collusion among the sources."[17] Second, sometimes what appears to be an inconsistency at first glance really isn't. If Matthew says that "Mary Magdalene and the other Mary" went to the tomb (Mt 28:1), and Mark says, "Mary Magdalene, and Mary the mother of James, and Salome" went to the tomb (Mk 16:1), we might at first think we have a contradiction on our hands. In actuality, there would only be a contradiction if Matthew said that Mary Magdalene and the other Mary went to the tomb *and, furthermore,* that no one else was with them. In some cases, apparent inconsistencies can be explained by supposing that the author of a given Gospel is not providing complete information. So one can accept as historical the main lines of the Gospels' resurrection narratives, while acknowledging some inconsistencies concerning details and viewing other apparent inconsistencies as *merely* apparent inconsistencies.[18]

Third, and most importantly, for present purposes it is not necessary to establish the general reliability of the Gospels, because the main argument of the previous chapter employed the minimal facts approach. Some reference to information found in the Gospel accounts was made in the course of examining hypotheses alternative to the resurrection, but the three core facts on which the argument primarily depends are sufficiently well established by the letters of Paul, the testimony of Clement and Polycarp, and other ancient sources.

TAKING STOCK

So, where are we? Faced with the difficulty of assessing all the various arguments and counterarguments, it's easy to start looking at the question "Did
Jesus rise from the dead?" merely as an intellectual issue, a problem to be
analyzed or a puzzle to be solved. We can examine claims about the resurrection like a scientist holding an alleged moon rock at arm's length, turning
it over this way and that and subjecting it to various tests to verify its au-
thenticity. Fair enough. But if we *only* do this, we've missed something. The
early disciples' claims do more than present us with an intriguing puzzle.
They also place before us a personal invitation of immense existential sig-
nificance. On one possible explanation of the available facts, the disciples
were wrong about the resurrection, and the invitation they offer (the invitation to follow the way of Jesus) is a merely human one. But on another
possible explanation of the facts, the disciples were right about the resurrection, and it is God himself who has given each one of us a personal invitation to draw closer to him by following Jesus. So the question before us
isn't just "What should I think?" but "What should I do?" What should I do
in response to what well may be the voice of God?

The interpersonal nature of the issue should therefore be kept in mind as
we take stock of the evidence available to us. Still, take stock we must. It is
reasonable to ask: how strong is the evidence for Christianity?

With a question as big as this, there is no widely agreed-upon procedure
one can use to weigh and balance the various pieces of competing evidence,
the numerous arguments and counterarguments that have been made. Yet
this much seems right: the cosmological argument and the fine-tuning argument make it plausible that a necessarily existing, intelligent being designed our universe. The existence of God is by no means unlikely. When
the beauty and existential resonance of Christian doctrine and historical
arguments for the resurrection are added into the mix, we should grant that
there is a good chance that Christianity is true. How high of a chance? Ultimately, each person must answer this question for him- or herself. In my
own view, the chance is very high—as I see it, the arguments we've examined
in part two of this book are by themselves sufficiently strong to justify belief
in Christian theism. But the reader need not agree with me on this point: for
our purposes here, there is no need to establish that Christianity is very

probably true. This is because, given the Pascalian argument of part one, all that is needed for a serious Christian commitment to be reasonable is the judgment that Christianity has at least a 50 percent chance of being true. And the evidence for Christianity is strong enough to meet that more modest goal. So if you are willing to grant that Christianity is as likely as not, then it is rational for you to commit to living a devout Christian life.

Suppose you agree. Suppose you agree that there's at least a 50 percent chance that Christianity is true, and that it's therefore rational for you to commit to living a Christian life. Even so, making a commitment can be scary. One may justifiably be hesitant at the prospect of making a major commitment merely on the grounds of an abstract argument. Fortunately, there's something more concrete to which we can turn: the lives of others who have said yes to the divine invitation. Serious commitment to authentic Christian discipleship can be a path to a deeply meaningful, morally upright and existentially fulfilling life—an abundant life. In part three, we'll hear the stories of three exemplary believers who illustrate this fact.

SAYING YES
to GOD

13

DIETRICH BONHOEFFER

ON AN ORDINARY DAY IN November 1931, twenty-five-year-old Dietrich Bonhoeffer and an elderly Protestant minister slowly climbed the stairs of a tall school building.[1] Looking down over a bannister from above, a mob of fifty boys yelled, hollered and dropped objects on the pair below. The group of boys was a confirmation class at Zionskirche, a Protestant church in a particularly rough area of north Berlin. At that time, attendance at confirmation class was less a voluntary choice of children or their parents and more of a state-sponsored expectation. The elderly minister had found the class too difficult to control and had brought in the recently ordained young pastor to take over. Bonhoeffer's close friend (and later biographer) Eberhard Bethge describes the confrontation:

> When they reached the top, the minister tried to force the throng back into the classroom by shouting and using physical force. He tried to announce that he had brought them a new minister who was going to teach them in the future and that his name was Bonhoeffer, and when they heard the name they started shouting "Bon! Bon! Bon!" louder and louder. The old man left the scene in despair, leaving Bonhoeffer standing silently against the wall with his hands in his pockets. Minutes passed. His failure to react made the noise gradually less enjoyable, and he began speaking quietly, so that only the boys in the front row could catch a few words of what he said. Suddenly all were silent. Bonhoeffer merely remarked that they had put up a remarkable initial performance, and went on to tell them a story about Harlem [Bonhoeffer had recently visited New York]. If they listened, he told them, he would tell them more next time. Then he told them they could go. After that, he never had reason to complain about their lack of attentiveness.[2]

Bonhoeffer soon got to know his students well, visiting them at their homes and meeting their parents. Writing to a friend, he spoke of the difficulties with which many had to contend: "Their home conditions are generally indescribable: poverty, disorder, immorality. And yet the children are still open; I am often amazed how a young person does not completely come to grief under such conditions; and of course one is always asking oneself how one would react to such surroundings."[3]

Bonhoeffer had grown up in very different surroundings, enjoying a happy and privileged childhood. His father was a renowned university professor of psychiatry and neurology, and his mother, a teacher before marrying, supervised the education of the eight Bonhoeffer children at home until they were seven or eight years of age, when they were sent on to public school. For most of Dietrich's childhood the family lived primarily in Berlin, but they also spent many idyllic weeks at their country home in the mountains. Servants and governesses assisted Dr. and Mrs. Bonhoeffer in raising their children and running their household. Dietrich's confirmation candidates were living in a much harsher reality. After a few months Bonhoeffer decided to move into the working-class neighborhood in which Zionskirche was located:

> Since New Year I've been living here in north Berlin so as to be able to have the young men up here every evening. In turns, of course. We eat supper and then we play something—I've introduced them to chess, which they now play with great enthusiasm. . . . At the end of each evening I read them something from the Bible and after that we have a short spell of catechizing, which often becomes very serious. The instruction went in such a way that I can hardly tear myself away from it.[4]

Bonhoeffer purchased a large bolt of cloth before the confirmation ceremony so that the boys could have suits for the occasion. In his sermon on the day of the service, he addressed his charges:

> Dear Confirmation Candidates! When in the last days before your confirmation I asked you many times what you hoped to hear in your confirmation address, I often received the answer: we want a serious warning which we shall remember all our lives. And I can assure you that whoever listens well today will receive a warning or two by the way; but look, life itself gives us enough and too many serious warnings today; and so today I must not make

your prospect for the future seem harder and darker than it already is—and
I know that many of you know a great many of the hard facts of life. Today
you are not to be given fear of life but courage; and so today in the Church we
shall speak more than ever of hope, the hope that we have and which no one
can take from you.[5]

DER FÜHRER

In the years to come that hope would be tested. World War I had been hard
on the German economy, and reparation payments to the victors added
further strain after the war. Germany soon faced crippling budget deficits,
to which it responded by printing money. This, in turn, resulted in hyper-
inflation in 1923. Loans from banks in the United States helped revive the
German economy in the mid-1920s, but when the US stock market crashed
in 1929, American banks demanded repayment. The severe economic shock
led to massive unemployment in Germany (up to 30 percent by 1932). People
were desperate for a change, and Adolf Hitler promised to provide it.
Germany held a presidential election on March 13, 1932, the very day Bonhoeffer's students were confirmed. The retired general Paul von Hindenburg
won, with 49 percent of the vote, but Hitler came in second, with 30 percent.
And his party, the Nazis, held many seats in the German parliament. By early
1933 Hitler had been appointed chancellor of Germany (the number-two
position in the government), and in the months that followed he consoli-
dated power through all manner of intrigue, deception, intimidation and
violence. By the end of 1934 he was both chancellor and president, presiding
over a police state complete with censorship of the press and a ban on other
political parties. Soldiers now swore an oath of loyalty to Hitler himself,
rather than to the German constitution.

Bonhoeffer's family was suspicious of Hitler from the beginning, and the
young pastor soon began to see a disturbing intrusion of Nazi ideology into
the state-supported German Evangelical Church in which he served. The Nazi
government passed legislation that made it illegal for individuals of Jewish
descent to work as government employees. Assisted by pressure from the
Nazis, a movement referred to as the "German Christians" supported an application of this law to the German Evangelical Church itself, with the eventual
result that Jewish converts to Christianity and ethnically Jewish Protestant

pastors were barred from working for the church. Bonhoeffer strenuously opposed this unjust and unbiblical policy (one wonders how the German Christians came to terms with the fact that, by their lights, neither Peter, nor Paul nor Jesus himself would have been judged fit for ecclesiastical service). Eventually the controversy led to a rift within the church, with World War I war hero Martin Niemöller, Bonhoeffer and other like-minded pastors becoming leaders in what became known as the Confessing Church. An August 1934 letter of Bonhoeffer's indicates his awareness that fundamental values were at stake: "It must be made quite clear—terrifying though it is—that we are immediately faced with the decision: National Socialist [i.e., Nazi] or Christian."[6]

In 1935 Bonhoeffer accepted an offer to organize and lead a seminary for the training of pastors associated with the Confessing Church. Over the next few years he became a thorn in the side of those within the German Evangelical Church who were sympathetic to the Nazis. Step by step Bonhoeffer was censured for his efforts to resist the Nazi takeover of German churches. Pastors in the Confessing Church were increasingly critical of Hitler's regime, and before long the Nazis had had enough. In 1937 they arrested or imprisoned over eight hundred Confessing Church leaders, including Niemöller, who would not be released from Dachau until 1945, when the concentration camp was liberated by Allied troops. Bonhoeffer's seminary was shut down by the Gestapo, though he continued the work illegally in a remote area of northeastern Germany. In January 1938, he and a group of other pastors were arrested by the Gestapo but were released after seven hours of interrogation. Things had gotten serious.

War

Hitler had won a series of risky gambles since his rise to power in 1934. In March 1936, in flagrant violation of the Treaty of Versailles, he moved German troops into the Rhineland, a demilitarized section of western Germany bordering France. The dictator later remarked that the two days following this move were "the most nerve-racking in my life. If the French had then marched into the Rhineland, we would have had to withdraw with our tails between our legs, for the military resources at our disposal would have been wholly inadequate for even a moderate resistance."[7] A quick, decisive military response would likely have been disastrous for Hitler, but the

French sat on their hands, as did the British. Soon Hitler made a pact with Mussolini, formerly an obstacle to German designs on Austria. In November 1937 the Führer called together his top military officials for a four-hour meeting. To the public he had been preaching peace, but to his military commanders he outlined his plans for war: the German race needed "living space," and lands to the east would provide it. Of the six individuals listening to Hitler's plans that day, three voiced their opposition. All three were soon relieved of their commands. By March 1938, Austria was under Nazi control; by March 1939, German troops had marched into Prague; in September 1939, Hitler invaded Poland. As German troops converged on Warsaw from the north, south and west, they left burnt-out houses and synagogues in their wake and murdered non-Aryan civilian noncombatants en masse. The Führer wasn't merely a dictator; he was a man possessed by hate and a criminal of the most dangerous kind.

Unbeknown to him, the dictator had narrowly avoided a potential coup from within Germany in early fall 1938. Initially convinced that Hitler's intention to attack Czechoslovakia would lead to a large European war that the Germans would be bound to lose, a considerable number of German generals had made plans to arrest Hitler on the announcement of the invasion of Czechoslovakia. But when it became clear that the French and British themselves wanted primarily to avoid war and had no real intention of coming to Czechoslovakia's aid, the rationale for the coup dissipated. The reason to depose Hitler was to avoid war, but the British and French would see to that goal, even if Germany did muscle out the Czechs. The British and French policy of appeasement took the wind out of the conspirators' sails, the coup was never attempted, and Hitler emerged stronger than ever. Why hadn't the leaders of the German Army stood up to Hitler earlier? His initial actions to build up the military had been too much to their liking, and by the time they realized the full extent of his ambition, it seemed to be too late. In December 1938 Baron von Fritsch, one of the generals who'd been sacked by Hitler for opposing war, explained his assessment of the situation to a friend, who summarized von Fritsch's views: "This man—Hitler—is Germany's destiny for good and for evil. If he now goes over the abyss—which Fritsch believes he will—he will drag us all down with him. There is nothing we can do."[8]

CROSSROADS

But not all shared von Fritsch's fatalism. Whether or not Hitler could be successfully overthrown from within Germany, there were some brave Germans willing to try. An important figure in the clandestine resistance movement was Admiral Wilhelm Canaris, head of the military intelligence department of the German armed forces (the Abwehr). A trusted member of his staff, Hans von Dohnanyi, was compiling a file detailing the crimes of the Nazis. Dohnanyi was the husband of Dietrich Bonhoeffer's sister Christel and a frequent visitor at the home of Dietrich's parents. Thus the magnitude of the Nazi's atrocities became known among the Bonhoeffer clan far sooner than they were known to the world at large. The Nazi persecution of Jews within Germany had already moved Dietrich to great restlessness and anger, but he hadn't joined the conspiracy against Hitler in any particularly active way.[9] Like Dohnanyi, Dietrich's older brother Klaus *was* already actively involved, and Klaus's wife, Emmi, pressed Dietrich on his position: what was he prepared to do?[10]

In early 1939 Bonhoeffer learned that all men of his age were required to register for military service. This put him in a difficult situation—if he were called up to fight and complied, he would be contributing to the evil cause he opposed, but if he were called up and refused, he would be executed. His refusal might also lead to further persecution of the Confessing Church with which he was associated. Adrift in these troubled waters, a life raft floated into view: with help from theological colleagues in the United States, he obtained an invitation to teach at Union Theological Seminary and work with German refugees in New York. Friends in the Confessing Church were supportive, hoping that, kept safe from war, Bonhoeffer would one day be able to return and rebuild the Protestant church in Germany, when the days of the Nazis were over. In June 1939 Bonhoeffer left for New York.

Even as he was still aboard ship in the Atlantic, Bonhoeffer was conflicted. Had he abandoned his friends and country in its time of greatest need? His doubts intensified on arrival in the United States; his friends and family were risking their lives, and he was being pampered at Union. Within days he was reproaching himself, "It is cowardice and weakness to run away here now."[11] After little more than a week in America, Bonhoeffer made his decision and broke the news to his disappointed would-be employer: he was going back

to Germany. "I must go back to the 'trenches' (I mean of the church struggle),"
he wrote to an American friend.[12] By July he was back on ship, returning to
his homeland. What lay ahead, he didn't know.

The American trip had accomplished at least this much: Bonhoeffer had
been granted a year's deferment of his military service. He continued to
carry out duties as a pastor with the Confessing Church, but gradually his
freedom to speak in public, publish and travel was being taken away by the
Nazis. In 1940 his brother-in-law Dohnanyi had an idea: Bonhoeffer could
join the Abwehr (military intelligence). Ostensibly he would continue his
work as a clergyman and theologian. Secretly he would be working for Hitler's armed forces as an informant. More secretly still, he would be part of
the Resistance, using his now officially sanctioned ability to travel to gather
and pass on information for the conspirators against Hitler. This would solve
his predicament about the draft and, more importantly, give him an opportunity to take a more active role in the effort against the Nazi regime. By the
end of the year Bonhoeffer was a member of the staff of the Munich Military
Intelligence Office.

AGENT BONHOEFFER

In October 1941 Bonhoeffer learned of the forced deportation of Jews living
within Germany to ghettos and concentration camps. With a colleague in
the Confessing Church, he compiled reports on the deportations for
Dohnanyi to pass along to the leaders of the Resistance. Concerned to save
some of his Jewish friends, Admiral Canaris came up with a plan to get a
group of Jews to safety in neutral Switzerland. The plan was called Operation
Seven, because initially the group numbered seven, but as time went on that
number grew to fourteen. The idea was to designate the adults in the group
as agents of the Abwehr and then allow them to leave Germany for Switzerland on the official (but false) pretext that they would say good things
about the Nazis to the Swiss. (Dohnanyi had made clear the real purpose of
the operation to the Jewish participants.) An obstacle appeared from the
Swiss side: Swiss neutrality meant that accepting German Jews into the
country was extremely difficult. Bonhoeffer and two colleagues in the Confessing Church appealed to their ecclesiastical contacts in Switzerland to
intervene, with Bonhoeffer enlisting the successful intercession of famous

Swiss theologian Karl Barth. A final snag was solved by Dohnanyi and the Abwehr: money had to be provided for the support of the Jewish refugees once they arrived in Switzerland. In the grand scheme of things it was a small success, but it meant a great deal to the fourteen people saved from a concentration camp.

The months that followed saw Bonhoeffer embark on a number of international trips for the Abwehr, including one to Sweden in spring 1942 for the secret purpose of getting information to the British about the conspirators' need for support. But it was too late for British Prime Minister Winston Churchill to be much interested in sorting out the good Germans from the bad, and Bonhoeffer's efforts on this score came to naught. In April 1943 things got worse: the Gestapo arrested both Dohnanyi and Bonhoeffer. How much did the secret police know? Bonhoeffer played dumb.

It was Bonhoeffer's good fortune that he was not put in the custody of the SS but was instead sent to Berlin's Tegel prison, which was under the ultimate control of none other than Bonhoeffer's uncle, General Paul von Hase. This allowed Bonhoeffer somewhat greater liberties within prison than he otherwise would have had, liberties he put to good effect. Before long he was secretly exchanging messages through his family with Dohnanyi, who was being held at a different facility. Biographer Eric Metaxas explains how:

> They had . . . worked out ahead of time how to communicate if any of them was imprisoned, and they now used these methods. One involved putting coded messages in the books they were allowed to receive. Bonhoeffer got many books from his parents and would send them back when he was finished with them. To indicate there was a coded message in the book, they underlined the name of the book's owner on the flyleaf or inside cover. If *D. Bonhoeffer* was underlined, the receiver knew there was a message. The message itself was communicated through a series of the tiniest pencil marks under letters on pages in the book. Every three or every ten pages—the number seemed to vary—a barely visible pencil dot would be put under a letter on that page. Ten pages later another letter would be marked with a dot. These marks would begin at the back of the book and proceed toward the front, so in the course of a three-hundred-page book one might have room for a thirty-letter communication. These were usually extremely important and dangerous messages, such as what Dohnanyi had communicated to his

interrogator, so that Bonhoeffer could corroborate that information and not get tripped up or caught contradicting something Dohnanyi said.[13]

Another method used was to slip tiny notes in between the cardboard and metal in marmalade jar lids (Bonhoeffer and Dohnanyi were both allowed to receive packages of food from family). Before long it became apparent that the Nazi interrogators knew rather little about Bonhoeffer's and Dohnanyi's real activities on behalf of the Resistance. Scrutiny focused on Dohnanyi. Apparent financial irregularities relating to Operation Seven raised suspicions, but with Canaris covering for his alibis, there was little unambiguous evidence against him. Bonhoeffer was accused of attempting to avoid military service but was able to parry the accusation effectively enough. And he managed to avoid revealing anything dangerous when questioned about Operation Seven. There was cause for hope: if the pair could continue to throw interrogators off the track and let the trial slowly fizzle out, each might be given a minor sentence, or they might be acquitted entirely. Besides, a successful coup could eliminate Hitler at any time.

Dohnanyi himself had been involved in one such attempt before his arrest, code-named Operation Flash. The plan was to hide a time bomb in the airplane that would carry Hitler back to Germany after a visit to Smolensk, Russia, on the eastern front in March 1943. The bomb would explode midflight, and the appearance of accident (rather than assassination) would smooth the transition to a new Germany. Canaris had Dohnanyi and another member of his staff fly to Smolensk to deliver the bomb. Shortly before Hitler's return flight, another of the conspirators, General von Tresckow, casually asked a member of Hitler's staff to carry some brandy back to a colleague in Germany. The man obliged and the "brandy," in actuality the cleverly contrived bomb, was loaded onto the plane, the fuse having just been activated. But the bomb malfunctioned and never detonated; Hitler made it home none the wiser but unharmed.

While Bonhoeffer was in prison, a more elaborate plot was being organized.

VALKYRIE

Count Claus von Stauffenberg was a handsome career Army officer in his midthirties who had begun to have serious misgivings about the Nazis as early as 1939. While fighting in Russia he was recruited into the conspiracy by von Tresckow but later sustained serious injuries in a battle in North Africa, losing an eye, one hand and two fingers on the other hand. After this he could have easily bowed out of both the army and the Resistance. Instead he requested a return to active duty and secretly took up a leadership role among the conspirators, helping to craft a detailed plan to assassinate Hitler, arrest key Nazi and SS leaders, and return Germany to sanity with the help of sympathetic officials (including Bonhoeffer's uncle Paul von Hase). A crucial component of the scheme was the co-opting of Operation Valkyrie, a plan already in place for the defense of Hitler's regime against the possibility of an internal uprising. Ironically this plan, which Canaris had persuaded Hitler to approve, was the perfect cover for the conspirators' takeover of the German state after Hitler's (intended) assassination. The Valkyrie plans allowed for the German Home Army (stationed within Germany rather than on the western or eastern fronts) to take control of key cities. As co-opted, the Home Army would be used to fight the SS and other pro-Nazi forces and protect the new German government installed during the coup. But the first step was the assassination of Hitler.

On July 19, 1944, it was decided that the time had come. Stauffenberg had been summoned to a July 20th meeting at the Wolf's Lair, Hitler's headquarters in East Prussia. On the night of the 19th, Stauffenberg worked late to finish the report he was to present to the Führer, then returned home, stopping at a Catholic church to pray. Early the next morning he boarded a plane to the Wolf's Lair; hidden in his briefcase were two time bombs.

Stauffenberg arrived to find that his 1 p.m. meeting had been moved up to 12:30 p.m. Shortly before the meeting he asked whether there was somewhere he could change his shirt, and in privacy set to work activating the bombs with the help of his aide. But the pair were interrupted at a crucial moment, and in their haste they stumbled, twice over: first, they only had time to activate one of the two bombs; second, the unactivated bomb was not placed in the briefcase with the activated one.[14] This meant that the explosion would be only half the intended strength.

The fuse mechanism allowed for an approximately ten-minute delay before explosion. After entering the meeting room, Stauffenberg placed his briefcase under the large oak conference table, about six feet from the Führer's legs, then listened to the briefing on recent Russian advancements.

Shortly after 12:37, Stauffenberg slipped out, putatively to take an important phone call to get updated information for his report—he was scheduled to speak next. Instead, he quietly left the building. At 12:42 the bomb detonated.

From a few hundred yards away, Stauffenberg saw the meeting room explode. Convinced that Hitler was dead, he bluffed his way through the three security checkpoints encircling the Wolf's Lair, drove back to the airfield and flew to Berlin for phase two of the coup. But all the careful planning had hit a snag: although four people had been mortally wounded by the explosion, Adolf Hitler was not among them. After recovering from the initial shock, Hitler was euphoric, concluding that fate was on his side. While Stauffenberg was in the air returning to Berlin, the other conspirators unwisely dragged their feet, initiating Operation Valkyrie to seize control of Berlin only after Stauffenberg arrived at 3:45 p.m. and stirred them to action. After a series of unfortunate failures of nerve by parties on the fence and several important missteps by the conspirators, the coup was quickly put down. Stauffenberg was dead by midnight. And the hunt for anyone and everyone connected with the plot was begun.

BUCHENWALD AND FLOSSENBÜRG

The Nazis used arrest and torture to ferret out those involved in the conspiracy, eventually making some seven thousand arrests. These included thousands of friends and relatives of the conspirators, including children. As Nazi understanding of the plot grew, renewed suspicion fell on Dohnanyi and the Abwehr, and thus also on Bonhoeffer. Canaris was arrested. Then, on September 20th, some of Dohnanyi's hidden files on Nazi war crimes were discovered outside Berlin. Dohnanyi's and Bonhoeffer's position became extremely perilous. After eighteen months in the comparatively luxurious Tegel prison, the pastor was moved to a five-by-eight-foot cell at the Gestapo headquarters in Berlin. While there he was the subject of intense interrogations, but it appears that he was able to largely keep secret the real (treasonable) purposes of his activities for the Abwehr. After four months he was moved to Buchenwald concentration camp.

Over fifty thousand people were killed at Buchenwald before Allied troops arrived to find the survivors in April 1945. Bonhoeffer was spared the worst of the camp's conditions and housed with sixteen other high-profile prisoners in the basement of a building originally used for Buch-enwald staff. Among the others imprisoned there were Captain S. Payne Best, a captured British intelligence officer; Josef Müller, a close friend of Bonhoeffer's and fellow former Abwehr agent; Vassily Kokorin, a Soviet air force officer; and Dr. Sigmund Rascher, a German physician who had per-formed horrifically cruel medical experiments on prisoners for the Nazis at Dachau but who had subsequently run afoul of his superiors. The pris-oners were given sufficient food to keep them alive and the opportunity to leave their small cells each day for a time, not to go outside but to walk up and down the corridor between the cells. Sometimes allowed to do this in groups, the prisoners managed to have significant contact with one another as the weeks ticked by.

On Easter Sunday, April 1, 1945, the inmates at Buchenwald could hear American artillery in the distance. The camp might be liberated at any time. Then again, the prisoners might be executed at any time. The Nazis were sometimes moving prisoners in advance of invading armies, sometimes simply killing them. On April 3 the prisoners from Bonhoeffer's building were crammed into the back of a large truck outfitted to run on a generator powered by a wood fire. As smoke filled the prisoners' compartment, Dr. Rascher exclaimed, "My God, this is a death van; we are being gassed!"[15] The Nazis had indeed used such vans in their euthanasia programs, but this was not one of them. As the van rolled slowly through the night, the air became more breathable, and the prisoners and three guards made their way to Flos-senbürg, a concentration camp near the Czech border. The camp had a reputation as a place of death, so it was with much relief that they were turned away—the camp was full. The van continued to travel south, and the prisoners were eventually deposited in a prison in Regensburg. It turned out that many of the families of those involved in the Stauffenberg plot were being held there. The opportunity to exchange information and support was much cherished. "Bonhoeffer spent most of the time talking through the small door opening to the widow of Carl Goerdeler [a key figure in the conspiracy] and telling her all he could about her husband's last days at the Gestapo prison [back in Berlin]."[16]

On Sunday, April 8, Bonhoeffer was separated from the rest of the group: two men came to correct an oversight and take him back to Flossenbürg.

The diaries of Admiral Canaris had been discovered, and it seems that when the new and incriminating information they contained was brought to Hitler's attention in early April, the Führer took a special interest in the case.[17] Orders were given to execute Canaris and several others connected with him, including Bonhoeffer. A hasty trial was conducted at Flossenbürg. On the morning of April 9, at the age of thirty-nine, Dietrich Bonhoeffer was hanged. His corpse was burned. A mere two weeks later, Allied troops arrived and liberated the remaining prisoners.

FAILURE AND SUCCESS

How should we view the short life of Dietrich Bonhoeffer? It's easy to conclude that in this case, the bad guys won. In a different set of circumstances Bonhoeffer could have had a long, happy life and a successful, meaningful career in his native land, either as an academic theologian or as a pastor. The events of the war took those possibilities away. He still could have lived a long, fruitful life in America, but his conscience intervened. After his return to Germany in 1939, he was prohibited from public speaking, from publishing and from carrying out the ordinary pastoral work he loved and at which he excelled. Never married, he left behind a grieving fiancée upon his death. Most of his attempts to assist the Resistance, for which he risked and ultimately lost his life, failed in their long-range goals. Bonhoeffer's life could easily be viewed as a tragedy. But while his life did possess an element of the tragic, he himself did not see things this way. Captain Best noted that at Buchenwald Bonhoeffer was actually "cheerful," and that while other prisoners complained, Bonhoeffer didn't:[18] "Bonhoeffer was different; just quite calm and normal, seemingly perfectly at his ease. . . . His soul really shone in the dark desperation of our prison."[19] Another British prisoner at Buchenwald, Hugh Falconer, reported that Bonhoeffer

> was very happy during the whole time I knew him, and did a great deal to keep some of the weaker brethren from depression and anxiety. He spent a good deal of time with Wasily Wasiliew Kokorin . . . who was a delightful young man although an atheist. I think [Bonhoeffer] divided his time with him between instilling the foundations of Christianity and learning Russian.[20]

Cheerful . . . in a concentration camp. Why? How? Another comment of Best's suggests an explanation: "Bonhoeffer was all humility and sweetness;

he always seemed to diffuse an atmosphere of happiness, of joy in every smallest event in life, and of deep gratitude for the mere fact that he was alive. . . . He was one of the very few men I have ever met to whom his God was real and ever close to him."[21] Bonhoeffer lived in the world, but he also lived in the presence of God. And the presence of the God who loves us can bring a peace the world cannot give. While Bonhoeffer deeply valued the good things of earthly life, he also believed that the ultimate goal of human existence is not the attainment of temporal goods but union with God and others, now and in eternity. Thus Bonhoeffer could say to Payne Best, as he was leaving him for the last time, "This is the end—for me the beginning of life."[22] At this parting, the day before his execution, Bonhoeffer also asked Best to convey a message to a good friend, Anglican Bishop George Bell: "I believe in the principle of our Universal Christian brotherhood which rises above all national interests, and that our victory is certain."[23] Victory and success for the Christian is not measured by years of life on earth, or by fame or pleasure or power. To be close to God and to love others is to succeed, and by that measure Bonhoeffer was a success indeed. In a personal letter to Bonhoeffer's family after the war, Best wrote: "He was, without exception, the finest and most lovable man I have ever met."[24]

Bonhoeffer's faith inspired him to stand up against evil. It encouraged him to draw close to his fellow human beings and to God, who gave him strength and peace even in the face of death. Adolf Hitler died a mere three weeks after Bonhoeffer, by his own hand. Death will come for all of us, but the person who loves God need not fear this. The crucial question is not "How can I avoid pain and death?" but "How shall I live? And what shall I do with the time that is allotted to me?"

14

JEAN VANIER

IN MAY 1940 HITLER'S FORCES swept into Belgium and northern France. As Dietrich Bonhoeffer watched from within the Third Reich, an eleven-year-old boy living in France fled south with his mother and siblings. The boy was Jean Vanier, whose father, Georges, was the diplomatic minister representing Canada to France. Jean, three of his siblings and his mother, Pauline, were picked up near Bordeaux by a British Navy destroyer, then transferred to a merchant ship and evacuated to Wales. After Georges Vanier had rejoined the family, they made the dangerous passage across the Atlantic and returned to Canada.[1]

Less than two years later, Jean surprised his parents with a request. He asked for a meeting with his father in his office, where young Jean presented him with some paperwork: the forms necessary to apply to the Royal Navy College in England. Jean wanted to become an officer in the British Navy, at that time the most powerful navy in the world, and he had somehow learned that the college took cadets as young as thirteen. His father's response made a lasting impression, as Jean later explained: "His answer to me was, 'I trust you. If that is what you want to do, you must do it.' My father's trust in me confirmed my trust in myself. When he said, 'I trust you,' he gave me life; he gave me permission to trust my intuitions and to just do what seemed right. I knew that if he trusted me, I could trust myself."[2] For her part, Pauline Vanier was deeply concerned about her son's plan. German submarines attempting to isolate the United Kingdom were sinking both British Navy ships and merchant vessels by the score, so Jean's journey back across the Atlantic would be perilous enough. On top of this, his destination (England) was being bombed by the German air force. Georges was not swayed: "You know, we mustn't clip that child's wings. We don't know what he may become in later life."[3]

After being accepted by the Royal Navy College, Jean traveled in a troop ship to Liverpool, along with a regiment of Canadian men going to the war. He then took a train to London to stay briefly with his older sister Therese, who had already come back to England and would go on to do important work for the Free French organization. But no one was home at Therese's apartment when Jean arrived, so when she and her friends did return around nine in the evening, they found the thirteen-year-old Jean sleeping on the doorstep surrounded by his baggage. In due course Jean traveled to the Royal Navy College (in the southwest of England) and began the term, learning seamanship and sailing in addition to the standard academic work for boys of his age, and playing tennis and rugby. Later he would be trained in navigation and gunnery. In September 1942 the buildings of the college were bombed by German planes, but the cadets weren't hurt, as it was still a week before the start of the upcoming term. Jean did well at the college and was placed in the Alphas, the top twelve members of his cohort. He was too young to be involved in combat, but he was in Paris in 1945 to see concentration camp survivors from Buchenwald, Dachau and Auschwitz "coming off the trains like skeletons, their faces tortured with fear, anguish and pain, still wearing their white-striped uniforms."[4] In the years that followed Jean served on several ships. When his father heard of a naval report that the young man "showed good qualities as an officer but could tend to lack respect for his seniors," his reaction was, "As long as he shows respect for those under him, he'll be all right."[5]

Jean had had a religious upbringing—both Georges and Pauline Vanier were devout Catholics. The couple regularly spent thirty minutes a day together in silent prayer and placed great importance on the religious instruction of their children. In his later years in the navy Jean began to make the Christian religion more deeply his own, praying the breviary and attending daily Mass when possible. By the age of twenty he was an officer serving on Canada's only aircraft carrier, but he began to feel that it was time to move on. When he expressed to his mother some interest in becoming a priest, she introduced him to Father Thomas Philippe, a Catholic priest of the Dominican order in France. Jean corresponded with Father Thomas and two other priests while still in the service. Eventually Jean felt that he should leave the navy and requested permission from his military superiors to resign. The chief of naval staff wrote to Georges Vanier, now the Canadian ambassador to France, expressing his regret that the navy was losing such a promising young officer. Ambassador Vanier replied: "[Jean's] aspiration transcends the human level. Knowing him as I do, I feel sure that he is answering to the Master's call. As you have been kind enough to ask me for my comments, I can only say that this is a matter between God and him in which man if possible should not interfere."[6] Though Jean didn't know exactly what he would do next, he did know *who* he was following: "When I left the Navy in 1950 my deepest desire was to be a disciple of Jesus and live the Gospel message—I didn't know whether it would be through the priesthood or another way, but I knew that I would know as time went on."[7]

EAU VIVE

After the war, Father Thomas Philippe had arranged, with the help of his family, for the purchase of several buildings within walking distance of the Saulchoir, the House of Studies of the Paris Province of the Dominicans (the Catholic religious order of which Thomas Aquinas had been an early member). During occupation the buildings had been requisitioned by the German military, but now they would house a mixed group of seminarians and laypeople studying philosophy, theology and Christian spirituality. The students came from all over the world and included Germans, Americans, Arabs and Asians as well as French, and some non-Christians as well as Christians. The community, which was open to both women and men, was called Eau Vive ("Living Water"). The residents lived simply, focusing on study, prayer, community life and manual work on the property. Many took courses at the Saulchoir, and in the summer Eau Vive hosted classes with high-profile visiting scholars, including philosopher Jacques Maritain.[8] It was to Eau Vive that Jean came in September 1950. He was just turning twenty-two. His experience of mentoring by Father Thomas was to be one of the great formative influences of his life:

> My first meeting with Père Thomas was deeply moving. I suppose that because of my innocence or freshness I needed a master, a teacher, a spiritual father. Listening to him, simply being with him, I felt transformed and I felt

a presence of God. He was an authentic man. I learned from him that to pray is not just to say prayers but to be prayerful, to remain quietly in the presence of God, to simply be in communion with Jesus.[9]

Jean was still thinking about becoming a priest, but given his background he knew relatively little about philosophy and theology. He accordingly took courses with the Dominicans at the Saulchoir, which would have included heavy doses of Aristotle and Aquinas. His time in community at Eau Vive was fruitful and peaceful . . . until 1952, when Father Philippe was summoned to Rome. This was a period before the Second Vatican Council, when a number of debates were taking place within the Catholic Church concerning how the church should respond to modern social conditions. There were fears that Father Thomas was too radical, not sufficiently orthodox. His permission to say Mass and hear confessions was revoked (for a time), and he was told that he must leave Eau Vive. The censure was painful for the priest, in his middle age and no doubt full of energy and ideas. But he was committed to the church and accepted his period of exile, pouring his energies into prayer and writing. He had such confidence in Jean Vanier that he asked the young man to take over leadership at Eau Vive, which Jean did for four years. During this period Jean also took two years of philosophy courses at the Institut Catholique de Paris. But there continued to be tension between some within the church hierarchy and Eau Vive, and in 1956 the Holy Office in Rome asked Jean to leave the community. When a certain Father Cayré, who had helped to push Jean out, expressed surprise "at the apparent lack of resentment with which Jean agreed to go, remarking that he had thought the young man was very attached to Eau Vive, [Jean's] response was unhesitating, 'Of course, but I am even more attached to Jesus.'"[10]

Jean spent the next year at a Trappist Abbey in Bellefontaine, France, "rising early in the morning to pray, then studying in his room, following the liturgical readings, doing some manual work in the garden, walking and reflecting."[11] His future was uncertain, but in the meantime he could make progress on his doctoral dissertation; he'd picked the ethics of Aristotle as his topic. In the years that followed Jean lived an often solitary existence, residing for a time in a small house near Fatima, Portugal, and continuing his life of study and prayer. A severe case of hepatitis slowed him down, but in 1962 he successfully defended his doctoral thesis, cum maxima laude, at the Institut Catholique on "Happiness as Principle and End of Aristotelian Ethics." Now well into his thirties, he was still listening for his calling in life.

Vanier's dissertation on Aristotle was well received, and before long the chairman of the philosophy department at St. Michael's College in the University of Toronto came across it and was impressed. He invited Vanier to teach ethics at St. Michael's for the spring semester 1964. The topic of the course was to be justice, but once Vanier had begun the semester, he realized that the students weren't particularly interested in what he had to say on that topic. So he redesigned his course and instead discussed friendship, love, sexuality and atheism. The classroom was soon filled to overflowing. This sort of midstream course redesign is surprisingly rare in academia. It bespeaks a special sensitivity to and awareness of the interests and concerns of one's students, and a willingness to go the extra mile for their sake. Vanier had never taught before, but he had a huge natural talent for it. His years of study and contemplation gave him a rich store from which to draw. He was invited "to give talks to the whole college and the hall would be packed to bursting point."[12] St. Michael's College was quick to offer him a permanent position. Georges and Pauline Vanier were no doubt glad to have their son closer to home—they had for several years been back in Canada, and in 1959 Georges had been appointed governor general of the country by Queen Elizabeth II.

Imagine for a moment that you and your spouse are a "power couple" in your society, active and important. After several years of religious soul-searching, your son has recently finished his PhD and completed his first semester teaching at a prestigious university. His classes have been a huge success with the students, and his career holds great promise. Then he tells you he's leaving academia completely. He's decided to move to another country and devote himself to taking care of two men with intellectual disabilities. Permanently.[13] How would you feel about this?

Raphaël and Philippe

Jean Vanier's decision to move back to France to care for two mentally handicapped men must have seemed crazy to the external observer. Certainly his mother was strongly opposed to the idea at first. But although Jean had loved teaching and interacting with students, he didn't feel it was meant to be his life's work.[14] His thoughts were elsewhere. He had stayed in contact with Father Thomas Philippe after the latter's removal from Eau Vive. In 1963 Father Thomas had moved to Trosly-Breuil, a village of about a thousand people to the north of Paris, where he had been invited to serve as the chaplain of Le Val Fleuri, an institution for men with mental handicaps. Jean had visited Father Thomas that year and had begun to get to know the residents of Val Fleuri. Jean later described his reaction: "Each one had so much life, had suffered so profoundly and thirsted so deeply for friendship. Within each gesture and each word was the question: 'Will you come back?' 'Do you love me?' Their cry of pain and their thirst for love touched me deeply."[15] Jean returned to France after he had completed his teaching at St. Michael's in spring 1964. Encouraged by Father Thomas, he began to visit different institutions for the intellectually disabled. He was overwhelmed by what he saw at St. Jean les Deux Jumeaux, an asylum near Paris that housed eighty men in a space intended for forty:

> Huge concrete walls surrounded the buildings made of cement block; eighty men lived in dormitories with no work. All day long they just walked around in circles. From 2 to 4pm there was a compulsory siesta, then time for a walk all together. . . . I was struck by the screams and the atmosphere of sadness, but also by a mysterious presence of God.[16]

One man at the asylum spat at everyone who approached him. Life in such institutions was often lonely and chaotic, and sometimes even violent. Many persons with intellectual disabilities were not well cared for in France at this time; some were in institutions, others in the care of their families but segregated from society. Vanier once "encountered a teenager on a farm chained up in a garage."[17] But the French government was trying to find solutions and was supportive of new ventures on behalf of the mentally handicapped. Father Thomas gently suggested to Jean that perhaps he could do something.

Encouraged by the psychiatrist who was chairman of the board of directors of Val Fleuri, Jean decided to open a house and welcome a small number of intellectually disabled men to live with him. With the financial help of his parents and friends, he purchased a simple, somewhat run-down house in Trosly-Breuil. It had one water faucet, no bathroom and a wood stove for heat.

Madame Martin, the director of St. Jean les Deux Jumeaux, supported Jean's idea and suggested three men in particular from the group of eighty under her direction. Raphaël Simi and Philippe Seux had both been placed in the asylum after the death of their parents. Raphaël had a vocabulary of about twenty words and often communicated by grunts. His impaired balance left him shaky on his feet. Philippe "talked a lot but frequently about the same things and lived to a large extent in his own dream world."[18] The third man, Dany, could not hear or speak and suffered from serious emotional problems. The men were invited to stay with Jean for a month's holiday, after which point they would be asked whether they would like to remain.

In early August 1964 things were ready at the house Jean had bought, which he would soon name L'Arche (French for "the ark"). Madame Martin brought Raphaël, Philippe and Dany, along with a large meal, and she joined the three men, Jean, Father Thomas, the psychiatrist from Val Fleuri and his wife, and other friends for an opening dinner. After the guests left, Jean was on his own with his three charges. "I was completely lost," he recalled, "especially with Dany. He couldn't hear and he couldn't speak. It was crazy taking him."[19] Vanier's biographer Kathryn Spink describes the first night:

> In a state of total insecurity, Dany began to hallucinate. He ran out into the quiet streets of Trosly-Breuil and made menacing gestures at the uncomprehending passers-by. The night of 5-6 August was a memorable one for Jean. Failing to find the electricity meter, although there was one in the house as he was to discover a few days later, he and his companions spent the first night in darkness and turmoil with Dany constantly on the move and Jean Vanier unable to get any rest."[20]

It became clear to Jean that he could not manage with Dany in the house, and the next morning, with sadness, he called Madame Martin to ask her to take him back to the asylum. He then settled in to his chosen life's work, getting to know Raphaël and Philippe and doing what he could to provide them with a good life. Decades later Jean reflected on why he had chosen to start L'Arche:

> When I welcomed Raphaël and Philippe there wasn't a specific or rational reason—it just seemed obvious. They were crying out for relationship, and I could provide it. Practically everything I did with L'Arche was intuitive, based

on the sense that this is what should be done. There was a beauty in these disabled men that was being crushed at the large, dismal, violent institution in which they had been put. These men were persons and precious to God, and so it seemed right, even evident, for me to do something about their unjust situation. Though I could not do anything on a large scale, at least I could live with a few of them and help them to find a decent life and the freedom to be themselves. This search for justice flowed naturally from my faith in Jesus: my faith in the Gospel message revealed the value and beauty of men and women with severe disabilities. People often ask me the reasons for starting L'Arche, but I didn't have reasons, I just trusted and loved.[21]

THE EARLY DAYS OF L'ARCHE

Raphaël, Philippe and Jean did the chores of everyday life together— shopping, cleaning, cooking. They laughed and had fun. They prayed together. The two disabled men were able to help in the garden, where land was cleared and vegetables were planted. Friends of Jean came to help renovate the house, and women in the village began to befriend the new community, bringing food from time to time. Philippe, who was twenty-four, repeatedly asked about his mother. Although both his parents were dead, no one had told him about his mother's death. Jean asked an uncle of Philippe's to take him to his mother's grave and help him accept her death. "He threw himself on his mother's grave and howled and howled in a way that you could hear for miles around, and I think those howls were not only because his mother, the only person he had ever loved, was dead but because no one had treated him as her son."[22] Soon Jean's mindset began to shift, and he found himself focusing less on doing things for Raphaël and Philippe and more on listening to them. Without having sought their opinion, he had been taking the two men to a 7:30 a.m. Mass every morning. As Spink relates,

> One morning Philippe asked [Jean] why he should [get up to go to Mass]. Only then did Jean Vanier realize that in order to remain there and not return to the institution, Philippe would have agreed virtually to anything, even to going to Mass when he did not want to. Yet the Holy Spirit could only express itself in freedom. The realization dawned that the more fragile a person's liberty was, the more it must be respected and protected. . . . It was a principle absolutely fundamental to the communities that would follow.[23]

Late in August a cousin of Father Thomas came to live at L'Arche and help out. In September the psychiatrist at Val Fleuri asked Jean to take in a third mentally handicapped man, Jacques Duduit. In December a fourth disabled man was welcomed, Jean-Pierre Crépieux. The group was getting bigger. And becoming a family. Vanier's goal from the beginning was to create a family environment for the disabled men he was living with, an environment in which they would be encouraged to grow and develop, but most of all one in which they would be respected and loved for who they were. They had been ignored, looked down on, laughed at and abandoned, and they carried with them deep wounds of rejection. In their hearts they harbored a powerful longing for acceptance and love, as all persons do. L'Arche was designed to be a place where persons with and without intellectual disabilities would form one community and find this acceptance and love. In an early letter Vanier explained:

> Our first role is to love the disabled, to love them just as they are. . . . On the level of reason they may be deficient, but often on the level of the heart, they are very rich. Our role is to discover, respect and love each person. We want to create a family rather than a school or a workshop where there are educators and those to be educated, those who are superior and those who are inferior. We want to create a family where there is peace, love and friendship.[24]

In March 1965 there was turnover in the staff at Val Fleuri and Jean was asked to become the new director. The institution housed over thirty intellectually disabled men and, once again, Jean found himself with more than he could easily handle. One of the inmates needed injections for diabetes; Jean practiced first on an orange. But things began to improve. Volunteers from the village chipped in. At a conference for professionals working with the disabled, a kindly psychiatrist took Jean under her wing, helping him understand more fully the psychological needs of the men under his care. Before long she was coming each week to provide valuable professional care. Val Fleuri included workshops in addition to living space, and the men took pride in their productive labor, which was an important part of both the original L'Arche community and Val Fleuri. Philippe prepared samples for a ceramics company and made woolen cushions; Jacques and Jean-Pierre wired electrical fixtures and simple electronic games. Raphaël continued to prefer work in the garden.[25]

The life of the community was not all work, though. In 1966 Jean arranged for a special trip, funded in part by the men's own earnings and in part by donations from generous benefactors. The group included forty disabled men and about twenty assistants; they traveled in individual cars through various cities in France and Italy, with the trip culminating in a pilgrimage to Rome. They were given special seats in St. Peter's Basilica for the Easter vigil Mass, and had an audience with Pope Paul VI, who asked for their prayers and addressed them with words of encouragement:

> Seeing you all together makes us realize that you are a small group united by love and an active will to help one another. You are a community in whose midst Jesus is happy to live. If some of you may think that you are not amongst those who have had the greatest luck in life, know that God loves you perhaps more than others. At any rate, we affirm that for us you are cherished sons whom we are very happy to receive.
>
> God calls all of you, in spite of your difficulties, to be saints, and He reserves a special role for you in his Church. So continue to live with courage, doing the best you can, loving each other and being brothers for one another. Live united like one big family, knowing that each one gives and receives more than he thinks.[26]

Jean explained the value of such trips and pilgrimages in a letter to friends and benefactors:

> Trips like these . . . give us new hope and, for some, are the beginnings of a whole new way of life, a life of deeper peace, more open to the world, to society and to others. . . . [Most of the disabled in the community] have no "worldly" hopes for the future. They cannot hope to advance in the professional world nor to found a family. Life could become monotonous if their hearts and spirits were not stimulated by holidays and trips, opening them up to the world around them.[27]

As another component of the effort to provide a rich and full human life for all the members of the community, numerous leisure activities were organized; by 1967 there were clubs for painting, photography, stamp collecting, plasterwork and basket weaving. Some of the men learned to play the guitar, some the recorder. Friends of the community would occasionally visit to show films. On the weekends there were bicycling trips, sometimes fishing, and folk dancing lessons taught by an American volunteer who had joined the community. Something special had begun.

THE GROWTH OF L'ARCHE

Without trying, L'Arche began to grow. People with intellectual disabilities who lived with their families in the area started coming to the workshops at Val Fleuri during the day. Parents, social workers and staff at psychiatric hospitals in France requested placements for intellectually disabled men and women in their care, and the L'Arche community purchased more of the old stone houses in Trosly-Breuil so as to be able to welcome new residential members. The French government provided crucial financial support. Jean returned to Canada at least once a year to lecture at St. Michael's, and before long he was being invited to speak at retreats in both Catholic and ecumenical settings in Canada and France. As he spoke about L'Arche at these retreats, people he met became interested in the movement, and some came to live with the community in Trosly-Breuil as assistants. By 1968 there were seventy-three people in L'Arche houses; by 1970 there were 112; by 1972, 126.[28]

In 1969 a married couple from Canada who had spent a year in Trosly-Breuil opened Daybreak, the first L'Arche community in North America. In 1970 a young woman from India who had been an assistant in Trosly-Breuil and a German woman whom Jean knew in Montreal traveled to India and, working with Vanier and a local board of directors, opened a L'Arche community in Bangalore (in south-central India). Asha Niketan (House of Hope) was located in a simple house outside the city. Water came from two wells on the property. The first two disabled members of the community were Joseph, a twenty-three-year-old Catholic with Down syndrome, and Gurunathan, a twenty-five-year-old Hindu who spoke little but was very welcoming and attentive to others. They had never worked before and took pleasure in learning to grow vegetables in the garden. Later, simple assembly work for a local factory helped support the venture. The community grew and included a local man who served as the gardener, his wife and their seven-year-old son. Prayer, games of soccer and time to listen to music on a tape player were parts of daily life. Meals were simple: beans, rice, vegetable soup, an egg or a piece of fish. Beds were made of wooden planks topped by a thin cotton mattress. In a letter written during the first days of the community, Jean—visiting India from France—described the daily schedule:

> We go to Mass at 6:15am. Following Mass we have a half-hour prayer in the community with Joseph and Guru. There is breakfast, work, lunch at 12:30, siesta, work, dinner at 7:15, prayer and we are in our rooms by 9:00. The rhythm is quite slow, poor and close to nature. We eat with our hands as we sit on the floor. There is no television or radio, not even a newspaper, no books, just fresh air, healthy food, work, prayer, rest and a deep unity among us, and the shining faces of Joseph and Guru.[29]

Within a year a half-dozen or so additional persons with disabilities had joined the community. Tomato plants, cabbage, spinach and one hundred banana trees had been planted, and two buffalo contributed milk. A typical day now included relaxation and breathing exercises in the morning and an hour and a half of recreation (songs, dances and games) before dinner.

Soon Jean was traveling internationally for several months a year, to give retreats and talks (including many at prisons) and to help support the new L'Arche communities that began to spring up. By 1975 there were twenty-eight L'Arche communities in nine different countries. Sometimes opportunities for new communities would seem to appear out of thin air. Vanier describes the beginnings of Asha Niketan-Nandi Bazaar, a L'Arche community in southwest India:

> We have been offered a large property of about sixty acres . . . on a hill near a village overlooking the sea—extraordinarily beautiful, full of silence. . . . The story of this property is quite a long one. Mr. Pramanand's father first saw it in 1938 when the English requisitioned, without compensation, his machinery and his factory in the south of Kerala which at that time was making soap. He had no money, but he wanted to buy this new property. The first seven acres cost five hundred rupees; he agreed to the price, still without any money. On the morning of the day fixed for him to buy the land, he received a letter and five hundred and twenty-one rupees from a man in Mangalore (in Mysore) whom he did not know. The man said he had had a dream in which he was told to send him the money. Mr. Pramanand's father bought the land and little by little began to build this new factory which closed up in 1959. He believed that the land belonged not to him, but to God. After the death of his father, Mr. Pramanand had been looking for a work of God to which he could give

this property. One day while travelling by train he saw a newspaper lying beside him, which he picked up and read. There was a long article on Asha Niketan-Bangalore. He wrote directly to Gabrielle.[30]

Today this community numbers ninety members, and includes three homes, a daycare center, work training units and an outreach program.[31]

As the number of communities increased through the '70s and '80s, so did the need for structure and governance, so that the far-flung L'Arche houses could support each other and so that new communities could be started in a way suitably informed by the mistakes and successes of the past. Vanier intentionally began to ease out of a leadership role, focusing instead on writing and speaking, as well as living the everyday life of L'Arche. He is now back in Trosly-Breuil, where he resides in one of the L'Arche homes. Well into his eighties, he still speaks widely and was recently awarded the prestigious Templeton Prize. As of 2015, the International Federation of L'Arche includes 147 communities in thirty-five countries.[32]

THE GIFT OF L'ARCHE

Jean Vanier started the first L'Arche home as a response to the needs of a small number of persons with intellectual disabilities. He was the helper; they were the helped. But rather quickly he began to realize that the helped were helping him to grow as a human being. This is a persistent theme in the reflections of nondisabled assistants who live in L'Arche homes: the mentally handicapped "humanize" the other members of the community.[33] Vanier explains,

> Believe it or not, it has been this life together [with the disabled] that has helped me become more human. Those I have lived with have helped me to recognize and accept my own weaknesses and vulnerability. I no longer have to pretend I am strong or clever or better than others. I am like everybody else, with my fragilities and my gifts.[34]

For those who have gifts of intelligence, competence, beauty and strength, it is so natural to approach life as an arena for competition and striving. Because we desire the approval of others, we become focused on achieving the things that will bring us approval. This in turn can lead us to focus on ourselves and on "getting ahead," on accomplishing the goals we have set for ourselves. But this can carry a cost. Personal relationships get pushed to the side as we concentrate on tasks and goals. What's more, when we don't question our natural tendency to prize intelligence, beauty, strength and competence, we tend to look down, subtly or not so subtly, on those who lack those qualities. And we begin to value ourselves only for the excellences and good qualities we possess. But we all have some weaknesses, some inabilities. We all sometimes fail in ways that bother us. So long as we value ourselves for our abilities, then, there will be parts of ourselves and our histories that make us feel inadequate, that make us feel lacking in value. We therefore hide those parts, from others and even from ourselves. Sometimes in this situation we put up subtle barriers, steering clear of conversations, interactions and relationships that might bring another person close enough to see our weaknesses. Yet if I do not share who I am with anyone, I cannot be close to anyone.

What Jean Vanier and many others at L'Arche communities have found is that life with the disabled can take one into another realm, into a whole different way of approaching life. The vulnerability and lack of status that the intellectually disabled person often displays mean that one is not likely to think of oneself as being in competition with that disabled person and that one will probably experience less fear of judgment by that person. One feels one's weaknesses less and has less of a need to hide them. The masks can begin to come off. Perhaps more importantly, relationship with the disabled allows one to recover the truth that the primary value of a person does not come from excellent qualities or accomplishments. I am valuable because I am a human being. Once this is internalized on a deep level, I begin to see myself in a new way. I don't feel the same compulsion to succeed or be approved, and I can accept my weaknesses and failures. I therefore become a more open person and can connect more deeply with others.

Vanier writes that there is a mysterious power "hidden in those who are powerless . . . they attract and awaken the heart."[35] L'Arche taught him "a way of putting people first, of entering into personal relationships." He continues:

> This way of approaching each individual, of relating to each one with gentleness and kindness was not easy for me. I joined the navy when I was very young, just thirteen, a highly impressionable age. All my training was geared to help me to be quick, competent, and efficient, and so I became. As a naval

officer, and even later, after I had left the navy, I was a rather stiff person, geared to goals of efficiency, duty, prayer, and doing good to others and to philosophical and theological studies. My energies were goal-oriented.

From the beginning, in 1964, l'Arche has been truly a learning experience for me. It has brought me into the world of simple relationships, of fun and laughter. . . . [The life of people with intellectual disabilities] is not a life centred on the mind. So it is that the people with intellectual disabilities led me from a serious world into a world of celebration, presence, and laughter: a world of the heart. . . . Power and cleverness call forth admiration but also a certain separation, a sense of distance; we are reminded of who we are not, of what we cannot do. On the other hand, sharing weaknesses and needs calls us together into "oneness."[36]

An early chronicler of L'Arche summarizes a number of personal characteristics that various disabled individuals brought to their communities:

Simplicity of spirit; affection and freedom to genuinely manifest that affection; candidness; openness to life, to people, to God; capacity to make people feel welcome; tendency to be concerned only with the essentials in life and in people; joy and an eagerness to give joy to others; generosity; capacity to live fully in the present moment; sense of wonder; sensitivity; unquestioning faith.[37]

Of course life in a L'Arche community is not all roses. Vanier writes of the frustration and anguish he sometimes felt in exasperating situations. But even then, the experience of being forcefully confronted with his own limitations in patience and generosity was an opportunity to acknowledge those limitations, accept himself for who he was and begin "to work with [my limitations] in order to diminish their power over me."[38]

A CHRISTIAN LIFE WELL LIVED

What does a devout Christian life look like? What does it mean to go all in and follow Jesus with one's whole being? There are many answers to these questions, as many answers as there are people, who find themselves in different situations, with different gifts and opportunities. Bonhoeffer gives us one inspiring picture. Jean Vanier gives us another. When in his early twenties he left the navy, his path forward was clouded with uncertainty. When in his thirties he set aside a blossoming academic career and instead devoted his life to caring for two virtual strangers, his choices must have seemed incomprehensible to some. But from the vantage point of the end of the story, we can see what a beautiful path Jean found simply by listening to his heart and following Jesus. In his statement when accepting the Templeton Prize, he reflected on what it means to grow as a person:

> When those ingrained in a culture of winning and of individual success really meet [the intellectually disabled], and enter into friendship with them, something amazing and wonderful happens. They too are opened up to love and even to God. They are changed at a very deep level. They are transformed and become more fundamentally human.
>
> Let me [tell] you about Pauline. She came to our community in 1970, hemiplegic, epileptic, one leg and one arm paralyzed, filled with violence and rage. It was not easy to live in one of our small homes with her. Our psychiatrist gave us good insight and advice: her violence was a cry for friendship. For so long she had been humiliated, seen as hardly human, having no value, handicapped. What was important was that the assistants take time to be with her, listen to her and show their appreciation for her. Little by little she evolved and became more peaceful and responded to their love. Her violence disappeared. She didn't particularly like to work in our workshops, but she loved to sing and to dance. When she was quite a bit older I would go and visit her. Sometimes she would put her good arm on my head and she would say "poor old man." It takes a long time to move from violence to tenderness. The assistants who saw her initially as a very difficult person, began to discover who she was under her violence and under her disabilities. They also began to change. They discovered that for a person, growth was not primarily climbing the ladder of power and success, but . . . learning to love people as they are.[39]

15

IMMACULÉE ILIBAGIZA

IN EARLY APRIL OF 1994, Immaculée Ilibagiza traveled the one hundred or so miles from her university in southern Rwanda to the small town of Mataba, in the west of the country.[1] She was coming home. Though close to the equator, Rwanda's high altitude gives it a pleasant climate—daytime temperatures average in the seventies. Frequent rain keeps it green and lush. Mataba overlooks Lake Kivu, the large, picturesque lake that separates Rwanda from the Democratic Republic of the Congo (then called Zaire). Immaculée had the good fortune to be returning not only to a beautiful place but also to a close and loving family. Her parents, Leonard and Rose, both worked in education, Rose as a primary school teacher and Leonard as an administrator in the Catholic school system. Also home for Easter were her younger brother, Vianney, and one of her two older brothers, Damascene.

Leonard and Rose must have been pleased with their lives. They lived in a house Leonard had designed and built, with a cistern to catch rainfall and solar panels that provided electricity on sunny days. In addition to their full-time jobs, they grew crops in their fields and had cows and other animals. Often sought out by neighbors for advice on family or business problems, they were respected and appreciated members of the community. Their desire to instill a love of learning and a strong work ethic in their children was bearing fruit. Their oldest son, Aimable, was in Senegal doing postgraduate work, preparing for a career as a veterinarian. Damascene had a master's degree in history and was teaching high school in the capital city, Kigali. Immaculée had won a highly competitive scholarship to the National University. They had much to be grateful for.

Unfortunately, there was also much to be anxious about. Leonard had been thrown in prison a few years earlier, though not for any crime. Despite his efforts to the contrary, he was caught up in a complicated political conflict between the Hutu majority and the Tutsi minority, the two main ethnic groups in Rwanda. When German colonists arrived in the area in the late nineteenth century, the Tutsi minority was politically and economically dominant. Both the Germans and the later Belgian colonists supported the existing stratification between Hutu and Tutsi. Indeed, they seem to have intentionally solidified it, using the Tutsi monarchy and traditional Tutsi political leaders to exercise indirect rule.[2] In 1933 the Belgians instituted a policy calling for all Rwandans to be issued an ethnic identity card, which identified the holder as Hutu, Tutsi or Twa (a second minority in the country comprising about 1 percent of the population). Tutsis were given more favorable educational opportunities, and the Belgians replaced many Hutu chiefs with Tutsi ones, so that "by the end of the Belgian presence in Rwanda in 1959, forty-three chiefs out of forty-five were Tutsi as well as 549 subchiefs out of 559."[3] Later, in the 1950s, the Belgians responded to international pressure and instituted reforms that gave greater representation to the Hutu.[4] As decolonization loomed, Tutsi traditionalists feared a loss of power. In 1959, after the death of the Tutsi king under ambiguous circumstances, Tutsi militants beat up Hutu political opponents and threatened greater violence. Groups of Hutus responded by looting and burning Tutsi houses; soon the country was engulfed in chaos. The episode ended after Belgian military intervention and the creation of a Hutu-led independent republic. After a military coup in 1973, the political system became a dictatorship, led by Hutu Juvénal Habyarimana.

The majority of Leonard's life, then, had been lived in a climate of Hutu dominance. With some notable exceptions, life was peaceful, and if a Tutsi stayed out of politics he or she was likely to be left alone. But things had become unstable in the early 1990s. Thousands of Tutsis who had fled Rwanda since the fall of the Tutsi monarchy lived the precarious life of refugees in neighboring Uganda. Many joined the Rwandan Patriotic Front (RPF) and, seeking a return to their homeland, initiated an invasion of Rwanda in October 1990. In response, the Habyarimana regime mounted a defense against the RPF army and arrested between six thousand and thirteen thousand Rwandan civilians. These were deemed "accomplices" of the RPF and were mostly Tutsis, but also some Hutu opponents of the government. Some were tortured.[5] Leonard was one of those arrested, most likely for the simple reason that he was a prominent Tutsi. He avoided starvation in prison by bribing a guard to allow a relative to bring him food. Soon the initial RPF attack was repulsed, and things settled down. Within two weeks Leonard was home safe and sound.

By 1994, however, the situation had become increasingly tense. Hundreds of Tutsi civilians had been killed in 1992 as uncertainty over the war threatened the government's hold on power. A new radio station mixed popular music with violent anti-Tutsi propaganda. And the government was training a youth militia, the Interahamwe. Purportedly meant to help protect the country against the RPF invasion, in reality the Interahamwe's main activity seemed to be the harassment of Tutsi citizens.

As Immaculée's family enjoyed an evening meal together partway through her visit home, Damascene seemed preoccupied. He was processing something he'd seen that day and finally burst out, taking his family off guard: "I saw them, I saw the killers. I was on my way to Bonn's house, and we saw them in the distance. They were wearing the bright colors of the Interahamwe and were carrying hand grenades. They had *grenades.*"[6] Leonard tried to calm his son, but Damascene continued:

> They have a list of names of all the Tutsi families in the area, and our names are on it! It's a death list! They are planning to start killing everyone on the list tonight! . . . Dad, we have to leave, *please.* We have to get out of here while we still can. We can just walk down the hill, find a boat, cross Lake Kivu, and be safely in Zaire by midnight. But we have to leave now before it's too late.[7]

Despite Damascene's pleas, Leonard assured his family that the tension would blow over. He and Rose had rode out tense times before, and it was no doubt difficult to entertain the thought of abandoning their home and all they had worked for.

It was the evening of April 6, 1994. Within a few short hours, Rwanda's president would be dead, and Hutu extremists within the government would begin an all-out effort to consolidate their power. The Rwandan genocide was about to begin.

Attacked

Ethnic conflict was by no means a pervasive feature of Immaculée's early life. Hutus and Tutsis speak the same language and essentially share the same culture. Moreover, Immaculée's parents had shielded her from knowledge of Rwanda's divisive past. She was not even aware of the distinction between Hutu and Tutsi until fourth grade, when her teacher, Buhoro, took roll by ethnic categories on the first day of class. (Buhoro kicked Immaculée out of class for the day when she didn't know whether she was Hutu, Tutsi or Twa.) Now the distinction was about to become a matter of life and death. At 8:20 p.m. on April 6, President Habyarimana's plane was shot down while flying into Kigali. Within hours, radical elements within the government assassinated the prime minister and other moderate government officials and attacked international peacekeepers. Within a few days, they had pushed aside moderate leaders in the army and taken complete control of the government.

Back in Mataba, Immaculée's family learned of the president's assassination in the early morning of April 7. Unsure what to do, they stayed in their home and waited. By April 10, thousands of local Tutsis had congregated at and around their home, looking to Leonard for leadership in the crisis. When a group of about fifty Interahamwe militia attacked the crowd with knives and machetes, Leonard and a large group of the Tutsi men in the crowd repelled the assault. But they feared that more numerous and more organized killers would soon be on their way. The radio was full of news of Tutsi murders throughout the country. Concerned in a special way for his daughter, Leonard directed Immaculée to flee to the home of Pastor Murinzi, a Protestant minister who was the father of one of Immaculée's childhood friends, the uncle of her boyfriend, and a well-known local Hutu. After a terrifying five-mile journey to his home, Immaculée was received warmly by Murinzi—but not by everyone gathered at his large home. The first person Immaculée encountered upon walking into the living room was none other than Buhoro, her teacher from years before. Glad to see someone she knew, she greeted him warmly. In response, "He looked down at my hand and then up into my eyes before clicking his tongue in disgust and turning his back on me."[8] Stunned, Immaculée moved into a different room in the house and was relieved to find one of her closest friends from childhood, a young Hutu woman named Janet.

Immaculée was feeling uncomfortable at the Murinzis' and asked Janet to stay at her home. Janet avoided eye contact, rebuked her for suggesting that she would hide Tutsis and left.

Thankfully, there were more courageous individuals in the house. One of Murinzi's sons comforted Immaculée and escorted her to the room of one of his sisters. Later, Pastor Murinzi hid Immaculée and seven other Tutsi women in a bathroom in his home. Her family, she learned, had been scattered when the Tutsis gathered at her house were attacked in force. Damascene had fled to the home of his trusted Hutu friend Bonn.

A BATTLE WITHIN

While Murinzi had agreed to hide Immaculée and the other women, Immaculée was not without concerns about his reliability. Relatives had told her that he disliked her father and was jealous of his standing in the community. When Immaculée's younger brother, Vianney, arrived at Murinzi's shortly after Immaculée, Murinzi refused to shelter him, saying that it was too dangerous for him to be protecting men. Crushed with fear for her brother's life, Immaculée began to worry that Murinzi might have ulterior motives for hiding only women. Still, he had found an excellent place for them to hide; later he would conceal them further by sliding a large wardrobe in front of the door, obscuring the bathroom from sight. Spreading the story that they were no longer in the house, he kept their presence secret from all but a few of his children.

A few days later, a crowd of hundreds of killers arrived to search Murinzi's house. These weren't soldiers or Interahamwe militia but local Hutus, people Immaculée had grown up with. Unsettled by fears of the invading RPF army, and in many cases coerced with the threat of violence by government officials, ordinary people had became perpetrators of genocide. The noise and malevolent chanting of the searchers penetrated the bathroom. Immaculée was overcome by despair and fear. The killers searched extensively but overlooked the bathroom.

In the days that followed Immaculée experienced an intense inner struggle. Expecting a second search at any time, she began to feel crippling anxiety. She found relief in prayer. But as time passed and she learned the extent of the genocide from Murinzi, she become angry:

I was angrier than I'd ever been before—more than I believed was even possible. I was angry at the pastor for telling us such horrific details when our families were out there with nowhere to hide. I was angry at the government for unleashing this holocaust. I was angry at the rich countries for not stopping the slaughter. But most of all, I was angry at the Hutus—all of them. And as the pastor droned on about the horrible things being done to Tutsis, my anger grew into a deep, burning hatred.

I'd never done anything violent to anyone before, but at that moment I wished I had a gun so that I could kill every Hutu I saw. . . . I wanted to . . . set the whole country on fire. If I'd had an atomic bomb, I would have dropped it on Rwanda and killed everyone in our stupid, hateful land.[9]

Soon Immaculée had difficulty praying. When she would reach the line in the Lord's Prayer "Forgive us our trespasses as we forgive those who trespass against us," she would try not to think of the killers, knowing that she was unwilling to forgive them.

Eventually, a second group of killers arrived to search the house. As Immaculée heard them on the other side of the wall, she tried to pray. But she felt like a hypocrite, professing to love God while at the same time hating so many of the human beings He had made. She felt like she was "lying to God every time [she] prayed to Him."[10] She tried to pray for the killers but stopped, convinced that they deserved death, not mercy. In her memoir she recounts one of her prayers at the time:

Why do You expect the impossible from me? . . . How can I forgive people who are trying to kill me, people who may have already slaughtered my family and friends? It isn't logical for me to forgive these killers. Let me pray for their victims instead, for those who've been raped and murdered and mutilated. Let me pray for the orphans and widows . . . let me pray for justice. God, I will ask You to punish these wicked men, but I cannot forgive them—I just can't.[11]

Soon Immaculée's other prayers felt hollow. "A war had started in my soul, and I could no longer pray to a God of love with a heart full of hatred."[12]

LIGHT IN THE DARKNESS

Immaculée struggled with her anger and inability to forgive for no less than four days. Eventually, she had a powerful religious experience that enabled her to regain peace. One evening she heard screams and then the cries of a baby. The crying continued all night, then fell silent. Immaculée recalls,

> I prayed for God to receive the child's innocent soul, and then asked Him, *How can I forgive people who would do something to an infant?* I heard His answer as clearly as if we'd been sitting in the same room chatting: *You are all my children . . . and the baby is with Me now.* It was such a simple sentence, but it was the answer to the prayers I'd been lost in for days.[13]

Children can be cruel, sometimes even violent. But so often when they do something hurtful, they don't truly understand what they are doing. Focusing on her belief that the killers were children of God, Immaculée found herself able to wish not only that they would be punished but also that they would recognize the terrible wrongness of their actions and that they would turn from evil and back to the light of God. Immaculée prayed that God would forgive them. Doing so, she took a huge step toward letting go of her anger and regaining inner peace. Instead of allowing the killers to poison her heart with bitterness, she began to conquer a horrific situation with love.

ESCAPE

In mid-June Immaculée and the other Tutsi woman received important news: the French army was sending troops to Rwanda. The French had had close ties with the Habyarimana regime, and the extremist Hutu government in power during the genocide appeared to be welcoming the arrival of French soldiers, so some Tutsis feared the intentions of the French force. But Immaculée reasoned that the increased international attention that would come with a French presence could only be good for the Tutsis. Once on the ground, the French soldiers announced their intention to set up safe havens for surviving Tutsis. Over the initial objections of Murinzi, Immaculée and the others convinced him to try to make contact with the French and arrange for their transfer to a safe haven.

In early July, Murinzi learned that the French had a small unit close by and traveled to meet with them. They directed him to bring the group of Tutsi women that night. At 2 a.m. Murinzi woke his ten children and led the Tutsi women out of the bathroom. Addressing his children, he said: "There, but for the grace of God, go any one of you. If you have a chance to help unfortunates like these ladies in times of trouble, make sure you do it—even if it means putting your own life at risk. This is how God wants us to live."[14] Then, together with his sons, Murinzi led the Tutsi women through the night to the French camp. They passed a group of Interahamwe on the road, but their identity as Tutsis went unnoticed. A large group of Tutsis travelling on an open road, still alive after two months of genocide, was the last thing the Interahamwe expected.

Once their identity as Tutsis was verified by the French, the women were ushered into the camp. They broke down in tears. Soon they were transferred to a larger camp ten miles distant, where they received food, water and security, and were joined by about twenty other Tutsi survivors. After three months in hiding, Immaculée was safe.

Damascene

At the French camp, Immaculée gathered news about her family from some of the other survivors. Her mother Rose had been killed a few days after Immaculée had arrived at Murinzi's. She was hiding when she heard someone being attacked. Thinking it was Damascene, she rushed out into the open shouting for the killers to stop. It wasn't Damascene. The killers turned on her. Immaculée's father was shot a few days later, when he travelled to a local government official to beg for help on behalf of several thousand Tutsis gathered at a stadium. The official had his soldiers drag Leonard outside and execute him. Vianney was at the stadium and was killed when it was attacked.

Damascene outlived the others. His friend Bonn hid him under his bed during the early days of the killings and later in a hole he dug at the edge of his family's property. Damascene moved from Bonn's house to the hole only hours before a group of killers arrived to search the house. After three weeks, they decided that the best course of action was for Damascene to attempt an escape across Lake Kivu to Zaire. Bonn knew a Hutu fisherman who was helping Tutsis flee. The pair traveled to the lake in the dead of night but arrived too late—that night's boat had already departed. Rather than risk the return journey to Bonn's, Damascene hid out during the following day at the home of Nsenge, a friend of his and Bonn's who lived near the lake. Nsenge was courageous and loyal. Sadly, his brother Simoni was not. Before dinner Simoni summoned a group of killers, who captured Damascene, dragged him into the street and surrounded him. They asked for the whereabouts of Immaculée, beating him and threatening to kill him slowly if he refused to tell them. He refused.

Later Immaculée learned that one of the killers cried for days after the killing: "He talked incessantly about all the things he and Damascene had done together . . . playing soccer, singing in the choir, and being altar boys. He was haunted by the kindness my brother had shown him and all the other boys they'd known. [He] expressed his remorse to anyone who would listen."[15]

RETURN TO MATABA

In late August the French operation in Rwanda was drawing to a close. The RPF army had advanced across the country, with hundreds of thousands of Hutus fleeing before it. Along with a group of other Tutsis, Immaculée was unceremoniously dropped off by the French soldiers near the RPF front line. After a dangerous transition, they were taken in by the RPF soldiers.

One of the Tutsi refugees Immaculée had met at the French camp had a home in Kigali, the capital, and invited Immaculée and several others to move in. Against all probability, she secured a job working at the United Nations office in Kigali. A few months later, a UN peacekeeper offered to take Immaculée and a friend back to Mataba, to visit relatives. They flew by helicopter to an army camp near the village and then traveled into Mataba with a military escort. Immaculée couldn't help but enjoy the helicopter ride, and she felt good being able to ride into her village without fear. Her good spirits vanished when they arrived, however, as she saw places that reminded her of times with her family and observed the destruction of all the Tutsi homes in the area, including her own. Her family's belongings had been looted before a fire was set; all that was left were some partially collapsed stone walls and her father's burned-out car.

Friends of Damascene's showed Immaculée his grave; an eyewitness gave her a detailed account of his last moments. She was overwhelmed:

> The lump growing in my throat stopped my voice, so I waved for the soldiers to take me back to the camp.
>
> As we drove away from my home, past the unmarked mounds of dirt that covered Mother and Damascene, I felt the bitter, dirty taste of hatred in my

mouth. On the return trip I looked at the faces peering at us as we passed, and I knew with all my heart that those people had blood on their hands—their neighbors' blood . . . *my family's blood.* I wanted the soldiers to douse Mataba in gasoline and let me light the match that would reduce it to ashes.[16]

The battle between forgiveness and the desire for revenge had begun again. In her autobiography Immaculée describes her soul as being "at war with itself."[17] She raged with anger but simultaneously realized that her feelings of hatred were drawing her away from "the freedom of forgiveness." "I never felt lonelier than I did that night," she writes. "God was my truest friend, and these feelings were a wall between us."[18] After hours of internal struggle, Immaculée prayed: "Forgive my evil thoughts, God . . . take this pain from me and cleanse my heart. Fill me with the power of your love and forgiveness. Those who did these horrible things are still Your children, so let me help them, and help me to forgive them . . . help me to *love* them."[19] Immaculée was at peace again. Forgiveness isn't forgetfulness or naiveté, and forgiveness for someone in Immaculée's position is perfectly compatible with the desire that the perpetrators of genocide should be punished for the sake of justice and the good of society. It is not wrong to want those guilty of heinous crimes to be held accountable. But a desire for punishment and accountability is not enough. Immaculée could see that forgiveness offered the only chance to break the cycle of hatred her community was stuck in. And forgiveness and love could bring her deliverance from a lifetime of bitterness and anger.

Immaculée has since emigrated to the United States and is now a popular author and speaker. In her experience we see a shining example of someone who fully lived out Jesus' injunction to forgive "not seven, but . . . seventy-seven times" (Mt 18:22) and to love one's enemies (Mt 5:44). In the face of so much evil, Immaculée could have doubted God. Instead, she chose to trust in God's goodness. She is an illustration of what commitment to Jesus in the most difficult of circumstances can look like. Thankfully, most people will never experience the horror that Immaculée and her family went through. But we all have our trials, and everyone can find it hard to forgive. If following the way of Jesus helped Immaculée to survive, overcome and grow in the most difficult of times, following the way of Jesus can help us in our more ordinary struggles, too.

CONCLUSION

Taking the Wager

A PERSON WHO APPRECIATES the reasonableness of Christianity and feels drawn to the way of Jesus but who has not yet made a commitment to living a Christian life may wonder how best to proceed. In the concrete, how does one become a disciple of Jesus? Or, if one is already a Christian, how does one become closer to God?

It seems to me that five things are especially worth doing. First, find a Christian community and become involved in it. Which community? "You will know them by their fruits" (Mt 7:16). And the fruit of the Holy Spirit is "love, joy, peace, patience, kindness, generosity, faithfulness, gentleness, and self-control" (Gal 5:22-23). Since every Christian community is made up of human beings, no Christian community is without failings and problems. But some are healthier than others. Find one of the healthier ones.

Second, make time for regular prayer. Prayer is communication with God, and just as it is rare to become close to another human person without communication, it is rare to become close to God without prayer. Even fifteen minutes a day of prayer is much, much better than nothing.

Third, spend time reading and meditating on the Bible, especially the Gospels. In seeking to understand the meaning of the Bible, avail yourself of the tradition. For two thousand years Christians have pondered the Scriptures; much can be gained by listening to those who have gone before us.

Fourth, ask God for help in leading a life that is pleasing to him and then do your best to cooperate. A conversion toward God involves a turning away from sin, from all attitudes and actions that are opposed to what is good. To cooperate in one's own spiritual growth requires that one be willing to admit one's failings. A clear awareness that one is loved by God can help one feel the security to do this.

Fifth, go all in on the two greatest commandments: to love God and to love others as yourself. In the Gospel of John, Jesus says, "If you love me, you will keep my commandments. And I will ask the Father, and he will give you another Advocate, to be with you forever. This is the Spirit of truth" (Jn 14:15-17).

The wager has captured people's attention since it was introduced by Pascal in the seventeenth century. In part one of this book, I presented an updated formulation of the argument, both in a basic version and in a modified form. If Christianity has at least a 50 percent probability of being true, then it is eminently reasonable to commit to living a devout Christian life. This is clearly the case for those who would lose little, all things considered, by living a life of Christian commitment, and it remains true for those who would lose much if Christianity is false—for the risk of loss if Christianity is false must be balanced against the even greater goods at stake if Christianity is true. But does Christianity have a 50 percent or higher probability of being true? In part two I argued that it does, building the case on the cosmological argument, the fine-tuning argument, the moral beauty and existential resonance of Christian doctrine, replies to the arguments from divine hiddenness and evil, and an argument for the resurrection. Christian commitment is rational, and the abundant life to which Jesus calls us is beautiful, as the short biographies of part three have hopefully shown.

But each must judge by his or her own lights. In the *Pensées*, Pascal notes a simple truth: "Either God is or he is not." You can seek God or you can ignore him. You can wager for God, or against God. In the end, these are the only two options: to do nothing is to place one's bet on the possibility that God does not exist. To which view will you incline? "At the far end of [an] infinite distance a coin is being spun which will come down heads or tails. How will you wager?"[1]

NOTES

INTRODUCTION

[1]William James, *The Will to Believe and Other Essays in Popular Philosophy* (Cambridge, MA: Harvard University Press, 1979), 30.

[2]The number of journal articles and books by each of these authors is large, but see the following for a representative sample. On epistemology and the rationality of religious belief: Alvin Plantinga, *Warranted Christian Belief* (Oxford: Oxford University Press, 2000), or Plantinga's condensed and less technical version of this material, *Knowledge and Christian Belief* (Grand Rapids: Eerdmans, 2015). On the problem of evil: Eleonore Stump, *Wandering in Darkness: Narrative and the Problem of Suffering* (Oxford: Oxford University Press, 2010), and Peter van Inwagen, *The Problem of Evil* (Oxford: Oxford University Press, 2006). On a number of issues: Peter van Inwagen, *God, Knowledge and Mystery: Essays in Philosophical Theology* (Ithaca, NY: Cornell University Press, 1995). On arguments for the existence of God and the resurrection, respectively: Richard Swinburne, *The Existence of God*, 2nd ed. (Oxford: Oxford University Press, 2004), and *The Resurrection of God Incarnate* (Oxford: Oxford University Press, 2003).

[3]Somewhat less roughly, the epistemic probability of a proposition, relative to some set of background information, is the level of confidence a rational person having that background information would assign to that proposition. For a discussion of epistemic probability, see Alvin Plantinga, *Warrant and Proper Function* (Oxford: Oxford University Press, 1993), chaps. 8-9.

1 A CURIOUS OFFER

[1]On what counts as an extraordinary circumstance, see chapter three.

[2]The work is available in many English translations, including Blaise Pascal, *Pensées and Other Writings*, trans. Honor Levi (Oxford: Oxford University Press, 1995).

[3]As noted by Jeff Jordan in his excellent monograph *Pascal's Wager: Pragmatic Arguments and Belief in God* (Oxford: Oxford University Press, 2006), 19-25. Throughout part one I draw heavily on Jordan's work.

[4]From "Religious Belief," a lecture for the Sunday Essay Society in Cambridge in 1899, quoted in Paul Levy, *Moore: G. E. Moore and the Cambridge Apostles* (New York: Holt, Rinehart, and Winston, 1979), 214.

[5]F. M. A. Voltaire, "Pascal's Thoughts Concerning Religion" (letter 25, 1734), in *Letters Concerning the English Nation* (Oxford: Oxford University Press, 1994), 127.

[6]Abbe de Villars, *Traite de la delicatesse* (Paris 1671); trans. in James Franklin, "Two Caricatures, I: Pascal's Wager," *International Journal for Philosophy of Religion* 44 (1998): 110.

[7]Christopher Hitchens, *God Is Not Great: How Religion Poisons Everything* (New York: Twelve, 2007), 211.

[8]Ibid., 212.

[9]Franklin, "Two Caricatures, I," 109.

[10]I'm influenced greatly here by Jordan, *Pascal's Wager*.

[11]Skeptical of this claim? Google the St. Petersburg Paradox, and see chapter four.

2 PASCAL'S WAGER: THE BASIC ARGUMENT

[1]For Christianity to be true requires that Christianity make a determinate set of claims about reality, and of course different denominations disagree about what that set includes. In the context of the wager, I'm thinking along the lines of C. S. Lewis's "mere Christianity," that is, the core religious beliefs common to traditional Catholic, Orthodox and Protestant Christians.

[2]On issues of grace and free will, see chapter four.

[3]Blaise Pascal, *Pensées and Other Writings*, trans. Honor Levi (Oxford: Oxford University Press, 1995), 156 (S680).

[4]William James, *The Varieties of Religious Experience: A Study in Human Nature* (New York: Longmans, Green, 1903), 485-86.

[5]Michael Martin, *Atheism: A Philosophical Justification* (Philadelphia: Temple University Press, 1990), 243.

[6]Rodney Stark and Roger Finke, *Acts of Faith: Explaining the Human Side of Religion* (Berkeley and Los Angeles: University of California Press, 2000), 31-32.

[7]Harold Koenig, Dana King and Verna B. Carson, *Handbook of Religion and Health*, 2nd ed. (Oxford: Oxford University Press, 2012), especially 123-44 and 301-7.

[8]Ibid., 269. They immediately continue: "The only exception is based on cross-sectional reports from the NSFH-I, which find that dissimilarity of religious beliefs and practices between couples is associated with marital arguments and spouse abuse." Studies on this data set (the National Survey of Families and Households, wave 1) find that religiosity is associated with less spousal abuse generally speaking but more spousal abuse in those cases in which husband and wife exhibit large differences in religious belief and involvement. See the summaries of studies by Ellison, Bartkowski and Anderson (1999), Ellison and Anderson (2001), Curtis and Ellison (2002), and Ellison and colleagues (2007) in Koenig, King and Carson, *Handbook of Religion and Health*, 262-71.

[9]Koenig, King and Carson, *Handbook of Religion and Health*, 128-30.

[10]Ibid., 131.

[11]Chaeyoon Lim and Robert D. Putnam, "Religion, Social Networks, and Life Satisfaction," *American Sociological Review* 75, no. 6 (2012): 915.

[12]Ibid., 920. For more data on the size of the effect of religiosity on well-being, see Frank Newport, Sangeeta Agrawal and Dan Witters, "Very Religious Americans Report Less Depression, Worry," Gallup, Dec. 1, 2010, www.gallup.com/poll/144980 /Religious-Americans-Report-Less-Depression-Worry.aspx; Chaeyoon Lim, "In U.S., Churchgoers Boast Better Mood, Especially on Sundays," Gallup, March 22, 2012, www.gallup.com/poll/153374/churchgoers-boast-better-mood-especially -sundays.aspx; and Frank Newport, Dan Witters and Sangeeta Agrawal, "Religious Americans Enjoy Higher Wellbeing," Gallup, Feb. 16, 2012, www.gallup.com/poll /152723/religious-americans-enjoy-higher-wellbeing.aspx.

[13]Lim and Putnam, "Religion, Social Networks, and Life Satisfaction," 920.

[14]Koenig, King and Carson, *Handbook of Religion and Health*, 307-11.

[15]Alan B. Krueger, Daniel Kahneman, David Schkade, Norbert Schwarz and Arthur A. Stone, "National Time Accounting: The Currency of Life," in *Measuring the Subjective Well-Being of Nations: National Accounts of Time Use and Well-Being*, ed. Alan Krueger (Chicago: University of Chicago Press, 2009), 46.

[16]Ibid.

[17]Lim, "In U.S., Churchgoers Boast Better Mood."

[18]M. E. McCullough, W. T. Hoyt, D. Larson, H. G. Koenig and C. E. Thoresen, "Religious Involvement and Mortality: A Meta-Analytic Review," *Health Psychology* 19, no. 3 (2000): 211-22. The analysis examined forty-two studies, but many used the same data sets, hence the figure of twenty-nine studies mentioned in the text.

[19]M. E. McCullough, W. T. Hoyt and D. Larson, "Small, Robust, and Important: Reply to Sloan and Bagiella (2001)," *Health Psychology* 20, no. 3 (2001): 228-29.

[20]See Koenig, King and Carson, *Handbook of Religion and Health*, 477-78.

[21]Robert D. Putnam and David E. Campbell, *American Grace: How Religion Divides and Unites Us* (New York: Simon and Schuster, 2010), 452.

[22]Ibid., 446.

[23]Ibid., 448.

[24]Ibid.

[25]Ibid., 472-73.

[26]Richard Gale, *On the Nature and Existence of God* (Cambridge: Cambridge University Press, 1991), 352.

[27]The renunciation of luxury doesn't rule out the appropriateness of paying special attention to one's own family and community, and it doesn't rule out celebration or the consumption of things beyond bare necessity. But moral excellence and the message of Jesus do seem to require a much larger willingness to share one's goods with the needy than is standard in contemporary industrialized countries. For

more on this issue, see Thomas M. Crisp's forthcoming book *Into Shalom: An Ethics of Radical Discipleship.*

[28]Timothy Keller, *The Reason for God: Belief in an Age of Skepticism* (New York: Dutton, 2008), 275-76.

[29]Andrew Newberg and Mark Robert Waldman, *How God Changes Your Brain: Breakthrough Findings from a Leading Neuroscientist* (New York: Ballantine Books, 2009), 14.

[30]For now we're assuming that "Christianity is true" and "Naturalism is true" are the only two possible ways the world might be. I'll dispense with this false assumption in chapter four, where we'll see that the wager argument succeeds even when we take into account other possibilities.

3 OBJECTIONS TO THE WAGER: MORAL RESERVATIONS AND THE COST OF COMMITMENT

[1]Richard Dawkins, *The God Delusion* (New York: Houghton Mifflin, 2006), 104.

[2]William James, *The Will to Believe and Other Essays in Popular Philosophy* (New York: Longmans, Green, 1897), 6.

[3]Sam Harris, "The Empty Wager," *Washington Post*, April 18, 2007, www.samharris.org/blog/item/the-empty-wager.

[4]Antony Flew, *The Presumption of Atheism and Other Philosophical Essays on God, Freedom and Immortality* (New York: Harper & Row, 1976), 64. The principle to which Flew alludes is that you should follow the evidence as far as you can, but then "frankly and honestly . . . recognize the limits of your knowledge" (32), rather than, say, allowing practical considerations to affect one's beliefs.

[5]J. L. Mackie, *The Miracle of Theism: Arguments for and Against the Existence of God* (Oxford: Oxford University Press, 1982), 202.

[6]J. Brehm, "Post-decision Changes in Desirability of Alternatives," *Journal of Abnormal and Social Psychology* 52, no. 3 (1956): 384-89.

[7]On this point, see Thomas V. Morris, "Wagering and the Evidence," in *Gambling on God: Essays on Pascal's Wager*, ed. Jeff Jordan (Lanham, MD: Rowman and Littlefield, 1994), 47-60.

[8]D. T. Gilbert, E. C. Pinel, T. D. Wilson, S. J. Blumberg and T. P. Wheatley, "Immune Neglect: A Source of Durability Bias in Affective Forecasting," *Journal of Personality and Social Psychology* 75, no. 3 (1998): 617-38.

[9]Ibid., 633.

[10]In what follows I develop an analogy given by Peter Kreeft in *Fundamentals of the Faith: Essays in Christian Apologetics* (San Francisco: Ignatius, 1988), 48.

[11]One would still face the same risk of martyrdom if Christianity is true, but in that case martyrdom would not be an uncompensated, needless loss.

4 More Objections to the Wager: Other Religions and Christianity

[1]Section 98 (Al-Bayyina), verse 6, *The Qur'an*, trans. M. A. S. Abdel Haleem (Oxford: Oxford University Press, 2005).

[2]For example, even on the interpretation of Islam being considered, outcome 2 shouldn't say "eternal misery," because there is a chance that someone who commits to Christianity today might change their mind later and convert to Islam before death. And, perhaps outcomes 4 and 7 should not be "lower chance of eternal happiness" but should instead be whatever is in outcomes 2 and 8. For the purpose of addressing the objection at hand, though, it's not necessary to enter into any of these issues. To make the point I am working toward, all we'll need now is a rough-and-ready description of outcomes 1-9.

[3]Suppose you thought medicine A had a 50 percent chance of curing you, and medicine B had a 10 percent chance of curing you, and no other medicine or regimen had an appreciable chance of curing you. Then taking medicine A would be the action that maximizes your chance of being cured. Something analogous is true in the religious case, thus my claim that the policy of committing to the religion one thinks is most likely to be true is the policy that maximizes one's chance at eternal happiness. This holds true for all but the most unusual circumstances. For a discussion of such circumstances, see Michael Rota, "A Better Version of Pascal's Wager," *American Catholic Philosophical Quarterly*, forthcoming, note 34.

[4]I've argued that nothing in the many gods objection has challenged the conclusion that practicing Christianity is a better bet than practicing no religion at all. But what if practicing a religion (Christianity included) actually *reduced* one's chances of gaining eternal happiness? Some philosophers, e.g., Michael Martin, have raised a clever objection along these lines. For a discussion of this objection, see Rota, "A Better Version of Pascal's Wager," section III.

[5]See also Mt 25:31-46 and Rev 20:12-13.

[6]See John Calvin, *Institutes of the Christian Religion* III.21-23.

[7]Irenaeus, *Adversus Haereses* 4.39.2-3, translation from William G. Most, *Grace, Predestination, and the Salvific Will of God: New Answers to Old Questions* (Front Royal, VA: Christendom Press, 1997), 143.

[8]John Chrysostom, *Homilia de ferendis reprehensionibus* 6, translation from Most, *Grace, Predestination, and the Salvific Will of God*, 106.

[9]Jerome, *Commentarium in Epistulam ad Ephesios* 1.1.11, translation from Most, *Grace, Predestination, and the Salvific Will of God*, 108.

[10]See Most, *Grace, Predestination, and the Salvific Will of God*, 106-9, 143-50, 259-78, 302-3.

[11]Cf. Augustine, *De correptione et gratia* 2.3, the *Indiculus* (between AD 435 and 442) and the Council of Orange II (AD 529). Key texts from these last two documents are available in English translation in *The Christian Faith in the Doctrinal Docu-*

ments of the Catholic Church, ed. Jacques Dupuis, 7th rev. ed. (New York: Alba House, 2001), 797-804.

[12]See Eleonore Stump, "Augustine on Free Will," in *The Cambridge Companion to Augustine*, ed. E. Stump and N. Kretzmann (Cambridge: Cambridge University Press, 2001), 137-39.

[13]See Eleonore Stump, *Aquinas* (New York: Routledge, 2003), 389-404, and Most, *Grace, Predestination, and the Salvific Will of* God, 138-40, 155-56, 457-72.

[14]By "the human will" is meant the part of a human being that enables a human being to perform acts of choice. More generally, it is with the will that one intellectually desires something, chooses something or commands certain of one's powers (e.g., one's limbs to move or one's intellect to focus on this rather than that).

[15]Stump, *Aquinas*, 394.

[16]There may be more to the human contribution than just omitting resistance to grace. See Aquinas, *Summa theologiae* I-II.111.2. (Thanks to Lawrence Feingold for this point.) But since the ability to omit resistance is enough to rebut premise (1), I set to the side further exploration of human cooperation with grace.

[17]Aquinas, *Summa contra Gentiles* III.159. Translation is my own; Latin text from *S. Thomae Aquinatis Opera omnia*, ed. R. Busa (Stuttgart: Frommann Holzboog, 1980), vol. 2.

[18]Jordan, *Pascal's Wager*, 146.

[19]See Cyril of Alexandria, *In Epistolam ad Romanos* 8.30, in Most, *Grace, Predestination, and the Salvific Will of God*, 270-71, and Ambrose, *De fide* 5.6.83, in Most, *Grace, Predestination, and the Salvific Will of God*, 275. For a defense of this view from the Post-Reformation period, consult the work of Jacob Arminius.

[20]For a powerful defense of this view, see Most, *Grace, Predestination, and the Salvific Will of God*.

[21]See John Calvin, *Institutes of the Christian Religion* III.21-23.

[22]*Super I ad Corinthios*, chap. 15, lecture 2. Translation is mine; Latin text is from *S. Thomae Aquinatis Opera omnia*, vol. 6.

5 WHERE DID PHYSICAL THINGS COME FROM?

[1]Aristotle, *Physics* VIII, 4-6, and *Metaphysics* XII, 1-6; Maimonides, *Guide for the Perplexed* 2.1; Thomas Aquinas, *Summa contra Gentiles* I.13 and *Summa theologiae* I, question 2, answer 3. For contemporary versions, see chapter seven of Richard Swinburne, *The Existence of God*, 2nd ed. (Oxford: Oxford University Press, 2004), and Alexander R. Pruss, "The Leibnizian Cosmological Argument," in *The Blackwell Companion to Natural Theology*, ed. William Lane Craig and J. P. Moreland (Oxford: Blackwell, 2009), 24-100.

[2]For a helpful discussion of the different forms of cosmological argument that have been proposed, see C. Stephen Evans, *Natural Signs and Knowledge of God: A New*

Look at Theistic Arguments (Oxford: Oxford University Press, 2010), chap. 3.

[3]Cf. Richard Dawkins: "Particles and antiparticles wink in and out of existence like subatomic fireflies, annihilating each other, and then re-creating themselves by the reverse process, out of nothingness" (Richard Dawkins, "Afterword," in Lawrence Krauss, *A Universe from Nothing: Why There Is Something Rather Than Nothing* [New York: Free Press, 2012], 189).

[4]A. D. Bajkov, "Do Fish Fall from the Sky?," *Science* 109 (April 22, 1949): 402.

[5]Warren Booth, Coby Schal, Edward L. Vargo, Daniel H. Johnson and Sharon Moore, "Evidence for Viable, Non-clonal but Fatherless Boa Constrictors," *Biology Letters* 7 (2011): 253-56.

[6]When I teach this argument in my philosophy courses, students sometimes ask, "But what if the whole group of contingent beings is infinite . . . how could a group going back infinitely in time have a cause?" Their thought is that, because the group stretches back infinitely into the past, there is no time or "place" for a cause to be, no way for a cause to "get behind" the group, in order to cause it. This is an excellent question. In my view there is a way an infinite network of contingent beings could have a cause: if God is outside time, then God could eternally decree that there always be such an infinite group. But if that sounds just a bit too abstract, and you think that there couldn't possibly be a cause for an infinite network of contingent beings, then the thing to think is that there must not be any such infinite network of contingent beings. This much seems clear: *if* there is one, it's contingent, and so it must have some cause.

[7]Daniel Dennett, *Breaking the Spell: Religion as a Natural Phenomenon* (New York: Viking Penguin, 2006), 242.

[8]*Summa theologiae* I, q. 2, article 3. Translation is my own; Latin text from *S. Thomae Aquinatis Opera omnia*, ed. R. Busa (Stuttgart: Frommann Holzboog, 1980), vol. 2.

6 Why Is the Universe Just Right for Life?

[1]Brian Greene, *The Hidden Reality: Parallel Universes and the Deep Laws of the Cosmos* (New York: Alfred A. Knopf, 2011), 142.

[2]I'm helped in this section by: Greene, *Hidden Reality*; Luke Barnes, "The Fine-Tuning of the Universe for Intelligent Life," *Publications of the Astronomical Society of Australia* 29, no. 4 (2012): 529-64; Paul Davies, *Cosmic Jackpot: Why Our Universe Is Just Right for Life* (Boston: Houghton Mifflin, 2007); Leonard Susskind, *The Cosmic Landscape: String Theory and the Illusion of Intelligent Design* (New York: Back Bay Books, 2006); Raphael Bousso, "The Cosmological Constant Problem, Dark Energy, and the Landscape of String Theory," *Pontificiae Academiae Scientiarum scripta varia* 119 (2011): 129-51, arXiv:1203.0307; and Geraint Lewis and Luke Barnes, *A Fortunate Universe: Life in a Finely-Tuned Cosmos* (Cambridge: Cambridge University Press, forthcoming).

[3]A caveat: where matter is present in space, the gravitational attraction generated by that matter inhibits the expansion of space. So within our solar system, for example, space is not expanding (or not to any significant degree). But in the vast regions between galaxies where there isn't much matter, space is expanding, even as you read this sentence.

[4]Think of a field as a physical entity that exists at every point in space. A familiar example from everyday life is the magnetic field.

[5]A Planck mass is a unit of mass equal to about .00002 grams. A Planck length is a unit of distance equal to about 1.6×10^{-33} centimeters. To express the cosmological constant in Planck units, we can express it as a quantity of Planck mass per cubic Planck length.

[6]Cf. Bousso, "Cosmological Constant Problem."

[7]See Susskind, *Cosmic Landscape*, 82-83.

[8]If we express the amount of energy as a given amount of mass per given volume of space, using Planck units, the estimation leads us to expect that the cosmological constant should be somewhere around 1 Planck mass per Planck volume. So whereas the total cosmological constant is the tiny fraction 1.35 divided by 10^{123} Planck mass per Planck volume, the contribution to the cosmological constant from known fields would be expected to be around 1 Planck mass per Planck volume. See the discussion in Greene, *Hidden Reality*, 142-44; Susskind, *Cosmic Landscape*, 87; and Bousso, "Cosmological Constant Problem," section 1.2.

[9]Susskind, *Cosmic Landscape*, 11.

[10]Greene, *Hidden Reality*, 150-51.

[11]See Robin Collins, "Evidence for Fine-Tuning," in *God and Design: The Teleological Argument and Modern Science*, ed. Neil Manson (New York: Routledge, 2003), 178-99. For a more accessible exposition of the evidence for fine-tuning, see Martin Rees, *Just Six Numbers: The Deep Forces That Shape the Universe* (New York: Basic Books, 2000). For a technical discussion, see Barnes, "Fine-Tuning of the Universe for Intelligent Life."

[12]For references, see Barnes, "Fine-Tuning of the Universe for Intelligent Life," 531.

[13]See Collins, "Evidence for Fine-Tuning," 181-82.

[14]Lewis and Barnes, *A Fortunate Universe,* chap. 7. I draw on Lewis and Barnes's work heavily in this section.

[15]Lewis and Barnes, *A Fortunate Universe*, chap. 1, emphasis added.

[16]Figure from Luke Barnes, email communication with author, Feb. 26, 2015.

[17]For the 10^{53} figure, see Collins, "Evidence for Fine-Tuning," 181.

[18]John Leslie, *Universes* (New York: Routledge, 1989), 10.

[19]An example from Timothy O'Connor, *Theism and Ultimate Explanation: The Necessary Shape of Contingency* (Chichester, UK: Wiley-Blackwell, 2012), 100.

[20]Leslie, *Universes*, 10.

[21]This objection has been pressed most forcefully by philosopher of science Elliott Sober; see his "The Design Argument," in *Blackwell Guide to the Philosophy of Religion*, ed. W. E. Mann (Oxford: Blackwell, 2004), 117-47.

[22]An adaptation of an example from A. Eddington, *The Philosophy of Physical Science* (Cambridge: Cambridge University Press, 1939).

[23]Adapted from Leslie, *Universes*, 13-14.

[24]I'm helped here by Luke Barnes's excellent discussion of this objection in a podcast episode, "11 Responses to Fine-Tuning," *Conversations from the Pale Blue Dot*, May 19, 2010, http://commonsenseatheism.com/?p=8109.

[25]For an extended rebuttal of the anthropic objection, see Jonathan Weisberg, "Firing Squads and Fine-Tuning: Sober on the Design Argument," *British Journal for the Philosophy of Science* 56, no. 4 (2005): 809-21.

7 A Primer on Probability

[1]I'm influenced in this chapter by E. T. Jaynes, *Probability Theory: The Logic of Science* (Cambridge: Cambridge University Press, 2003).

[2]The proponent of the anthropic objection (see chapter six) makes a similar error, by including the wrong information in K. Let E be the evidence that the cosmological constant falls within the life-permitting range, and let K include the fact that the cosmological constant could have taken on any of a very wide range of values, of which only a tiny fraction are life permitting. H_D is the hypothesis that some intelligent being was involved in the production of our universe ("D" for designer). $H_{\sim D}$ is the hypothesis that no such designer was involved. (For one who accepts $H_{\sim D}$, the thing to think would be that our universe was produced by some blind physical process.) The anthropic objection starts with the correct observation that, because we are ourselves living beings that arose in the universe, we cannot expect to observe a non-life-permitting universe. If we are here to observe anything, then we *will* observe a life-permitting universe. All true enough. But the anthropic objector then goes on to assert that since we know we are here, the probability that our universe is life permitting given no designer and background knowledge is equal to 1, and so is no different than the probability that our universe is life permitting given a designer and background knowledge. That is, the objector thinks

$$P(E|H_{\sim D}\&K) = P(E|H_D\&K) = 1$$

and supports this claim by saying that because we know that we are here, existing in our universe, we must include "we are here able to observe something" in K. To see that this is a mistake, recall that the background knowledge is "background" relative to the acquisition of the evidence E, and so the background knowledge K is specifically meant to exclude E. We want to include in K everything relevant, except the evidence E. But if we include anything in K which necessarily implies

E, we will have failed at this goal. If we include "we are here able to observe something" in K, then the background knowledge will logically require that (E) our universe is life permitting. Anyone who knows K will also know E, and thus K will include E, contrary to the whole point of separating out the evidence from the background knowledge. See Jonathan Weisberg, "Firing Squads and Fine-Tuning: Sober on the Design Argument," *British Journal for the Philosophy of Science* 56, no. 4 (2005): 819.

[3]Recall from chapter six that, in order to answer the Star Trek objection, we have chosen to treat the life-permitting range of the effective cosmological constant as $\left\{\frac{-1}{10^{108}}, \frac{1}{10^{108}}\right\}$ in Planck units, rather than Weinberg's much narrower range of $\left\{\frac{-1}{10^{120}}, \frac{1}{10^{120}}\right\}$.

[4]Equation (1) says that $P(H_D|E\&K) = \frac{P(H_D|K) \cdot P(E|H_D\&K)}{P(E|K)}$

But it follows from some basic rules of probability that $P(E|K) = P(H_D|K) \cdot P(E|H_D\&K) + P(H_{\sim D}|K) \cdot P(E|H_{\sim D}\&K)$.

So (1) becomes $P(H_D|E\&K) = \frac{P(H_D|K) \cdot P(E|H_D\&K)}{P(H_D|K) \cdot P(E|H_D\&K) + P(H_{\sim D}|K) \cdot P(E|H_{\sim D}\&K)}$

To make the computation simpler, let $\alpha = P(E|H_{\sim D}\&K) = \frac{1}{10^{41}}$.
Then $P(E|H_D\&K) = \frac{1}{10^9} = \frac{10^{32}}{10^{41}} = 10^{32} \cdot \alpha$

Thus we have, $P(H_D|E\&K) = \frac{P(H_D|K) \cdot 10^{32} \cdot \alpha}{P(H_D|K) \cdot 10^{32} \cdot \alpha + P(H_{\sim D}|K) \cdot \alpha}$

The α terms cancel. And since H_D and $H_{\sim D}$ are contradictory propositions, $P(H_{\sim D}|K) = 1 - P(H_D|K)$. Substituting, we get

$P(H_D|E\&K) = \frac{10^{32} \cdot P(H_D|K)}{10^{32} \cdot P(H_D|K) + [1 - P(H_D|K)]}$

Finally, simplifying the denominator of this equation gives us equation (2) in the text.

[5]If we knew that the cosmological constant could not have had a different value, that knowledge would be included in K, and $P(E|H_D\&K) = P(E|H_{\sim D}\&K)$

[6]The following abbreviations for propositions will be helpful:

E = The effective cosmological constant falls within the life-permitting range.

H_D = An intelligent being was involved in the production of our universe.

$H_{\sim D}$ = It is not the case that an intelligent being was involved in the production of our universe.

N = For any value v, if the effective cosmological constant = v Planck units, then it is metaphysically necessary that the effective cosmological constant = v Planck units.

$H_{D \sim N} = H_D$ and $\sim N$

$H_{DN} = H_D$ and N

$H_{\sim D \sim N} = H_{\sim D}$ and $\sim N$

$H_{\sim DN} = H_{\sim D}$ and N

The background K includes the information that if the value of the cosmological constant is not metaphysically necessary, then physical theory indicates a very wide range of possible values for the cosmological constant. As earlier, we take as a premise that $P(E|H_D\&\sim N\&K) \gg P(E|H_{\sim D}\&\sim N\&K)$. But $P(E|H_D\&N\&K) = P(E|H_{\sim D}\&N\&K) = P(E|H_{\sim D}\&\sim N\&K)$; this is because K does not include E, and knowledge of N without knowledge of E doesn't provide any reason to think the value of the cosmological constant is one epistemically possible value rather than another. For ease of exposition let $\alpha = P(E|H_D\&N\&K) = P(E|H_{\sim D}\&N\&K) = P(E|H_{\sim D}\&\sim N\&K)$, and assume, as previously, that $P(E|H_D\&\sim N\&K) = 10^{32}\alpha$. The weakness of the necessity objection can be shown by comparing (a) $P(H_D|E\&K)$ as it was estimated before the necessity objection was taken into account, to (b) $P(H_D|E\&K)$ as it should be estimated after the necessity objection is taken into account. Before taking the necessity objection into account, we had:

$$(2)\ P(H_D|E\&K) = \frac{10^{32} \cdot P(H_D|K)}{1 + (10^{32} - 1) \cdot P(H_D|K)}$$

To take the necessity objection into account we need to allow for a non-zero epistemic possibility of N and then see how doing so affects $P(H_D|E\&K)$. First, note that $P(H_D|E\&K) = P(H_D\&\sim N|E\&K) + P(H_D\&N|E\&K)$. By Bayes' theorem, this sum equals

$$\frac{P(H_D\&\sim N|K) \cdot P(E|H_D\&\sim N\&K) + P(H_D\&N|K) \cdot P(E|H_D\&N\&K)}{P(H_D\&\sim N|K) \cdot P(E|H_D\&\sim N\&K) + P(H_D\&N|K) \cdot P(E|H_D\&N\&K) + P(H_{\sim D}\&\sim N|K) \cdot P(E|H_{\sim D}\&\sim N\&K) + P(H_{\sim D}\&N|K) \cdot P(E|H_{\sim D}\&N\&K)}$$

Using our assumption that $P(E|H_D\&\sim N\&K) = 10^{32}\alpha$, this simplifies to:

$$P(H_D|E\&K) = \frac{P(H_D\&\sim N|K) \cdot 10^{32} + P(H_D\&N|K)}{P(H_D\&\sim N|K) \cdot 10^{32} + P(H_D\&N|K) + P(H_{\sim D}\&\sim N|K) + P(H_{\sim D}\&N|K)}$$

Next, because the probabilities of any set of mutually exclusive and jointly exhaustive propositions must sum to 1, we have:

$$P(H_D\&N|K) + P(H_{\sim D}\&\sim N|K) + P(H_{\sim D}\&N|K) = 1 - P(H_D\&\sim N|K)$$

And so $P(H_D|E\&K) = \dfrac{P(H_D\&\sim N|K) \cdot 10^{32} + P(H_D\&N|K)}{P(H_D\&\sim N|K) \cdot 10^{32} + 1 - P(H_D\&\sim N|K)} = \dfrac{P(H_D\&\sim N|K) \cdot 10^{32} + P(H_D\&N|K)}{1 + (10^{32} - 1)\, P(H_D\&\sim N|K)}$

By the product rule,

$$P(H_D\&\sim N|K) = P(\sim N|H_D\&K) \cdot P(H_D|K)$$

$$P(H_D\&N|K) = P(N|H_D\&K) \cdot P(H_D|K)$$

Substituting these values gives us

$$(2)'\ P(H_D|E\&K) = \frac{10^{32} \cdot P(\sim N|H_D\&K) \cdot P(H_D|K) + P(N|H_D\&K) \cdot P(H_D|K)}{1 + (10^{32} - 1) \cdot P(N|H_D\&K) \cdot P(H_D|K)}$$

$(2)'$ expresses the posterior probability of the designer hypothesis, allowing for a non-zero epistemic possibility of N. Note that (2) is the special case of $(2)'$ where $P(N|H_D\&K) = 0$.

To get a feel for how little the necessity objection affects things, we can insert a sample value in for $P(N|H_D\&K)$ and compare the results of (2)' to the results in the text from (2). Let's be as generous as is reasonably possible to the necessity objection and assume $P(N|H_D\&K) = P(\sim N|H_D\&K) = \frac{1}{2}$. Then (2)' reduces to:

$$(2)''\ P(H_D|E\&K) = \frac{10^{32} \cdot (\frac{1}{2}) \cdot P(H_D|K) + (\frac{1}{2}) \cdot P(H_D|K)}{1 + (10^{32} - 1) \cdot (\frac{1}{2}) \cdot P(H_D|K)} = \frac{(10^{32} + 1) \cdot P(H_D|K)}{2 + (10^{32} - 1) \cdot P(H_D|K)}$$

In the text it was noted, from (2), that if a person starts out with a prior probability $P(H_D|K) = \frac{1}{2}$, her posterior probability $P(H_D|E\&K)$ should be well over 0.999999. If this same person then takes the necessity objection with great seriousness, allowing $P(N|H_D\&K) = P(\sim N|H_D\&K) = \frac{1}{2}$, then by (2)'' her posterior probability should still be well over 0.999999! The same is true if the person starts out with a prior probability $P(H_D|K)$ of 1 in 10, or 1 in 1,000, or 1 in 10,000. Only as we descend to lower and lower priors $P(H_D|K)$ can the necessity objection begin to make a difference. Equation (2) tells us that if a person starts out with $P(H_D|K)$ $= \frac{1}{10^{28}}$, then her posterior probability $P(H_D|E\&K)$ should be a bit over 0.999900. If the same person then takes the necessity objection into account according to (2),'' her posterior probability should still be over 0.999800. The necessity objection only makes an appreciable difference by the time we get down to a prior of 1 over 10^{31}, in which case the necessity objection lowers the posterior probability from about 0.909 to 0.833. But given the results of the cosmological argument in chapter five, it's unreasonable to assign a prior probability as low as that to the proposition that our universe was produced by a necessary being having intelligence, and so it's likewise unreasonable to assign a prior probability as low as that to the more general proposition (H_D) that our universe was produced by an intelligent being.

8 GOD AND THE MULTIVERSE

[1]Leonard Susskind, *The Cosmic Landscape: String Theory and the Illusion of Intelligent Design* (New York: Little, Brown, 2006), xi.

[2]This example of an argument in the form of constructive dilemma is not my own, but I cannot track down the source—I've been using it for years when teaching logic.

[3]On the existence of different kinds of creatures adding value to creation, consider the medieval theologian Thomas Aquinas: "For He brought things into being in order that His goodness might be communicated to creatures, and be represented by them; and because His goodness could not be adequately represented by one creature alone, He produced many and diverse creatures, that what was wanting to one in the representation of the divine goodness might be supplied by another. For goodness, which in God is simple and uniform, in creatures is manifold and divided; and hence the whole universe together participates in the divine goodness

more perfectly, and represents it better than any single creature whatever" (Aquinas, *Summa Theologica*, 2nd rev. ed., trans. Fathers of the English Dominican Province [Westminster, MD: Christian Classics, 1981], part I, question 47, answer 1).

[4]For more on this topic, see Timothy O'Connor, *Theism and Ultimate Explanation: The Necessary Shape of Contingency* (Chichester, UK: Wiley-Blackwell, 2012), chap. 5.

[5]An adaptation of an example from Luke Barnes.

[6]Although it's true that $P(E|H_B$ & John survives to observe whether or not his widget is red & K$) = 1$, the proposition *John survives to observe whether or not his widget is red* implies E, and so it can't rightly be included along with the rest of the background knowledge K. This was the mistake of the anthropic objection—see chapter seven, note 2. So $P(E|H_B\&K)$ still $= 0.01 << P(E|H_R\&K) = 0.99$. Note also a second disanalogy that is irrelevant: it doesn't matter that John existed before he was sent the widget, whereas human beings did not exist before the cosmological constant was life permitting. We could change the John story so that it is about John's mother, Jane, at a time before John's conception. If John, years later, learns the story of his mother's widget order, he will gain evidence that his mother ordered from Redd's and not Blue Velvet. The idea behind this second point is due to Jonathan Weisberg, "Firing Squads and Fine-Tuning: Sober on the Design Argument," *British Journal for the Philosophy of Science* 56, no. 4 (2005): 819n9.

[7]It's worth pausing here to dispel a possible source of confusion. Assuming, as we now are, that there is a multiverse, it will be certain, or nearly so, that somewhere in the multiverse there will be at least one universe with a life-permitting cosmological constant. Does that mean that, since K* includes the existence of a multiverse, $P(E|{\sim}D\&K^*)$ should be equal to one, or nearly so? Not at all, because our evidence E is not the proposition that there is at least one universe somewhere with a life-permitting cosmological constant; it is rather the much more specific proposition that a given particular universe, our universe, has a life-permitting cosmological constant.

To see the difference here, compare two experiments. In experiment 1, I will pick a number between one and ten but won't tell you which number I picked. Call the number I picked "n." I will then roll a fair, six-sided die ten times, and shout "Yes!" if and only if the nth roll lands six. Say that we carry out this experiment and I do shout "Yes!" How much was it to be expected beforehand that I would shout "Yes!"? Answer: ⅙. You don't know which number I picked, but it doesn't matter. I had to pick some number, and whatever number I picked, the probability that the corresponding roll would be a six is ⅙. In experiment 2, the setup is different: I will roll a fair, six-sided die ten times, and shout "Yes!" if and only if at least one of the rolls lands six. Say that we do the experiment and I shout "Yes!" How much was it to be expected that when we carried out the experiment you would hear such a shout? The answer turns out to be not ⅙, but a much higher number, about 0.84. The only way I won't shout "Yes!" is if none of the rolls end up landing six. The probability of that happening is $(\frac{5}{6})^{10}$, and so the probability of at least one six is $1 - (\frac{5}{6})^{10} \approx 0.84$.

In the first experiment, your evidence is that a given particular roll has landed six, while in the second experiment your evidence is that at least one of the ten rolls landed six. These are very different pieces of evidence. While a higher number of rolls (higher than ten) would increase the probability of a shout in the second experiment, a higher number of rolls would not increase the probability of a shout in the first experiment. Similarly, supposing that our universe is in fact produced, the assumption that there are many universes doesn't increase the probability that our universe (a given particular universe) will have a life-permitting cosmological constant. (On this point, see Roger White, "Fine-Tuning and Multiple Universes," originally published in *Nous* 34 [2000]: 260-76, and reprinted with a helpful postscript in *God and Design: The Teleological Argument and Modern Science*, ed. Neil A. Manson [New York: Routledge, 2003], 229-50.) The mere existence of our universe may well be equally likely on an atheistic multiverse as on a theistic multiverse, but its life-permitting character is much more likely on a theistic multiverse.

[8]In keeping with Jesus' description of God as a father, I'll refer to God with the masculine pronoun *he*. Strictly speaking, though, the divine nature is neither male nor female.

9 The Beauty and Existential Resonance of Christianity

[1]Plato, *Phaedo* 85 c-d, from *The Last Days of Socrates*, trans. Hugh Tredennick (Harmondsworth, UK: Penguin Classics, 1954). My use of this passage and the core insight of this chapter (that the content of Christian revelation is some evidence for its truth) are both inspired by Sandra Menssen and Thomas Sullivan, *The Agnostic Inquirer: Revelation from a Philosophical Standpoint* (Grand Rapids: Eerdmans, 2007).

[2]Because I'll be examining certain aspects of the content of Christian doctrine, this chapter will have a more theological feel than previous chapters.

[3]Particularly troubling are a set of texts in Deuteronomy and Joshua in which God appears to command the Israelites to kill Palestinian men, women and children living in the Promised Land (see, e.g., Deut 20:16). On this issue, see *Divine Evil? The Moral Character of the God of Abraham*, ed. Michael Bergmann, Michael Murray and Michael Rea (Oxford: Oxford University Press, 2011). I find particularly insightful the contribution of Richard Swinburne to that volume. For a different but complementary approach, see Richard S. Hess, "Appendix 2: Apologetic Issues in the Old Testament," in Douglas Groothuis, *Christian Apologetics: A Comprehensive Case for Biblical Faith* (Downers Grove, IL: InterVarsity Press, 2011), 673-76. Hess interprets the "towns" referred to in the key passages as military forts and argues against the view that the Israelites slaughtered noncombatants.

Another passage that has caused much confusion is Genesis 22:1-18, in which God commands Abraham to sacrifice his son Isaac, intervening to stop him only at the last minute. On this narrative, see the superb discussion by Eleonore Stump, *Wandering in Darkness: Narrative and the Problem of Suffering* (Oxford: Oxford University Press, 2010), chap. 11.

[4]This section and the next are informed by Thomas V. Morris, *Making Sense of It All: Pascal and the Meaning of Life* (Grand Rapids: Eerdmans, 1992). I'm also helped by Groothuis, *Christian Apologetics*, 418-37.

[5]Blaise Pascal, *Pensées*, ed. and trans. Roger Ariew (Indianapolis: Hackett, 2005), 46 (L149).

[6]Ibid., 32 (L116).

[7]An analogy from Groothuis, *Christian Apologetics*, 432-33.

[8]Augustine, *Confessions*, trans. F. J. Sheed (Indianapolis: Hackett, 1993), book 1, chap. 1.

[9]Pascal, *Pensées*, 45 (L148).

[10]Bertrand Russell, "The Free Man's Worship," in *The Collected Papers of Bertrand Russell*, ed. R. A. Rempel, A. Brink and M. Moran, vol. 12, *Contemplation and Action 1902–14* (London: Allen and Unwin, 1985), 66-67.

[11]Simon Blackburn, "An Unbeautiful Mind," *New Republic*, Aug. 5, 2002.

[12]Steven Weinberg, *The First Three Minutes: A Modern View of the Origin of the Universe* (New York: Basic Books, 1977), 154.

10 COUNTEREVIDENCE: DIVINE HIDDENNESS AND EVIL

[1]This is an adaptation of a parable of Søren Kierkegaard's (from *Philosophical Fragments*). I've adapted the parable so as to address the problem of divine hiddenness, but the idea of doing so is not my own—I first came across a similar use of Kierkegaard's parable years ago on a blog post but have not been able to track down the source.

[2]C. Stephen Evans has argued that if God exists, we should expect knowledge of God to be both widely available and easily resistible. A loving God would want to make knowledge of himself possible for all but would also want to refrain from compelling belief and relationship. And Evans argues that this wide accessibility and easy resistibility is exactly what we find: God can be known by many through various signs (like the contingency of the world, the order of the universe and the existence of moral obligation), but these signs can also be easily dismissed or reinterpreted. See his *Natural Signs and Knowledge of God: A New Look at Theistic Arguments* (New York: Oxford University Press, 2010), esp. 12-17.

[3]For a reply to the argument from hiddenness, see Peter van Inwagen, *The Problem of Evil* (New York: Oxford University Press, 2006), 135-51.

[4]Those of van Inwagen, *Problem of Evil*, and Eleonore Stump, *Wandering in Darkness: Narrative and the Problem of Suffering* (Oxford: Oxford University Press, 2010).

[5]Van Inwagen, *Problem of Evil*, 86.

[6]Ibid., 86-87.

[7]Ibid., 88.

[8]Ibid., 89, 95-112.

[9]Eleonore Stump, "The Problem of Evil," *Faith and Philosophy* 2, no. 4 (October 1985): 413-15.

[10]The will is the component of a human being that enables him or her to make choices. The will can be subject to dispositions (or inclinations) of various sorts, e.g., a person can be inclined to choose a concrete good, like pleasure, over an abstract moral good like keeping a promise.

[11]Stump, *Wandering in Darkness*, 395.

[12]Thomas Aquinas, *Super ad Thessalonicenses* I, prologue, trans. Stump, *Wandering in Darkness*, 398-99.

[13]Thomas Aquinas, *Collationes Credo in Deum*, sect. III, trans. Stump, *Wandering in Darkness*, 398.

[14]Aquinas, *Expositio super Job*, chap. 7, sect. 1, translation from *The Literal Exposition on Job: A Scriptural Commentary Concerning Providence*, trans. Anthony Damico (Atlanta: Scholars Press, 1989), 146. Quoted in Stump, *Wandering in Darkness*, 400.

11 HISTORICAL EVIDENCE FOR CHRISTIANITY: THE RESURRECTION

[1]Matthew S. McCormick, *Atheism and the Case Against Christ* (Amherst, NY: Prometheus Books, 2012), 12.

[2]William Lane Craig, *Reasonable Faith: Christian Truth and Apologetics*, 3rd ed. (Wheaton, IL: Crossway, 2008), 399.

[3]For arguments against the resurrection, see McCormick, *Atheism and the Case Against Christ*; Michael Martin, *The Case Against Christianity* (Philadelphia: Temple University Press, 1991); and Bart D. Ehrman, *How Jesus Became God: The Exaltation of a Jewish Preacher from Galilee* (New York: HarperOne, 2014). For arguments in favor of the resurrection, see N. T. Wright, *The Resurrection of the Son of God* (Minneapolis: Fortress, 2003); Michael Licona, *The Resurrection of Jesus: A New Historiographical Approach* (Downers Grove, IL: InterVarsity Press, 2010); and Craig, *Reasonable Faith*, chap. 8.

[4]Licona, *Resurrection of Jesus*, 468.

[5]The two- to three-year figure comes from Bart D. Ehrman, *How Jesus Became God*, 376-77n4. See also Licona, *Resurrection of Jesus*, 229.

[6]As Licona has pointed out in *Resurrection of Jesus*, 229n124.

[7]1 Clement 5, translation from Horace E. Hall, *Epistles of Clement and Polycarp*, Christian Classics Series VII (London: Unwin Brothers, n.d.).

[8]Polycarp, *The Epistle to the Philippians* 3.2, translation from Hall, *Epistles of Clement and Polycarp*.

[9]Bart Ehrman, *The Historical Jesus: Lecture Transcript and Course Guidebook. Part 2 of 2* (Chantilly, VA: Teaching Company, 2000), 162, quoted in Licona, *Resurrection of Jesus*, 600.

[10]Bart Ehrman, quoted in Robert B. Stewart, ed., *The Reliability of the New Testament: Bart D. Ehrman and Daniel B. Wallace in Dialogue* (Minneapolis: Fortress, 2011), 56.

[11]Bart Ehrman, *Jesus, Interrupted: Revealing the Hidden Contradictions in the Bible (and Why We Don't Know About Them)* (New York: HarperOne, 2009), 177-78.

[12]Bart D. Ehrman, *The New Testament: A Historical Introduction to the Early Christian Writings*, 5th ed. (New York: Oxford University Press, 2012), 316.

[13]This explanation involves a rejection of the second of Licona's three minimal facts—the disciples didn't really *believe* that Jesus was resurrected, although they did claim that he was.

[14]See Michael Cook, *Muhammad* (Oxford: Oxford University Press, 1983), 18-22, and Martin Lings, *Muhammad: His Life Based on the Earliest Sources* (Rochester, VT: Inner Traditions, 2006).

[15]Cf. Fawn M. Brodie, *No Man Knows My History: The Life of Joseph Smith the Mormon Prophet* (New York: Alfred A. Knopf, 1946).

[16]See Russell Miller, *Bare-Faced Messiah: The True Story of L. Ron Hubbard* (New York: Henry Holt, 1987).

[17]Richard Swinburne, *The Resurrection of God Incarnate* (Oxford: Oxford University Press, 2003), 70.

[18]See, e.g., Gerd Ludemann, *The Resurrection of Christ: A Historical Inquiry* (Amherst, NY: Prometheus, 2004), and Michael Goulder, "The Baseless Fabric of a Vision," in *Resurrection Reconsidered*, ed. Gavin D'Costa (Oxford: Oneworld, 1996), 48-61.

[19]For a much-expanded argument along similar lines, see Wright, *Resurrection of the Son of God*, particularly chap. 18.

[20]These arguments are mainly taken from Swinburne, *Resurrection of God Incarnate*, chap. 11.

[21]Swinburne, *Resurrection of God Incarnate*, 163-70.

[22]Ibid., 165. I interpret the structure of Swinburne's argument on 165-70 as follows: From very early on, the Christians celebrated the Eucharist on a Sunday. The best explanation of this fact is either that (a) they visited the tomb on Sunday and found it empty, and formed the belief that Jesus had risen on Sunday, then later decided to celebrate the Eucharist on that day in commemoration of the resurrection, or (b) Jesus appeared to the disciples on the first Easter Sunday, and at that time or during a later appearance communicated to them his intention that they celebrate the Eucharist on Sundays in commemoration of the resurrection. Now, it's clear that if (a), then the visit to the tomb on Easter Sunday was not a

late invention. But why does (b) imply that the visit to the tomb on Easter Sunday was not a late invention? Perhaps Swinburne's idea is that if (b), the disciples would have checked the tomb after the Easter Sunday appearance. Regardless, for my purposes the crucial chain of reasoning is this: (1) one of only a few viable explanations for the early Christian celebration of the Eucharist on Sundays is that some of the disciples discovered the empty tomb on a Sunday, and (2) this raises the probability that the disciples did discover the empty tomb, which in turn (3) counts against the suggestion that Jesus was buried in an unknown location, or not buried at all.

[23]Ehrman, *How Jesus Became God*, 160.

[24]Craig, *Reasonable Faith*, 399; Swinburne, *Resurrection of God Incarnate*, 29.

12 MIRACLE OR MYTH?

[1]E.g., Bart D. Ehrman, *How Jesus Became God: The Exaltation of a Jewish Preacher from Galilee* (New York: HarperOne, 2014), 173.

[2]Most of the arguments in this section are drawn from Richard Swinburne, "The Probability of the Resurrection," in *God and the Ethics of Belief: New Essays in Philosophy of Religion*, ed. Andrew Dole and Andrew Chignell (Cambridge: Cambridge University Press, 2005), 117-30. See also Richard Swinburne, *The Resurrection of God Incarnate* (Oxford: Oxford University Press, 2003).

[3]Anselm, *Cur Deus Homo*, and Aquinas, *Summa theologiae* III, question 1.

[4]For more on the atonement, see the forthcoming monograph of Eleonore Stump on that subject, provisionally titled *At-Onement*.

[5]See Swinburne, *Resurrection of God Incarnate*, 117-26.

[6]See Stephen T. Davis, "Was Jesus Mad, Bad, or God?," in Stephen T. Davis, *Christian Philosophical Theology* (Oxford: Oxford University Press, 2006), 149-71.

[7]Thomas Sheehan, "How Did Easter Originally Happen? An Hypothesis," in *The Resurrection of Jesus: A Sourcebook*, ed. B. B. Scott (Santa Rosa, CA: Polebridge, 2008), 108.

[8]Thomas Sheehan, "The Resurrection: An Obstacle to Faith?" in *Resurrection of Jesus*, 94.

[9]Ibid., 102.

[10]John Shelby Spong, *Resurrection: Myth or Reality?* (New York: HarperSanFrancisco, 1994), 233.

[11]Ibid., 257.

[12]As does Michael Licona, *The Resurrection of Jesus: A New Historiographical Approach* (Downers Grove, IL: InterVarsity Press, 2010), 400-436.

[13]N. T. Wright, *The Resurrection of the Son of God* (Minneapolis: Fortress, 2003), 318.

[14]Ibid., 282-84, 347-56.

[15]See ibid., 359.

[16]Still, what are we to make of the strange ending of Mark (Mk 16:8)? One possibility is that the original ending has been lost (see Swinburne, *Resurrection of God Incarnate*, 149-53). Another possibility is that Mark deliberately ended his Gospel abruptly as a literary technique designed to put his readers in the place of the disciples, to invite his readers to ask themselves, "How am *I* going to respond to these claims about Jesus?" On this point see the comments of Daniel Wallace in *The Reliability of the New Testament: Bart D. Ehrman and Daniel B. Wallace in Dialogue*, ed. Robert B. Stewart (Minneapolis: Fortress, 2011), 54.

[17]James Taylor, email to author, Aug. 4, 2015. Taylor adds that this idea is not original to himself. Craig attributes a similar point to eighteenth-century theologian Jacob Vernet in *Reasonable Faith*, 334.

[18]For a sophisticated reconstruction of how the several resurrection narratives in the New Testament might fit together, see chap. 9 of Swinburne's *Resurrection of God Incarnate*.

13 DIETRICH BONHOEFFER

[1]Information on Bonhoeffer's life is taken primarily from Eberhard Bethge, *Dietrich Bonhoeffer: A Biography*, rev. ed (Minneapolis: Fortress, 2000), and Eric Metaxas, *Bonhoeffer: Pastor, Martyr, Prophet, Spy: A Righteous Gentile vs. The Third Reich* (Nashville: Thomas Nelson, 2010). Information on background political and military events is taken mainly from William L. Shirer, *The Rise and Fall of the Third Reich: A History of Nazi Germany* (New York: Simon and Schuster, 1960).

[2]Bethge, *Dietrich Bonhoeffer*, 226.

[3]Letter to Erwin Sutz, in *No Rusty Swords: Letters, Lectures, and Notes,* ed. Edwin Robertson, vol. 1, *1928–1936*, Collected Works of Dietrich Bonhoeffer (New York: Harper & Row, 1965), 140.

[4]Ibid., 150.

[5]Mary Bosanquet, *The Life and Death of Dietrich Bonhoeffer* (New York: Harper & Row, 1968), 104, translated from Dietrich Bonhoeffer, *Gesammelte Schriften*, ed. Eberhard Bethge, 4:44-45.

[6]Dietrich Bonhoeffer, *London: 1933–1935*, Dietrich Bonhoeffer Works 13, ed. Keith Clements, trans. Isabel Best (New York: Fortress, 2007), 191-92, quoted in Metaxas, *Bonhoeffer*, 236.

[7]Paul Schmidt, *Hitler's Interpreter* (New York, 1951), 41, quoted in Shirer, *Rise and Fall of the Third Reich*, 293.

[8]Ulrich von Hassell, *The Von Hassell Diaries, 1938–1944* (New York, 1947), 23, quoted in Shirer, *Rise and Fall of the Third Reich*, 320.

[9]Metaxas, *Bonhoeffer*, 317.

[10]Ibid., 359.

[11]Dietrich Bonhoeffer, *The Way to Freedom: Letters, Lectures and Notes, 1935–1939*, ed. Edwin Robertson, trans. Edwin Robertson and John Bowden, Collected Works of Dietrich Bonhoeffer (New York: Harper & Row, 1966), 230.

[12]Ibid., 226.

[13]Metaxas, *Bonhoeffer*, 443.

[14]Roger Moorhouse, *Killing Hitler: The Plots, the Assassins, and the Dictator Who Cheated Death* (New York: Bantam Dell, 2006), 262.

[15]Metaxas, *Bonhoeffer*, 518.

[16]Ibid., 523.

[17]Bethge, *Dietrich Bonhoeffer*, 1022n50.

[18]Letter from Payne Best to S. Leibholz, March 2, 1951, quoted in Bethge, *Dietrich Bonhoeffer*, 919.

[19]Ibid., 920.

[20]Sabine Leibholz-Bonhoeffer, *The Bonhoeffers: Portrait of a Family* (New York: St. Martin's, 1971), 198-99, quoted in Metaxas, *Bonhoeffer*, 527.

[21]S. Payne Best, *The Venlo Incident* (Watford, UK: Hutchinson, 1950), 180, quoted in Bethge, *Dietrich Bonhoeffer*, 920.

[22]Best, *Venlo Incident*, 200, quoted in Bethge, *Dietrich Bonhoeffer*, 927.

[23]Bethge, *Dietrich Bonhoeffer*, 1022n54.

[24]Letter from Payne Best to S. Leibholz, March 2, 1951, quoted in Bethge, *Dietrich Bonhoeffer*, 920.

14 JEAN VANIER

[1]My main sources for biographical information about Jean Vanier's life are: Kathryn Spink, *The Miracle, The Message, The Story: Jean Vanier and l'Arche* (London: Darton, Longman, and Todd, 2006); Jean Vanier, *An Ark for the Poor: The Story of L'Arche* (Toronto: Novalis, 1995); Jean Vanier, *Our Life Together: A Memoir in Letters* (Toronto: Harper Perennial, 2007); and Bill Clarke, *Enough Room for Joy: The Early Days of Jean Vanier's L'Arche* (New York: Bluebridge, 2007).

[2]Vanier, *Our Life Together*, 2.

[3]Spink, *The Miracle, The Message, The Story*, 19.

[4]Ibid., 24.

[5]Ibid., 26.

[6]Ibid., 30.

[7]Vanier, *Our Life Together*, 3.

[8]See Spink, *The Miracle, The Message, The Story*, 35-38, and Charles Cunliffe, "The Life of L'Eau Vive," *The Tablet*, Oct. 18, 1952, 16.

[9]Vanier, *Our Life Together*, 3.

[10]Spink, *The Miracle, The Message, The Story*, 44.

[11]Ibid.

[12]Ibid., 56.

[13]Vanier, *Our Life Together*, 5, 11.

[14]Ibid., 4.

[15]Vanier, *Ark for the Poor*, 15.

[16]Ibid., 16.

[17]Spink, *The Miracle, The Message, The Story*, 60.

[18]Ibid., 62.

[19]Ibid., 61.

[20]Ibid.

[21]Vanier, *Our Life Together*, 5-6.

[22]Spink, *The Miracle, The Message, The Story*, 62.

[23]Ibid., 64.

[24]Jean Vanier, letter of Nov. 5, 1965, in Jean Vanier, *A Network of Friends: The Letters of Jean Vanier to the Friends and Communities of L'Arche*, ed. John Sumarah, vol. I, *1964–1973* (Hantsport, NS: Lancelot, 1992), 33.

[25]Vanier, *Our Life Together*, 19-20, 31.

[26]Pope Paul VI's speech to pilgrims from Le Val Fleuri and L'Arche, Holy Wednesday, 1966, quoted in Vanier, *Our Life Together*, 29.

[27]Vanier, letter of Sept. 10, 1966, in *Network of Friends*, 46.

[28]Vanier, *Ark for the Poor*, 34.

[29]Vanier, letter of Oct. 29, 1970, in *Our Life Together*, 79.

[30]Vanier, letter of Nov. 20, 1973, in *Network of Friends*, 195-96.

[31]Asha Niketan, accessed April 27, 2015. www.ashaniketancalicutnandhibazar.org.

[32]L'Arche International, accessed April 27, 2015. www.larche.org.

[33]See Clarke, *Enough Room for Joy*, 42.

[34]Jean Vanier, *Becoming Human* (Mahwah, NJ: Paulist, 2008), 2.

[35]Vanier, *Ark for the Poor*, 26.

[36]Vanier, *Becoming Human*, 88-89.

[37]Clarke, *Enough Room for Joy*, 48.

[38]Vanier, *Becoming Human*, 100.

[39]Jean Vanier, "Transforming Our Hearts" (Templeton Prize News Conference, British Academy, London, March 11, 2015).

15 Immaculée Ilibagiza

[1]Information on Immaculée Ilibagiza's story comes from her autobiography, *Left to Tell: Discovering God Amidst the Rwandan Holocaust* (New York: Hay House, 2006). As she notes, she has changed the names of individuals other than her family members.

[2]See Julius O. Adekunle, *Culture and Customs of Rwanda* (Westport, CT: Greenwood, 2007), 16-17, and Gérard Prunier, *The Rwanda Crisis: History of a Genocide* (New York: Columbia University Press, 1995), 23-40.

[3]Prunier, *Rwanda Crisis*, 26-27.

[4]Scott Straus, *The Order of Genocide: Race, Power, and War in Rwanda* (Ithaca, NY: Cornell University Press, 2006), 21.

[5]Ibid., 192.

[6]Ilibagiza, *Left to Tell*, 39.

[7]Ibid., 39-40.

[8]Ibid., 58.

[9]Ibid., 88.

[10]Ibid., 92.

[11]Ibid., 93.

[12]Ibid.

[13]Ibid., 93-94.

[14]Ibid., 134.

[15]Ibid., 155.

[16]Ibid., 196.

[17]Ibid.

[18]Ibid.

[19]Ibid.

Conclusion: Taking the Wager

[1]Blaise Pascal, *Pensées*, trans. A. J. Krailsheimer (London: Folio Society, 2011), 129 (S680/L418).

AUTHOR INDEX

SUBJECT INDEX

SCRIPTURE INDEX

Finding the Textbook You Need

The IVP Academic Textbook Selector
is an online tool for instantly finding the IVP books
suitable for over 250 courses across 24 disciplines.

---

www.ivpress.com/academic/
